THE IRISH PARLIAMENTARY TRADITION

THE IRISH PARLIAMENTARY TRADITION

Edited by Brian Farrell

With three essays on the Treaty debate

by F. S. L. Lyons

Gill and Macmillan . Dublin

Barnes & Noble Books . New York

a division of Harper & Row Publishers, Inc.

First published in 1973

Gill and Macmillan Limited
2 Belvedere Place
Dublin 1
and in London through association with the
Macmillan International Group of Publishing Companies
Published in the U.S.A. 1973 by
Harper & Row Publishers, Inc.
Barnes & Noble Import Division

Gill and Macmillan SBN: 7171 0594 6
Barnes & Noble ISBN: 06 492068 2
Printing history: 5 4 3 2 1

Jacket designed by Graham Shepherd

Printed and bound in Great Britain by
Bristol Typesetting Co. Ltd., Bristol, England

Contents

From War to Civil War in Ireland
Three Essays on the Treaty Debate
by F. S. L. LYONS

Contributors

BRENDAN BRADSHAW, SM
Bridges Research Scholar, Corpus Christi College, Cambridge

FRANCIS JOHN BYRNE
Professor of Early (including Medieval) Irish History, University College, Dublin

ART COSGROVE
College Lecturer in Medieval History, University College, Dublin

DONAL F. CREGAN, CM
President of St Patrick's College, Drumcondra, Dublin

BRIAN FARRELL
College Lecturer in Political Institutions, University College, Dublin

HUGH KEARNEY
Richard Pares Professor of History, University of Edinburgh

JOSEPH LEE
Fellow of Peterhouse, Cambridge

F. S. L. LYONS
Professor of Modern History, University of Kent at Canterbury

J. L. MCCRACKEN
Professor of History, New University of Ulster, Coleraine

OLIVER MacDONAGH
Professor of Modern History, University College, Cork

F. X. MARTIN, OSA
Professor of Medieval History, University College, Dublin

KEVIN B. NOWLAN
Associate Professor of Modern History, University College, Dublin

J. G. SIMMS
Lecturer in Modern History, Trinity College, Dublin

Preface

Two parliaments were created in twentieth-century Ireland. One, Dáil Éireann, apparently sprang from a revolutionary, illegal assembly in Dublin to become the legislature of a new Irish state claiming jurisdiction over the whole of the island and exercising jurisdiction over the greater part of it. Today it is recognised internationally as the parliament of Ireland. The other, the parliament of Northern Ireland, was established under a British statute (the Government of Ireland Act, 1920), survived for a half-century as an incongruous and disputed regional assembly for a fragment of Ireland within the United Kingdom. It was suspended by a British statute in 1972. Both assemblies adopted the conventions of the British parliamentary model, developed strong, disciplined parliamentary parties and accepted single-party cabinet government as the normal outcome of regular electoral contests. There is, then, an unexplained paradox : the 'revolutionaries' who repudiated the British connection in favour of an independent Ireland were able to establish and maintain a stable representative system; the loyalist inheritors of a legally constituted British parliament have failed.

This book was not specifically designed to resolve that paradox. It was planned essentially as an investigation of the historical roots of Irish representative government. In the process the seeds of contemporary Irish political stability and decay are analysed within a parliamentary context for the first time.

The purpose of this collection of essays is not to present a mere description, still less a justification of Irish parliaments and their leaders. It is intended to be explanatory and interpretative rather than factual and narrative; not a bland reconstruction of the course of Irish parliamentary history but an investigation cast in chronological form. Inevitably, in particular essays, it is necessary to describe events, but each essay is primarily designed as a contribution to solving the central questions posed by the persistence of the Irish parliamentary tradition : why, and to what extent, have the Irish people clung to a parliamentary mode of government? how far have Irish parliaments been 'representative'? how have they contributed to the establishment, development and prosperity of a separate Irish nation? can they be seen as reflecting and influencing, reinforcing or destroying, other more general values in Irish political culture? have they yielded to, or affected, other kinds of political leadership at critical points?

The questions could be multiplied. Basically they fall into three main groups. First, who were the political elite?—what was their relationship with the 'people'? how important was the consent of the governed? did the leaders share, advance or change the political opinion of their time? Second, *how* did they function?—was the preferred mode unambiguously parliamentary? were the institutions themselves modified in significant ways? was the Irish political practice similar to developments elsewhere—especially in Britain? Third, what degree of success can be attributed to these leaders?—how do their aims compare with their achievements?

This mode of investigation may be criticised as an attempt to impose a 'Whig interpretation' on Irish history—a gradualist but inevitable attainment of constitutional liberties through the development of representative and tolerant political institutions. There is no such commitment to the concept of an uninterrupted progress towards political perfection, although a certain pattern of political development through a series of critical steps or thresholds may be discerned. But a positive effort is made to offer a corrective to the selective and uncritical 'nationalist' interpretation which reduces the complex Irish historical experience to a linked series of militant uprisings in successive generations against 'seven hundred years' of British oppression and persecution. This latter version, with its insistence on the use of violence to achieve political ends and its emphasis on personalities rather than institutions, tends to be exclusive in its definition of 'the Irish people' and conservative —if not reactionary—in its commitment to an idealised and unchanging traditional political culture. Yet any objective assessment of the evidence obliges us to believe that a deep-rooted (and, on occasions, violent) opposition to British rule involved no rejection of its operational machinery and pragmatic norms. The value of stable representative institutions resting on an extended and fair franchise was recognised as early and as widely by the Irish as by the British.

Stated in these terms, it might seem that the emphasis in this book would fall on an institutional and narrowly 'political' range of issues. This, however, is not its exclusive concern, since the structures and conventions, the forms of governmental and political activity, depend upon the society in which they are found and the values on which it rests. The essays have, therefore, been cast within the broader context of Irish political culture so that they relate both to the political traditions and to the folk heroes, to the spirit as well as to the content of public laws and structures, to the manner and tone of political exchanges, to the expectations and the standards underlying both the formal and informal rules and conventions of social and political life.

The first sixteen essays in this book were originally delivered as the forty-eighth series of Thomas Davis Lectures, broadcast on RTÉ between January and April 1972. Fortunately, Professor F. S. L. Lyons agreed to the inclusion of his three essays on the Treaty debate (also broadcast on RTÉ, as the forty-seventh series of Thomas Davis Lectures in December 1971) in the present volume. To him and to the other contributors, in particular the Rev. Professor F. X. Martin, OSA, I owe a debt of gratitude for easing the editorial burden. Michael Littleton, of RTÉ, was an unfailing source of practical support, experienced encouragement and critical concern from the conception of the series right through to publication. Miss Rose Kenna of RTÉ was at all times helpful with scripts. Mary Dowey and Colm Croker of Gill and Macmillan have achieved a first in organising the publication of a Thomas Davis series within a year of the original broadcast; I am particularly indebted to Colm Croker for his indefatigable and scrupulous labours in bringing the book to press. My colleagues in the Department of Ethics and Politics, University College, Dublin, have all been generous with time and interest and my family tolerant as always.

Brian Farrell, November 1972

The Paradox of Irish Politics

BRIAN FARRELL

IT is difficult to dislodge established myths; hard to scale down accepted heroes to human dimensions. Traditions take on a life, reality and purpose of their own. A single version of events, a standard ordering of experience, quickly becomes hardened into orthodoxy : yesterday's propaganda becomes today's history and passes into tomorrow's politics. The move is imperceptible; its effects incalculable. Since the early 1920s just such a move has helped first to create, and subsequently to sustain, a one-sided and questionable view of how the Irish nation and the Irish state came into existence.

According to this view, the Irish political tradition has always been developed by protest, resistance and violence. These are the milestones that measure and mark the steps by which Ireland moved to nationhood. They have become the foundation stones of a widely held interpretation of the Irish historical experience. For some—especially in the North today—they remain as sign-posts of possible further political development.

The emphasis on the Easter Rising of 1916 is vital to this theme. It is seen as the only true seed-bed of contemporary Ireland; the central expression of authentic Irish nationalism; the single source of our independence. Its heroes are offered as models; their writings taken to enshrine our ideals; their protest in arms presented as the only effective procedure for achieving freedom. The new Irish state of the 1920s seems to spring so naturally and immediately from that week-long armed revolt that we have often lost sight of the many other contributions that were necessary for the establishment of modern Ireland.

This kind of emphasis on heroic action, on the rising against overwhelming odds, even on the hopeless failure is common among minority and oppressed peoples. It is documented in James Baldwin's evocations of the black American ghettoes and in Franz Fanon's larger canvas of racial imperialism. And it is understandable. Imperial states can celebrate their victories and their conquests; successful nations pile up their political triumphs; stable societies build the story of their past around the achievements of their statesmen and leaders. Subject peoples have no such solace. The defeated must proclaim the gallantry of failure; those denied redress seize violence as the only available tool; they chronicle past efforts in order to kindle new expectations from the ashes of old hopes. The reason for the emphasis is obvious: it provides a focus for agitation, for action and for coherent unity in the militant phases of a liberation struggle.

But this very fact makes it an insecure and uncertain base for the establishment and maintenance of a stable political regime. The heightened awareness of the past, the identification with its most militant moments, the exaltation of its heroes—all those factors which serve so well to stimulate protest and rebellion while freedom is being won—become a threat to that freedom and order in the newly independent state. And here we confront a central paradox of modern Irish politics: all our emphasis on the fight for Irish freedom, on the resort to arms by committed minorities against alien domination, on the series of challenges (so often defeated) to the established order—all of this provides no substantial explanation for the extraordinary degree of political stability which has been witnessed since the establishment of the state. It is a stability which critics say has led to stagnancy and worse. But it is a stability which is remarkable, if not unique, among the newly developed states of the twentieth-century world.

In the flush of victory after the First World War there was a great deal of optimism about the likelihood of political progress and development. The war itself was interpreted simply as a moral clash between the wicked and absolutist regimes of Central Europe and the virtuous liberal-democratic Allies. The war saw the end of four great empires on mainland Europe—Germany, Austria-Hungary, Russia and Turkey. The brave new world was quick to offer a confident answer to the question of how these ancient and now-fragmented territories should be politically organised; that answer was to impose a new framework of constitutional, representative government.

There were two main models—two working models—available for copy: the British parliamentary and cabinet model and the American presidential and federal system. These two models were adopted and adapted by a mushroom growth of new and newly organised states. Across Central Europe and the Balkans the effort was made to create political societies that would be reasonably secure, reasonably free and reasonably efficient. Russia went further in experimentation by organising a new state-system that would provide, at least in theory, a release from economic as well as political ills.

The experience of Europe in the inter-war years did nothing to justify the hopeful predictions of the constitution-makers. Yet, in the aftermath of the Second World War—as the British, French, Dutch and Belgian empires in Africa, the Middle East and Asia gave way before a new tide of nationalism—there were few original political solutions on offer. Once again the effort was made to 'export' parliament, to impose the formal constitutional rules and the elaborate political institutions of the West on the Third World. The history of these areas in the 1960s has again demonstrated the inadequacy of these old government formulae to resolve the problems of state-building.

This duplicated history of failure should also have reinforced a sense of the fragility, and indeed the relative scarcity, of so many aspects of political life which we take for granted. By and large, we are conscious of economic inequalities in the modern world. The gap between the rich nations of the West and the developing areas of Africa, Asia, Latin-America is spelled out in terms of gross national product, of average incomes, of living standards measured as units of food, shelter and education. This maldistribution of economic resources, both within and between states, is a central theme of our time, although it may well be that it is a theme whose magnitude and implications are not even yet properly appreciated.

The notion of inequalities in political resources is less clearly understood. Yet it too is a critical dimension in comparing states. Stable political structures require more than merely economic development if they are to survive. In particular, the complex of institutions and structures that we associate with liberal-democratic states requires a high level of political development. Indeed, that combination of free elections, alternation of parties in government, the existence of a free Opposition and independent courts is rare among modern states. With a fine disregard for the flourishing Scandinavian and Benelux democracies, there has been some tendency to claim that this kind of stable, representative system of government is an English 'export',[1] although there can be no doubt that the group of former British territories in North America, Australia and New Zealand form a conspicuously successful and compact group within the general category.

Ireland is an exception within that group for a number of reasons. It is a newer state, seen as the product of a relatively recent (and, for some, still unfinished) war of independence. Ireland is subject to the inherent political uncertainty, communal bitterness and sporadic violence of states with disputed territorial boundaries. It is apparently heir to a violent political tradition. In a word, Ireland has inherited a set of conditions that should have made a liberal-democratic regime difficult, if not impossible, to create and sustain. That point is clarified if you stop for a moment to consider the major problems that faced the new rulers of the Irish Free State as they set about the business of establishing a separate Irish policy in the early 1920s.

The new state was born into civil war. Ireland has shared that experience with other infant states. The cost can be counted in terms of numbers killed and the extent of physical destruction. Far more significant for the political future of such states is the damage to the social fabric inflicted by internal wars. All effective civic cultures rest to some extent on a bed of political trust, on a willingness to cooperate with others, on a basis of shared values. There may be substantial disagreement —on such matters, for instance, as the distribution of property, or the role of a major church—but there will tend to be agreement on procedures, an understanding on how change is to be achieved, on acceptance of the 'rules of the game'. This applies even to questions of changing those rules.

Civil war challenges that consensus. It destroys that civic trust. The very basis of authority in the state is questioned; the legitimacy of the regime is denied; the electoral, or some other orderly, method of resolving disputes is replaced by resort to violence. The dangers of this situation, especially for new states,

are obvious. The state itself may be encouraged to adopt authoritarian rather than representative rule; its opponents may be
confirmed in their belief that only an armed coup can secure
their demands. In Ireland the Civil War generated a bitter
cleavage which only gradually became integrated and institu-
tionalised into a political party system; a militant minority remained permanently estranged and, in successive generations
since, have posed an intermittent threat to political stability.

A second major threat—and, again, one that has confronted
many new states—was related to the existence of the political
barrier between North and South. Disputed boundaries produce
and reflect tensions not only between but also within states.
They create minority groups on each side who not merely seek
the downfall of the regime on the other side but also question
the legitimacy of the regime under which they live. Most citizens
in stable countries talk simply about 'the Government' and
mean their government—even in critical comment there is an
implication that the government is accepted. But these disappointed and frequently dispossessed groups qualify the term
—they speak of 'the Bonn Government', 'the Makarios Government', 'the Dublin Government'; the implication is obvious—it
is not *the* Government, not *their* Government, not a fully legitimate nor permanent regime.

Partly, of course, this mirrors a problem of identity. For
some people in the South to be Irish meant refusing to recognise the authority of the Irish Free State; in the course of time
the difficulty has resolved for most people. In the North it
remains a central and burning issue : people variously describe
themselves as British, Irish, Ulster. These divisions and doubts
can all be related to the fact that the extent of the boundaries
of the Irish state remain an issue of conflict. Nor, as recent
events have shown, is the problem confined to the North. Out-
breaks of trouble on one side of the border spill over into politics and lives of people on the other side. Since 1921 the border
has been another major challenge to the legitimacy and continuance of stable politics in Ireland.

A third major difficulty for the new Irish Free State and the
Stormont regime was posed by the existence within their areas
of control of distinct and entrenched minorities. In the North
that minority was populous, underprivileged and politically

disaffected. In the South the Protestant minority was small but economically privileged, associated with British rule, and a powerful symbol of alien cultural dominance. Yet it too was absorbed—as the civil war division was absorbed—into a stable representative system. This is not to say that the smaller religious minorities have yet been fully integrated into contemporary Irish society but, certainly by comparison with the North, the Republic comes close to the modern practice of a pluralist society.

There were, then, at the outset three outstanding threats to the establishment of normal liberal-democratic regimes : a civil war situation, a disputed border, and a disaffected minority. These were located within a broader context of relative economic underdevelopment. Of course it can be argued that by comparison with the new states of the Third World, Ireland started off with major advantages : a broad system of education, transportation and administration—all the necessary infra-structure of a modern state. However, there were also marked economic disadvantages at the outset—especially by comparison with other former 'white dominions'. And these conditions were confronted by new leaders who had little or no executive experience as they entered on the massive task of state-building. That work could scarcely have been accomplished if the central Irish political tradition had been so robustly rebellious, so chronically violent and so demanding of change as has been usually suggested.

The legends and the ballads sing of Emmet, the Fenians, the men of 1916 and the boys of Kilmichael. They stretch on from the days of the Black and Tans and the Civil War to the later days of the Patriot Game and Seán South of Garryowen. They continue to identify and promote a version of the Irish past associated especially with the political writings and actions of Pádraig Pearse.

And the point needs to be emphasised that Pearse wrote within and for a minority tradition. His work was selective. It was propagandist. Its purpose was not to explain the past but to *use* the past. Pearse wanted to make rebels of his readers and he selected his history with that precise purpose in view. He rejected and reduced some elements of the Irish past in order to construct an alternative tradition of progressive, militant,

revolutionary separatism. Pearse rejected Grattan and his ex-
periment with an independent parliament for Ireland; dismissed
O'Connell's injection of Irish claims into Westminster; ignored
Butt and Biggar; condemned the parliamentarians of his own
day. He made a partial exception of Parnell, whom he described
as a 'pale ghost' of separatism. Pearse traced his own tradition
—an amalgam of separatism, of non-sectarianism, and above all
of physical force—from Tone through Davis and Lalor and
Mitchel.

In a collection of essays commemorating Thomas Davis it is
surely appropriate to note how wide a gap separated the Young
Irelander from the Pearse who invoked his name. Davis was
a separatist. Certainly he was a vigorous apostle of non-sectarianism. But what of physical force? Pearse himself acknowledged that 'Davis would have achieved Irish nationhood by
peaceful means if he could.' Then he goes on to quote from
one poem and one essay to back his assertion that 'Davis was
ready to fight,' and so locate him within a physical-force tradition.[2] This is certainly a distortion of Davis.

Davis's slogan was not fight that you may be free but 'educate that you may be free'. In October 1844 when mobs in
Sackville Street protested a government award of coach con-
tracts, Davis was critical of direct action and asserted, 'We want
law and order—we are seriously injured by every scene or act
of violence, no matter how transient. Let us have no more of
this humbug.'[3] In an outspoken condemnation of agrarian outrages in Munster Davis's opening sentences echo Pearse's later
invocation of the cleansing power of blood only to reject it :
'The people of Munster are in want—will murder feed them?
Is there some prolific virtue in the blood of a landlord that the
fields of the South will yield a richer crop where it has flowed?'
In an essay on 'Moral Force' Thomas Davis wrote, with approval :

There are two ways of success for the Irish—arms and persuasion.
They have chosen the latter. They have resolved to win their
rights by moral force. For this end they have confederated their
names, their moneys, their thoughts, and their resolves. For this
they learn history, and forget quarrels.

The version of Irish history which Davis offered his readers was also far removed from that of Pearse. In a 'Chronology of Ireland' printed in his collected writings, by far the greatest number of entries refer to parliaments and acts of parliament. Among the very few early entries he listed :

B.C. 489   Ollamh Fodhla, the Irish Solomon, institutes the great Feis or Triennial Convention at Tara.
A.D. 164   King Fedlim the Legislator established the law of Eric.
554   The last triennial council held at Tara.

These entries may well refer to myths rather than history, but it is through their myths that a people often preserve and express their deepest values.

This argument should not be pushed too far : clearly Davis's vision of Irish history and Irish nationhood went far beyond 'those who saw in it nothing but a parliament in College Green'.[4] At the same time, Davis's account cannot easily be placed within the physical-force version of Irish nationalism articulated so fluently by Pearse before 1916 and accepted as national orthodoxy afterwards. Indeed, Davis's own most substantial contribution to the writing of Irish history was a parliamentary study—*The Patriot Parliament of 1689*. So it seems entirely proper, in a book recalling Davis's contribution to the development of Irish nationalism and published more than fifty years after the establishment of a separate Irish state, to look again at the course of Irish history and to attempt to trace within it a different, and arguably a dominant, political tradition. This is a tradition built around the development in Ireland of representative institutions of government.

On the face of it this may seem a perverse enterprise. It can be argued that for much of the time parliament in Ireland was the preserve of a privileged and largely alien minority. It was an engine of oppression against the majority. At best it was a weak and ineffective instrument of minority Irish interests against British domination. And there is substance to all these charges.

In Ireland the development of representative government has often been fractured; it has been frequently ineffective in its application and almost always incomplete in its range. Parliament has failed to identify problems in time, failed to cope with present needs, failed to provide for future demands.

But it has never been abandoned. A renewed recognition of this traditional commitment to basic democratic values and representative institutions may be the necessary and neglected key to unlock a fuller, more central and less negative understanding of the Irish political tradition.

This parliamentary thread is a much more complex, confused and insecure guide than the single searing torch with which Pearse sought to illuminate all aspects of the Irish historical maze. It offers no simple certainties and proffers few unquestioned dogmas. The Irish parliamentary tradition is not marked by any steady and unbroken progress towards greater freedom and greater participation in government but stumbles on by a series of doubtful fits and uncertain starts. Its major actors have not been legendary heroes and villains cast in an epic mould, but everyday men of affairs—creatures, like the rest of us, in whom there was room for good and ill, for calculating self-interest and for nation-wide largeness of heart; men in whom the petty and the proud, the mean and the magnificent, the narrow bounds of practical realities and the wider horizons of great political visions were mixed.

Obviously, violence, protest and physical force form part of this Irish political culture. But one can also discern other strands—a rejection of absolutist claims to rule, an emphasis on the representation of local demands and interests, an attachment to equity and to the rule of law. These give force and meaning to the fabric of government; they are central to a deep core of constitutionalism in Irish life; and they are reflected in the fact that in its origins and throughout its development the modern Irish state of the twentieth century has preserved a parliamentary form and operated parliamentary norms.

The essays in this book attempt to trace this back even before the introduction of formal parliamentary institutions following the Anglo-Norman conquest. A re-examination of early Irish kingship shows that the society into which the Normans inserted their alien parliament had at least some framework of representation, consultation, opposition and answerability shoring up the more visible symbolism of royal rule.

The essay on the original Celtic political system is followed by an examination of the role of parliament from Norman times through to the foundation of the Irish Free State. It is a record that compares strangely with the contemporaneous development in Britain. England progressed from Tudor monarchy through the burgeoning of a Stuart absolutism which was punctured by two revolutions that identified parliament as the effective political arena of control and command. Ireland, by comparison, saw her own parliamentary tradition—in part product of old Celtic assemblies, in measure a fragmented Anglo-Norman instrument—steadily eroded and used in the sixteenth century to impose a Reformation settlement. In the seventeeth century efforts to summon an Irish parliament were resisted. Under Charles I the Anglo-Irish were ready to pay handsomely for 'Graces' which included the privilege of parliament. Under Wentworth the Irish parliament was a rapidly used rough instrument to impose a 'thorough' policy of control from the top. While England experimented with Cromwell's rule, in Ireland the Confederation of Kilkenny preserved the flicker of the parliamentary tradition alight, but for a quarter of a century after the Restoration Parliament of Charles II was dissolved by Ormond in 1666 no legal Irish assembly met. Again it was an illegal body, the 'Patriot Parliament' of 1689 which indicated that some tradition had survived and which was to become a symbol of resistence for Anglo-Irish constitutional nationalism in the future. But in the short term that Parliament was rejected. Under William there was yet another round in that chronic reshuffle of land ownership in Ireland ushering in a miserable eighteenth century in which Irish parliamentarians were slow to share their privilege and power. Through that century an assertive line of Anglo-Irish nationalism can be traced from Molyneux through Swift and Berkeley to Flood, Grattan and the Irish Volunteers but in the main society remained divided, distrustful and desperately poor. The legislative independence of Grattan's Parliament promoted the expansion of Dublin as a capital city, but far more important was the contemporary population explosion which, in the absence of industrialisation, created a vast rural slum, a string of congested districts, along the west coast. It was out of the West, coming from Kerry and asserting itself first in Clare, that new political leadership and change arose; O'Connell, unlike his English contemporaries, was a political leader operating in a transitional society that was still closer to the traditional than to the modern end of the scale of development. O'Connell marks the true beginnings of the modern Irish political tradition, which is one of the reasons he has been singled out by the dominant school of 'republican' nationalists as a symbol of British influence in Ireland—as an 'Uncle Tom' figure.

This kind of ideological condemnation of the Irish parliamentarians of the last century ignores and evades another facet of Ireland's successful 'importation' of British parliamentary institutions. It is evident that 'geography and history combine to make the British influence the most important in determining the pattern of much of Irish political thought and practice.'[5] The 'republican' tradition portrays this influence as both antagonistic and negative and therefore blames the parliamentarians for encouraging and promoting that influence.

But this is to ignore the very real Irish contribution to the making of British traditions. The relations between these two islands was always, to some extent, reciprocal and Ireland's experience of parliamentary politics derived not merely *from* but *within* the Westminster model. The burgeoning Irish nationalism of the nineteenth century affected the development of British democracy. In the last century, precisely as Britain itself was moving from the rule of a hereditary oligarchy to a more representative system of government, Ireland and its problems, its leaders and their tactics, played a major and sometimes critical role in Westminster. More governments were defeated on Irish issues than on any other topic debated in the Commons.

The Irish influence was creative as well as destructive. Indeed to this very day the shape of British parliamentary institutions bears the imprint of that Irish presence. If Westminster is the mother of modern parliaments, Ireland can claim to be as much midwife as offspring. O'Connell brought the power of organised mass democracy into British politics; Biggar's obstructionism helped to precipitate the procedural changes in Standing Orders that have ever since allowed the executive to control the business of parliament; Parnell gave an object lesson in the advantage of disciplined party votes in the House of Commons; the intransigence of the House of Lords on Irish Home Rule helped to sign the death warrant of its own power to oppose the policy of a cabinet. In the period from the Act of Union into the early years of the present century the 'Irish Question' and its advocates in parliament came to play an increasingly decisive role in internal British politics. The final achievement of 'normal' two-party stable government in Britain demanded the expulsion of the Irish representatives as an alien body.

This leads to the most fundamental and controversial assertion to be made for the Irish parliamentary tradition: that it was through parliament and largely within parliament that Ireland grew to both nationhood and independence.

Part of the legacy of 1916 has been the development of a sharp distinction—amounting to a contradiction—between the separatist and the parliamentary tradition in Ireland. The rhetoric of an old propaganda war has become confused with, and superimposed upon, the course of events. The idea of a distinct Irish nation and the achievement of its independence has been presented as the unique creation of Pearse's separatist, 'republican' tradition. Yet that minority line could scarcely claim a monopoly of separatism or of nationality. The actual development of the modern Irish community from a feudal society of depressed peasants owes as much to the parliamentarians as to the militants. The range of reforms achieved through parliament stretch from Catholic Emancipation to the Land Acts, the introduction of an educational scheme and of modern administration, the beginnings of electoral reform and of social welfare. The plight of nineteenth-century Ireland echoed Bishop Berkeley's query of a hundred years earlier: 'Whether there be any country in Christendom more capable of improvement than Ireland?' The parliamentarians might well have claimed to give a persuasive answer to his subsequent query: 'Whether my countrymen are not readier at finding excuses than remedies?'

Of course, this is not to suggest that the Irish parliamentary tradition has not been affected—perhaps the better word is infected—by the other, more militant tradition of violent protest and rebellion. Indeed, a deeply ambiguous attitude towards violence and towards those who favour the resort to arms has frequently marked Irish political leaders. On many occasions, it can be shown, the parliamentary presentation of the Irish case has been most formidable when backed by a strong under-current of extra-parliamentary agitation and support. Nor should it be forgotten that in terms of militancy and suffering, the 'republican' side have no monopoly of the record: O'Connell and Parnell, John Dillon and Griffith also served their time in jail and were also battered on the pillory of British public opinion for speaking out in defence of Irish interests and claims.

Nowadays, the ambivalence towards the threat of force and the political effectiveness of force is seen by many as the off-shoot of the enforced division of this island. A longer per-spective on the development of the Irish political tradition suggests deeper roots. Force has often been the only means of protest left to an oppressed people, the only weapon against privilege (itself supported by institutional violence), the only communication available to leaders denied a hearing. It has blossomed sporadically and tragically; it has rarely been domin-ant or desired by a majority. It has been contained in the past by a widely based and firmly founded attachment to consti-tutional procedures and representative values. It is hoped that this present critical examination of the Irish parliamentary tradition, in all its strengths and weaknesses, will help to estab-lish the capacity of the Irish system and the commitment of the Irish people not merely to contain but to eradicate that violence in the future.

King and Commons in Gaelic Ireland

FRANCIS JOHN BYRNE

THE present parliamentary institutions in Ireland derive much more from those of the United Kingdom of Great Britain and Ireland than from the medieval Irish parliament which reached its apogee in the days of Grattan. Still less have they any connection with the assemblies of Gaelic Ireland, although we have adorned them with the names of *Oireachtas, Dáil* and *Seanad*, and the head and members of government with the titles of *Taoiseach, Tánaiste* and *Aire*. Nevertheless, the existence of such native terms does demonstrate that collective decision-making was a part of Gaelic polity, and an examination of their origin may help us to appreciate the constitutional side of a culture which is often portrayed as violent and anarchic.

Of course a moment's thought will show us that an anarchic society is a contradiction in terms. Gaelic society was tough and conservative and has a recorded history of over a thousand years during which it converted to its own ways both Roman Christianity and Norman feudalism. It offered much satisfaction to some: it was cosy and familiar, rooted in the soil, at home in the local landscape and best suited to the economy of many districts.

In common with most human societies it was graded and stratified: everyone knew his place, but everyone also knew his fellows. Because it was so local—tribal if you like—all relationships, whether economic or political, were intensely personal. They were cemented by the reciprocal giving of rent, tribute and gifts. Patronage was sought, accepted and expected. Hospitality rather than punctuality was the politeness of its princes. A good name was the highest treasure and satire dreaded as the plague. Violence was commonplace, but restricted in scope. Those who take the sword shall perish by the sword, and the chief practitioners of violence—the royal dynasts—were its principal victims. Royal families proliferated and periodically pruned their own branches, thereby preserving the balance of nature and preventing great social change or revolution. The dynastic principle affected all the higher grades of society, from the ecclesiastical families of coarbs and erenaghs through the hereditary learned families of poets, lawyers and historians, down to the skilled craftsmen. Among the commoners land-holding was the badge of freedom, though cattle might be held in fief from a lord, and the land must remain in the male kindred and not be alienated by marriage, sale or gift.

This picture is generalised and takes no account of the changes which did affect even so conservative a society over a period of ten centuries. An adequate treatment of the Gaelic system at any period is beyond the scope of this essay.[1] But it is worth pondering whether there does not lurk, beneath all our anglicisation, a considerable latent inheritance from the Gaelic past.

The king or *rí* was the pivot of the community, the *tuath*. Although there were over-kings who had several tribal kings subject to them, and great provincial kings over these again, the essence of early Irish kingship was local. The high kings were themselves first and foremost kings of their own *tuatha*: they reigned but did not rule over others. There were as many as one hundred and fifty petty kings in early Ireland and a fluctuating number of great provincial kings. The high kingship of all Ireland was claimed by the Uí Néill of Tara as early as the seventh century, but they did not make it a reality until the middle of the ninth. In the eleventh century an elaborate theory and history of the high kingship was developed by the men of learning and this ideal became a potent ambition for the great kings of the twelfth century; but a monarchy, in the sense of a single ruler who had abolished all subordinate kingships, was never dreamt of nor thought desirable.

In fact, however, by the twelfth century the O'Briens in Munster, the MacMurroughs in Leinster, and the O'Connors in Connacht had made themselves rulers of their own provinces and their sub-kings appear rather in the role of officers of a semi-professional army than as kings leading their own peoples into battle on behalf of a mere overlord. The petty kings had lost political importance and are commonly referred to by the lower title of *tigerna* (lord) or *toísech* (leader). Increasingly from the ninth century onwards the over-kings attempt to put in their own nominees in the subject kingdoms and even to intrude members of their own dynasties. Such action always met with resentment and opposition, but while it was common practice in the twelfth century we have hints that it had not been unknown in the archaic period, though the process had been disguised by the manipulation of pedigrees.

The seventh-century brehon laws gave a full description of a society still in a tribal state, though even then they were probably archaic. The tribal king has very few governmental functions : he is essentially a war-leader, though he can only summon his people to a hosting on certain occasions and for a limited period and he has no army but their amateur forces. He presides at the *óenach* or assembly of all the *tuath*; he neither makes nor enforces law, but takes hostages and pledges from the people binding them to observe the traditional laws. With their consent he can promulgate certain new ordinances, notably church laws such as the *Cáin Phátraic*, and emergency regulations in time of plague, famine or invasion. His main function is to represent the *tuath* in its dealings with the outside world, whether in war or in peace. He makes treaties of peace or *cairdde* with the kings of other *tuatha*, or becomes the tributary of an over-king by a contract very similar to that between a client and his lord and personal in nature.[2] Meetings of this nature are usually referred to by the name of *dáil*; summit meetings between high kings, of which the annals tell us, may be called *ríg-dála* or *mór-dála*. In pagan times the king represented his people also in their dealings with the Otherworld, for there can be little doubt that Irish kingship was sacral.

Sacral kingship is attested over wide areas of Europe, the Near East and Africa, and its introduction to Ireland must ante-date the coming of the Celts, for as late as the sixteenth century Irish kings were most often inaugurated at sacred sites associated with neolithic burial mounds.

Sacral kingship is sometimes misunderstood. It gave the king certain priestly functions but did not mean that he was divine or considered to be a god either in his lifetime or after his death. Still less did it imply any 'divine right of kings'

Rather did it place the king in the front line of danger. His inauguration was a symbolic marriage with the goddess and he was held responsible for the fertility of the country. He could be a scapegoat. We have no explicit traditions that Irish kings were ever sacrificed, as were the early Swedish kings of Uppsala, but many of the Old Irish death-tales of early and prehistoric kings have an eerie atmosphere which suggests that such a memory lay just beneath the surface. Early Irish warfare was ritualistic and, as in a game of chess, normally ended with the death of one of the opposing kings. For this reason the frequency of royal deaths in battle or by assassination is not a fair guide to the instability of society. In archaic terms a violent death was almost the only positive act which public opinion approved of in a king. The earliest Irish tract on kingship, which in its first version is quite pagan in tone, in effect expects the king to do nothing; his Truth or Justice (*fír flathemon*), which is reiterated upon as his essential credential, really consists in his presiding as a symbol of the status quo over a rigidly hierarchical society.[3]

From the eighth century onwards we find churchmen, particularly the Culdees, urging kings to act as defenders of Christian principles and to reform society. The conversion of Ireland had owed little to the influence of the kings, who stood to lose their sacral aura by the new religion, and the early Irish synods were confided to the clergy. But in 780 the annals tell us of a meeting of the synods of the Uí Néill and the Leinstermen at Tara where there were many scribes and anchorites under the presidency of Dublitter of Finglas, a leading Culdee. This had been preceded by a campaign in the course of which the high king Donnchad had devastated the churches of Leinster. The synod evidently ended in a treaty of peace. By 804 the peace was over and the new high king Aed mac Néill was poised for war on the Leinster border at Dún Cuair near Enfield, where there was a meeting of the senators of the Uí Néill under Condmac, Abbot of Armagh. It may have been then that Aed became the first king of Tara to receive ecclesiastical consecration, whence his epithet Aed Oirdnide, 'the ordained'. The church of Armagh, having established its primacy in Ireland, was propagating the idea of a high kingship which would be its secular counterpart and the guarantor of its privileges. It was at Armagh in 851 that a *ríg-dál* was held where the king of Ulster for the first time acknowledged the suzerainty of the high king of Tara, Máelsechnaill mac Máele Ruanaid.[4]

The annalist who recorded the assemblies of 780 and 804 in Latin has confused the terms for synod and senate. The Old Irish word *senod* derives from the former, but in fact these meetings combined secular and religious functions. The ecclesiastical consecration of kings became fashionable at the end of the eighth century in imitation of the Carolingian practice. But in Ireland it was never more than a veneer—an optional extra to the pagan rites. These were normally carried out by the *fili*, the chief poet, whose inaugural ode was no mere praise-poem but actually invested the king with princely qualities by means of formulaic incantation. The king could lose his rank if formally satirised by the poet, who was the lineal descendant of the Celtic druids. Even where the poet was displaced by the church the ceremony became secularised again when carried out in the later middle ages by the hereditary coarbs, and the poet's white hazel wand remained the symbol of royal authority. Sometimes the greater rulers were inaugurated by their chief sub-king or by the head of the former royal family whose territory they had taken over, as when O'Neill in the sixteenth century was inaugurated by O'Kane and O'Hagan at Tullaghogue.

Attempts to Christianise kingship and society may not have been totally successful but they gave the kings new notions of power and authority. The period of the Viking wars brought closer connections between church and state which were not always to the advantage of religion, and the disturbances of the ninth and tenth centuries gave the kings a splendid opportunity to make use of their emergency powers and so create prerogatives based on a series of precedents. It is significant that some of the great provincial assemblies fell into decay at this period.

The *óenach* or assembly was the great annual gathering of the rural *tuath* on the occasion of some festival: many of the *óenaige* were held at the harvest-home of Lugnasad and lasted for a week.[5] Although the word *aonach* now means 'a fair', the Old Irish *óenach* was much more than this. It was very like the Icelandic *thing*. The king presided here over his people, and their laws and traditions were rehearsed. An old law tract says :

'It is the peoples (*tuatha*) who adopt the law; it is the king who confirms it.' Furthermore, 'it is the people's right that the king do not pledge them to hold an assembly which the whole *tuath* does not proclaim, but only those dwelling in the vicinity.' The king is said to have higher dignity than the *tuath*, but only because it is the *tuath* that has raised him to the kingship.[6]

We must not be too credulous as to the democratic nature of the assembly. Only the freemen had a voice, and they were all clients of one or other of the nobles, who in turn might be in clientship to the king or to a member of his dynasty. As in most medieval assemblies votes were weighed rather than counted.

The *óenach* provided an opportunity for the transaction of all sorts of business, law-suits, barter, match-making and general jollification. Games, and especially horse-racing, were an essential feature. In Latin writings the *óenach* is variously referred to as an *agon regale* (royal games), a *circus*, a *theatrum*, or a *spectaculum*. The games were funerary in origin, for the site of the fair was the pagan tribal cemetery. The story-telling which took place had a purpose, for the function of myth and legend was instruction rather than entertainment: the whole *óenach* was a recreation and renewal of the traditions of the tribe, providing the cohesion necessary in a scattered community. Even when a subject tribe had suffered defeat and loss of territory it clung to its *óenach*. The Ciarraige of central Connacht had by the eighth century been split into three geographically separate groups by the expansion of the dominant Uí Briúin Aí, but continued to meet at their old place of assembly, *Cara na Trí Tuath* (Carranadoe in Roscommon). Nenagh takes its name from the Oenach Téite of Ormond, which may have been the original assembly of the Múscraige.

Inter-tribal matters were discussed and the prestige of the high kings displayed at the great provincial assemblies of which the most famous were the Oenach Carmain and the Oenach Tailten or 'Fair of Teltown'. To preside at these was the prerogative of the kings of Leinster and Tara respectively. The annals tell us that the Oenach Tailten was not held in 873—an event without precedent—and that it was again neglected in 876, 878, 888, 889. This implies that it was an annual event, contrary to the later and more legendary accounts. The decline of the *óenach* was due to a number of causes rather than directly to the Viking wars, for this was a period of relative respite from their raids.

A primary cause was the increasing divarication of the Northern and Southern Uí Néill, between whom the high kingship of Tara now alternated regularly. In 916 the fair was revived by Niall Glúndub on his accession: his short reign and his death fighting the Dublin Norse at Islandbridge indicate his ambition to be a national monarch. But after the 'black fair of Donnchad' (*dub-óenach nDonnchada*) in 926, when the high king was attacked at the assembly by Niall's vigorous and ambitious son Muirchertach of the Leather Cloaks, the Oenach Tailten fell into total abeyance. The following years were marked by increasing alienation between the Northern and Southern Uí Néill even while they were in process of developing a real high kingship of Ireland. In 1007 the Fair was revived somewhat artificially by Máelsechlainn, who had recently been forced to acknowledge Brian Bóruma as high king of Ireland, having received no help from his northern cousins. An elaborate poem written for this occasion by Cúán Ua Lothcháin gives the pagan elements of fertility kingship a slight Christian veneer. He describes how the fair was founded in honour of the funeral games of the mythical goddess Tailtiu, making mention of the numerous grave-mounds on the site, and refers to the fact that Máelsechlainn was grandson both of the high king Donnchad and of Muirchertach who had broken up his assembly:

Four score years all but one year, Tailtiu lay deserted, alas how long! and the green of Cormac without a chariot.
Until there came in his serried array the king's comely-bearded grandson, and the son, who drinks heady mead, of the daughter of the king who thwarted the fair.
The king of Tara, chosen thence, Máelsechlainn of secure Slemun —like the river Euphrates rises on high the one champion of Europe . . .
He brought the cornfield of the Gaels out of danger, he brought Ireland out of shipwreck, he raised the Fair of Tailtiu from the sod . . .
Too little he counts it, what he has given us of good; little, what he has given us of corn, of milk, of malt . . .
Too little he thinks it, all that he contrives for our profit; too

little all the fish, the honey, the mast; too little, that we hold, when the corn-rick is roofed, an *óenach* for every *tuath* . . .

He desires, though our life here should be long before going otherwhere, that he should bring us into the house of God after achieving his design.

Christ be with Máelsechlainn of the sages! Christ with him against misfortune, against tribulation! Christ with him to protect and prosper him against war, against battle![7]

However, Cúán reproaches seven named kings for not attending the Fair, and he tactfully avoids all mention of Brian, whom Máelsechlainn had accompanied the previous year on a victorious circuit of the North. It is clear that Máelsechlainn could not have been holding the Oenach Tailten as a national assembly, unless we interpret the event as an attempt to rebel against Brian, and of this there is no hint elsewhere.

But during the next hundred years the scholars came to regard the now obsolete Oenach Tailten as a national assembly of all Irish kings under the high king of Tara. It was in this sense that it was again revived by Toirdelbach Ua Conchobair in 1120 when he made his unexpectedly successful bid for the high kingship of Ireland. The Fair was celebrated for the last time by his son Ruaidrí Ua Conchobair in 1168, when we are told that the attendant horses and cavalry covered an area over six miles in length.[8]

The decline of these great fairs as really live institutions rather than as occasions for political propaganda is part and parcel of the break-up of Old Irish society noticeable in the ninth and tenth centuries—a phenomenon which is only indirectly a result of the Viking wars. Recent evidence has made it more and more clear that in the seventh and eighth centuries the great monasteries had already become centres of trade and commerce: some of them developed their own fairs. In 800 the king of South Brega was killed when his horse threw him at the *óenach* of St Mac Caille of Lusk. We know that a fair was held at Roscrea on the feast of SS Peter and Paul, and the *óenach* of Colmán Ela was famous from an early date: presumably it was held at his monastery of Lynally, in a border district easily accessible from Munster, Leinster, Meath and Connacht. When later the Norse established their trading centres the market or *margad* (the very word is a borrowing

B

from Old Norse) must have replaced the *óenach* in many areas as the occasion for commercial transactions. At the same time the increasingly arbitrary powers exercised by the over-kings shows that they no longer had to rely so fully on popular assent, while the depression in the status of the ordinary freeman meant that his voice was of no account. A generation or more before the Anglo-Norman invasion the hosting of all the freemen had been replaced by a military aristocracy capable of sustaining long campaigns.

The *airecht*, later *oireacht*, was originally an assembly of the freemen to transact public business. From it derives the word *oireachtas*, which means both 'assembly, meeting' and 'sovereignty, power, nobility'. *Airecht* itself comes from *aire* 'a freeman', cognate with the Sanskrit *arya* which gives us the term Aryan, frequently used to describe the Indo-Europeans until brought into disrepute by the Nazis. In the ancient laws every freeman is an *aire*, and this sense is retained in the word *bóaire*, the typical strong farmer who is not a noble. But from quite early times the title of *aire* was restricted to the nobility, and it was from this class that the king's *airecht* was formed.

Airecht also has a wide range of meanings for different types of law-court: most legal disputes were submitted to a brehon for private arbitration, though in later times we hear of lords directing that a case be heard by a particular brehon.[9] Unlike the full *óenach*, an *airecht* could apparently be held as occasion demanded. Such assemblies were normally convened on a specified hill or *tulach*—a custom referred to in the laws themselves as well as in literature and attested at the very end of the Gaelic regime by Finglas, Chief Baron of the Exchequer, who says, 'Divers Irishmen doth observe and keep such laws and statutes which they make upon hills in their country firm and stable, without breaking them for any favour or reward.'[10]

The usual Irish way of indicating the submission of one king to another is to say that he went into his house. But in 1093 the Annals of Inisfallen record that Muirchertach Ua Briain made an expedition into Connacht, on which occasion the Síl Muiredaig, that is to say the O'Connors and their relations, 'came into his *airecht*'. Such a use of the word *airecht* to denote the immediate circle of chiefs under the authority of a paramount king became commoner as Gaelic society became less democratic and as feudal ideas infiltrated in the later middle ages. From the thirteenth century onwards the Irish lords were able to employ Scottish gallowglasses and other professional troops and became even less dependent upon popular favour and more able to impose their will upon their sub-kings. By the middle of the fourteenth century we find the word *oireacht* being used both of the sub-kings (*uir-ríogh*)—the English confused the two words and referred to both as 'urraght'—and of the territory over which, through them, the over-king held sway. Thus Oireacht Uí Chatháin was O'Kane's country in County Derry, and the barony of Iraghticonor represents the lordship of O'Connor Kerry. The *oireacht* of O'Donnell or O'Neill in the sixteenth century consisted of the chief men of their own kindred together with their subordinate chieftains and the captains of their gallowglasses.[11]

In theory Irish kingship was elective, although eligibility was confined to one particular kindred. We have no account of the details of election in the early period, whether it was by popular acclaim, a vote of the nobility, or an agreement between the rival claimants within the royal family. No doubt, as in most medieval kingships, all elements were present, but in practice the office must normally have gone to that member of the royal family who had most clients to support his claim. To avoid the bloodshed which so often ensued when rivals had equal forces, recourse was had to the election of a *tánaise* or heir-apparent during the life-time of a king. In the Elizabethan period, at any rate, the *tánaise*, like the king, had a special demesne granted to him in virtue of his office. The English were so struck by the custom that they used the word 'tanistry' for the whole Irish system of succession to land and office. Naturally, kings desired, and sometimes secured, the direct succession of their sons, but this was a tendency strongly resisted by other members of the family, as too long a monopoly of the fruits of office by any one branch would doom the others to relative obscurity. Thus the nomination of a *tánaise* could be a means whereby a rival branch of the family could stake its claims to the succession the next time round : the *tánaise* might well be leader of the opposition rather than deputy to his king.[12]

Even in the later middle ages the kings, though by no means

democratically elected, could not afford to override the vested interests of the establishment: the numerous members of their own kin, all eager to replace an unsatisfactory ruler, the clergy, and the learned classes. These formed the main resistance to Henry VIII's policy of surrender and regrant which tempted the kings to exchange their independent but limited power and wealth for the feudal privileges of full tenure under the king and assured succession to their eldest sons.

Yet at the height of the Nine Years' War O'Neill and O'Donnell acted in high-handed fashion. In 1595 Fenton reported to Burghley, 'O'Donnell has made a MacWilliam, an O'Dowde and a M'Dermode of such as were of his own faction, being persons base and far off from that dignity,' and we can read in detail the admiring account by Lughaidh O Cléirigh of how Red Hugh O'Donnell surrounded the ancient ring-fort of Eas Caoide where MacWilliam should be elected with his picked household troops and gallowglasses and chose Tibbot son of Walter Ciotach Burke to be proclaimed as MacWilliam, carrying the other claimants, 'older in years and greater in repute than he', off in captivity to Tír Chonaill, and how again in 1600 in a less bellicose but even more unscrupulous manner he took advantage of O'Neill's hospitality to proclaim his own nominee Cúchonnacht as Maguire.[13]

O'Donnell's right to have any say in these elections was based on extremely dubious historical claims to overlordship. But these were times of war and stress. Perhaps the fairest and shortest account of a typical election in later Gaelic Ireland is Sir Henry Sidney's comment on the failure of Conn son of An Calbhach to defeat the nomination of Red Hugh's father in 1567: 'This Chon looked to be the captain of the country, but the bishops and other landlords of the same elected Sir Hugh to be O'Donnell.'[14]

The Coming of Parliament

F. X. MARTIN, OSA

THE invaluable heritage bequeathed by medieval Europe to the modern world in a wide range of human activity was largely derived from the classical world of Greece and Rome, from Byzantium, from the Jews and Arabs, and was passed down through the Renaissance and Reformation to our own time. While the distinctive stamp of individuality which the men of the middle ages gave to each of these legacies is clearly discernible, the medieval era was not merely a period of transmission. There are at least two institutions—parliament and the university—which are peculiarly medieval. They were original contributions, one might say 'creations', of the medieval world. Both have become the birthright of practically every modern state. There is a close, and at times an intimate, connection between them.

Ireland was unfortunate in the circumstances in which these two institutions came to the island. There were several attempts to found a university at Dublin during the fourteenth and fifteenth centuries but they fizzled out due to a variety of causes—lack of money, the indifferent attitude of the English officials in Dublin and Westminster, the unsettled political condition of the country. Eventually, when a university was founded in 1591 it was an institution alien in religion and culture to the Gaelic Irish, alien even to much of what was held dear by the Anglo-Irish. It took more than three centuries for Trinity College, Dublin, to adapt itself to the soil in which it was rooted.

The history of parliament in Ireland is somewhat happier, though it too resisted due recognition of the rights of the Gaelic Irish in the medieval period. But, even during that time, the Anglo-Irish gradually became conscious of their separate identity from the English, and it was their efforts in parliament which set an example and demonstrated methods later used by the separatists to achieve independence.

One of the most insidious dangers in writing history is to read our ideas back into earlier periods. This is particularly true of the history of parliament, be it in England or Ireland. In neither country did parliament begin as a democratic institution in the modern sense of the word, any more than Magna Carta was a democratic document. Political parties and regular parliamentary opposition were undreamt of in medieval times. If this is borne in mind, the early development of parliament in Ireland will be not merely understood but appreciated.

How much do we know about the origins of parliament in Ireland? Undoubtedly it owed a great deal, indeed its very characteristics, to England; but parliament, despite a popular belief to the contrary, was not a development peculiar to England. The system of representation, which was to become an essential feature of parliament, was already firmly established in France, Italy and Spain by the thirteenth century. Nevertheless, it is true that it was from England that parliament came to Ireland and it is only against that immediate background that its origins and evolution are intelligible.

Every sensible monarch had need to consult with at least a selected number of his leading nobles. This was the royal council. Naturally, the first men the king turned to for advice and help were the friendly great barons, men of noble blood, considerable substance and assured loyalty. They had to be men he could depend on in a crisis, men with whom he had a fundamental bond of interests. The very nature of the feudal relationship between lord and vassals meant that their counsel had to be sought in affairs pertaining to common interests. This will immediately explain why—apart from many other reasons —the Gaelic Irish princes were unlikely to find a place in the medieval Irish council and parliament. What had they in common with a monarch who never visited the country, who could not speak their language, who belonged to a different culture, who administered a system of law utterly alien to the brehon legal code, and whose agents in Ireland could profit only at the expense of the native Irish?

But parliament was something more than a royal council.

The king found it convenient to call in not only the great barons but also representatives of other sections of the community, particularly when it was judged necessary, as in times of war and national crisis, to introduce further taxation and propose new laws affecting personal rights, property and income. Parliament in England began as a formal gathering before the king of groups of people, or their representatives, who were summoned to talk or parley—hence the word 'parliament'—with His Majesty. Initially, therefore, it was an expanded version of the royal council, men the king wished to consult, even if he had no intention of following their advice. Parliament was an occasion for doing justice, for hearing petitions from the king's subjects; in order to cope with these affairs he reinforced his council with representative people who were likely to ease his task. In England, by the year 1260, this representation took the form of two knights elected by the freeholders of each county, and of two burgesses (or citizens) from a number of towns.

In Ireland, the system of shiring, or division into counties, proceeded slowly. By the year 1307—a century and a half after the coming of the Normans to Ireland—there were as yet only twelve counties, Dublin, Kildare, Meath, Carlow, Louth, Waterford, Cork, Tipperary, Limerick, Kerry, Connacht and Roscommon.[1] There were also those four areas, the 'liberties'[2] as they were called, Kilkenny, Wexford, Trim and Ulster, which were under the control of the Anglo-Irish. Each one of the counties and liberties could be called upon to send representatives for consultation with the king's chief agent, the justiciar.

The towns were a further source from which the justiciar could draw members to attend his council and parliament. The first towns in Ireland had been founded by Norsemen, but these were constructed on the coast, and it is the Normans who must be given the credit for spreading towns and villages throughout the country. A number of the more important towns, such as Cork, Drogheda and New Ross, might be expected to send two representative burgesses to the parliament.

The barons and knights of the shire who attended the council, and its later development, the parliament, might cooperate with the royal officials or they might seek to promote the welfare of the Anglo-Irish (as they tended to do increasingly), but it would run against their very grain to lend themselves to decisions which would benefit the native Irish. There could, in any case, be little sympathy for the Gaelic Irish in a council dominated by the justiciar and his English officials, whose first duty was to look to the king's good.

The overwhelming majority of the townsfolk were Anglo-Irish, which meant that they, like the knights of the shire, were men committed to either the royal or the Anglo-Irish interest.

The royal and Anglo-Irish interests, however, were not necessarily identical. Though the king might, and in certain circumstances did, see the advantages in favouring the Gaelic chieftains, this could never make sense to the colonists whose very existence was constantly in threat from the natives.

Since the coming of the Normans to these islands, the king in England, as also his justiciar in Ireland, had always found it necessary to consult the council. It was an obvious method of government, a very limited sharing of power. But parliament was another story. It was only with the victory of the English barons in 1258 that Henry III was forced to accept at Oxford the provision that there would be three parliaments a year 'to treat of the common business of the realm and of the king' and to be attended by the councillors. The name 'parliament' was officially adopted; the assembly was organised and given a constitution; and the history of parliament dates from that year, 1258.

It was specifically stated then that provisions of Oxford were also to be applied to Ireland, and an apparent consequence of the events at Oxford was the Parliament which met at Castledermot, Co. Kildare, in mid-June 1264. This is the first assembly in Ireland to which the term 'parliament' can be applied with some certainty. Unfortunately, the evidence is so fragmentary that we know little of its proceedings. The justiciar Richard de la Rochelle, and his council were present as an essential feature of the parliament and, although twenty-six knights were also in attendance, there is no reason to suppose they were elected representatives of the commons. Further meetings of parliament were held at irregular intervals—five more are recorded before the year 1289, and thereafter they met regularly and frequently. Yet, it is not until the Parliament of 1297 that we find mention of knights representing counties and liberties; they were joined in 1299 by representatives of the towns, and the Parliament of 1300 saw both knights of the shire and town representatives present. Already by the year 1275, it had been stated officially on more than one occasion that certain royal ordinances had been issued on the advice of Edward I and of 'the whole community of Ireland'. Although, of course, 'the whole community' meant only the Anglo-Irish, and in particular the lords and prelates, the phrase indicates that a fundamental principle of representation—namely consent of, or at least consultation with, the governed within the limits of the Anglo-Irish world—was being accepted by the royal administration.

It was in the closing years of the thirteenth century that parliament in Ireland rapidly evolved into the form which it preserved substantially for the rest of the medieval period. While this must be seen as a development parallel with the evolution of parliament in England, there was the additional fact that one strong Welshman, John Wogan, played a decisive part in Irish parliamentary affairs. Appointed justiciar in 1295, he ruled for sixteen years, but it was not merely the unusual length of his period as governor of the country which gave him an advantage. He was endowed with keen intelligence and commonsense, was dedicated to the interests of his king, indefatigable in the council-chamber and equally vigorous in the field (though not always successful in these military affairs). He had a practical purpose in summoning parliaments—he wanted men, money and supplies for the king.

Edward I, still consumed with ambition in his old age, was at war on three fronts—with the Scots, the Welsh and the French. In 1295 he directed Wogan, then newly-appointed justiciar, to raise a force of ten thousand men. It was a tall order and could not be fulfilled without the full cooperation of the Anglo-Irish community. This explains why Wogan summoned a Parliament to Dublin in 1297, calling on the great barons, the bishops and a number of monastic prelates to attend. He also summoned the sheriffs of the counties of Dublin, Louth, Kildare, Waterford, Tipperary, Cork, Limerick, Kerry and Roscommon, as well as the corresponding officials—the seneschals—from the liberties of Meath, Wexford, Carlow,

Kilkenny and Ulster. In addition, he enjoined that each sheriff and seneschal should see that his county or liberty would organise, with the consent of that area, the election of two representatives fully empowered to act on behalf of their community. This latter injunction embodied the beginning of genuine representation; it was further extended when representatives of the towns were summoned to the Parliament of 1299 and when both counties and towns had their representatives at the Parliament of 1300. Such composition of the parliament had apparently become established practice by the time parliament met in 1310.

Nobody can deny that a change took place with the Parliaments of 1297, 1299, 1300 and 1310, but historians have differed sharply on its significance. Those of the older school—Orpen, Curtis and Maude Clarke, still under the influence of William Stubbs—saw these parliaments, particularly that of 1310, as the Irish equivalent of the English 'Model Parliament' of 1295, when the royal summons drew barons, bishops, abbots, earls, knights, burgesses, and even representatives of cathedral chapters and parishes into one assembly. The English parliamentary historian Stubbs had formulated a theory in his *Constitutional History of England*, published in 1873–78, in which he saw a conscious 'grand design' on the part of Edward I so that the whole nation could participate in the government of the realm. A reaction against this view as applied to Ireland was perhaps inevitable, but it gained almost irresistible force when it was led by Richardson and Sayles, the two greatest living experts on the medieval Irish parliament. They appeared to deliver the *coup de grâce* when, in 1952, they pronounced in inexorable tones that 'For such a view, it need hardly be said, there is no contemporary warrant, and it involved an introduction into the thirteenth century of ideas of a later age.'[3] It is true that Curtis, in particular, may have been too enthusiastic about the parliaments of these years, especially in his *History of Medieval Ireland*, published in 1923, but his fault was perhaps more in the terms he used than in the substance. Yet, however much Richardson and Sayles may dismiss the allegedly democratic composition of these parliaments, there are certain aspects which cannot be lightly swept aside.

It was patently true that the representation was not democratic in the modern sense, but was rather representative oligarchy. Yet one cannot overlook the fact that the Parliament of 1310 was, within the context of the Anglo-Irish world, the most representative the country had ever seen. It should be remembered that the Anglo-Irish then controlled almost three-quarters of Ireland: by 1307 the king's writ was being observed in as remote a spot as Dunquin, Co. Kerry. The Gaelic world, within its limitations, had never summoned such a representative assembly. When Wogan issued his writs for a Parliament to meet at Kilkenny in February 1310, he called together eighty-eight barons, as well as bishops, prelates, two knights of each shire, and two representatives from a number of towns, 'having full power on behalf of the said communities to parley, treat, and ordain with the justiciar, the council and the nobles of the land, upon certain matters'.

It is true that parliament was still mainly judicial and not legislative, that the justiciar's council dominated the assembly, and that the representatives summoned from the shires and towns were expected to listen and agree, not to debate and query. But, though they did sing dumb on these occasions, they were there as representatives of their various communities, and inevitably the day came, a bare generation later, when they were not content to sit and nod assent to taxation and other legislation, but were to debate and query and even to oppose the justiciar. This development constituted a measure of popular participation in governmental affairs and, though it was still confined to the Anglo-Irish, it was, many centuries later, to be adopted and adapted by the native Irish in their struggle for independence.

If, on the other hand, it is necessary to modify the severe criticism which Richardson and Sayles levelled at Curtis and Maude Clarke for reading too much into the Parliaments of 1297, 1299, 1300 and 1310, it is likewise necessary to point out how unreal are the strictures of the nationalist commentators who denounce these parliaments because they did not include representatives of the Gaelic Irish. There is no evidence that the native Irish wished or sought for such representation; even at this stage they did not think in terms of a national representative assembly. The question of their attendance never arose in 1297. Indeed, parliament in that year stated curtly that those Anglo-Irish who insisted on wearing Irish garb and long locks of hair would be treated as Irish. Yet this must not be taken as a declaration of racial war between the two peoples. The Anglo-Irish were on the defensive, anxious to preserve their colony intact; the Statute of Kilkenny was already in the air. That the King of England neither despised nor underestimated the Gaelic Irish is evident from the summons to Wogan in 1301 when the justiciar was ordered to appear with all the faithful nobility of Ireland: royal orders for support were sent to a hundred and eighty leaders in Ireland, including O'Connor, O'Brien, O'Neill, McCarthy and seventeen other Gaelic princes. And they rallied to the king's support. At least in a crisis, the King of England was willing to accord some recognition to the Irish.

If the colonists were on their guard against the native Irish, as was indicated in the Parliament of 1297, they were likewise conscious that they were a middle nation, distinct from the English. Their attitude blazed forth in a spurt of indignation at the Parliament of 1324 when the assembly was discussing the fascinating case of Dame Alice Kyteler, the much-married Kilkenny lady who was accused of being a witch.[4] Her principal accuser was Richard Leatherhead, the English Franciscan Bishop of Ossory, while a principal protagonist in her favour was Sir Arnold le Poer, Seneschal of Kilkenny. Le Poer, riled beyond measure by the Bishop's pursuit of Dame Alice, denounced Leatherhead at a session of the parliament in Kilkenny as an Englishman, a foreign intruder who dared to describe the Irish as heretics and to disregard Ireland's title, 'Island of Saints'. Le Poer was obviously playing on the prejudices of his listeners when he attacked the Bishop in these terms, but it is highly significant that they made sense to an Anglo-Irish audience. In the account of the public confrontation between le Poer and Leatherhead, we are also incidentally given an unexpected picture of the Irish parliament in one stage of evolution. We are told that, while the justiciar and his council were meeting in private, the barons, the bishops and the representatives of the shires and towns were assembled in the hall, where they were addressed by both le Poer and Bishop Leatherhead. Plainly, the important business was being conducted by the justiciar and his councillors behind closed doors while the other members of parliament were allowed to indulge themselves in more colourful and less important affairs.

The power structure of the parliament is incidentally illustrated by one of the most celebrated of medieval Irish documents, the Remonstrance of the Gaelic princes to Pope John XXII in 1317.[5] This outspoken condemnation of English rule in Ireland cites examples of the discrimination by English and Anglo-Irish against the natives of the country. It refers in particular to a statute passed at the Parliament meeting in Kilkenny in 1310 forbidding monasteries in the colony to receive Irishman into their communities. Elsewhere in the document the Gaelic princes state that they had recourse in vain for redress of this and other wrongs to the king and his council. These two statements shed a shaft of light on what had already become established practices—the importance of parliament in formulating legislation, and the fact that, in the ultimate analysis, the real power nevertheless remained in the hands of the king (or the justiciar) and his council. Parliament was not regarded as *the* power in the land.

While the Remonstrance criticises the behaviour of the English in Ireland, the main brunt of the attack is explicitly directed against the Anglo-Irish. They are described as a 'middle nation . . . differing so widely in their principles of morality from those of England and all other nations that they may be called a nation of the most extreme degree of perfidy. . . By their scheming they have alienated us from the King of England, hindering us from holding our lands as voluntary tenants under the Crown'. It was the Anglo-Irish, weakened by the Bruce invasion, assailed on every side by the resurgence of the native Irish, treated with suspicion by the royal officials from England, who now organised the Irish parliament so that it became a powerful critic of English administration in Ireland. The Gaelic Irish were, in their own words, willing to become loyal subjects of the Crown. A new pattern was thus introduced into Irish history, one with momentous consequences. All patriotism, be it Anglo-Irish or Gaelic, has a hard core of self-interest, and while it is true that this was the principal motive of the Anglo-Irish, it is equally a fact that parliamentary opposition to government in the English interest begins with the colonists of this period.

The Anglo-Irish were not without reason for their resentment. Though they had loyally supported the young King Edward III in his war with the Scots, His Majesty and Council in England decided in May 1338 that none but native Englishmen should hold legal offices in Ireland, and that a thorough inquiry was to be made into all grants of lands and liberties granted by the King and his father. Such an inquiry would jeopardise many lands held by the Anglo-Irish. Resentment came to a head when an adjourned session of parliament was being held at Kilkenny in November 1341. The Anglo-Irish decided to go over the head of the justiciar, Sir John Morice, whom they despised as a low-born English knight, and appeal directly to the king. They sent two envoys to Edward III in which they expounded their case with vigour and cogency. They made no bones about the lamentable condition of the country, and laid the blame square and straight on the shoulders of the king's ministers.[6]

A third of the country, previously in the hands of the king's subjects, had fallen to the natives. The royal castles at Roscommon, Rindown and Athlone, as well as Bunratty, had been lost. Gone also were the wardships in Connacht and Ulster, with other royal estates and castles. But the real evil, they averred, was not pressure from the Gaelic Irish but the corruption of government officials. Ministers heavily in debt would not meet their responsibilities and the burden fell on the people; ministers were accumulating offices and fees; they did private deals with the native Irish and prevented the colonists from recovering their lands; money services were being levied needlessly, sometimes irregularly, and without the consent of those concerned. Absentees were the curse of the country, leaving their properties undefended but squeezing all possible profit from them. The rights of His Majesty's subjects were being overriden roughshod; nobles of the land were seized without due process of law, imprisoned and detained at the whim of royal officials. Persons indicted of felonies in Ireland were being summoned to answer the charges in England.

But for all their sharp complaints, the petitioners took their stand firmly on the rock of loyalty to the monarch. They declared bluntly : 'Scots, Gascons and Welsh have often levied war against the Crown, but your loyal English of Ireland have ever been true subjects and, please God, will always be so.' They went on to comment that the reward for the faithful Anglo-Irish subjects had been a succession of grasping officials sent from England, ignorant of Irish affairs, intent only on lining their pockets by oppressing the king's loyal followers. They pointedly asked how it was that these officials, who arrived with empty purses in Ireland, could, even in the space of one year, wax fat in substance while His Majesty grew not one penny the richer.

The Parliament of 1341 at Kilkenny and the petition which was sent from it to Edward III were interpreted by the historian Edmund Curtis as part of a patriotic process. He saw the rebellious Earl of Desmond as the inspiration of what he described as the 'Patriot Party'. It is easy to decry his view, but it is only fair to remember that he qualified his statement with the comments that

The Patriots of the fourteenth century, like those of the eighteenth century were loyal to the Crown, but hostile to English ministries; they were strong in protest but feeble in suggestion; they were preoccupied with their class interest, that of an ascendancy bent on the domination of Ireland; and they said nothing about the native race whose emancipation they alone could achieve.[7]

The fiery yet respectful petition to Edward III owed its impetus to the fact that it had behind it the burning resentment of the entire Anglo-Irish colony. It was not sent, as Curtis believed, by the notoriously turbulent Maurice, Earl of Desmond, but was brought to the king by the chancellor of Ireland, and was addressed from 'the prelates, earls, barons and the commonalty of the land of Ireland'.[8] The feelings of the Anglo-Irish were expressed in their annals :

The land of Ireland stood at this moment at the point of breaking for ever from the hands of the King of England.[9]

Edward took the point and replied on 14 April 1343, conceding most of the issues contested by the Anglo-Irish. Curtis, for all his minor errors, had seized on an essential point when he described the indignant petition from parliament in 1341 as 'this first remonstrance of the Anglo-Irish against domination from England'.[10]

Much of the petition of 1341 to Edward III was devoted to

taxation and other such exactions. The problem of local and parliamentary taxation becomes increasingly important in the development of the Irish parliament. Taxation was first operated on the basis of negotiation between local communities and the king, and the practice of parliamentary taxation on a national basis does not appear to have been seriously attempted until the Irish Parliament of 1300, when representatives of counties and towns were summoned specifically for this purpose. But even then, the justiciar, John Wogan, found that the most acceptable and, therefore, the most profitable system would be to conduct a series of individual bargains with urban and rural communities, as also with the clergy of each diocese. (The Irish have always preferred the individual and particular approach.)

If money and supplies were to be sought from the colonists, it was inevitable that, in return, they would demand more power, as well as recognition of their 'rights and liberties'. This became evident when a tough and shrewd justiciar, Sir Thomas Rokeby, set about governing the country in 1349. He resolutely fought the Gaelic Irish, notably the O'Briens of Thomond, but was willing to make agreements with them. He found it still more important to make agreements with the Anglo-Irish. A Parliament was held at Kilkenny in October 1350, with Rokeby presiding, at which twenty-five ordinances were enacted for the government of the country. The most important was confirmation for Ireland of Magna Carta. The confirmation was almost common form, but in the circumstances and with the ordinances it guaranteed the position of the Anglo-Irish; and the government of the colony was largely in their hands from 1355 to 1361, with Maurice of Desmond, Maurice of Kildare and James of Ormond each in turn playing his part as justiciar.

There has been so much concentration upon the Statute of Kilkenny of 1366 that it is not generally realised that its most striking provisions had already been promulgated by the king's great council of Ireland in 1351 when Rokeby was justiciar. In this he undoubtedly had the support of the majority of the Anglo-Irish. However much a Desmond, a Kildare or an Ormond might flirt with Gaelic culture and associate with Gaelic princes (and princesses), he remained at heart a colonist, conscious of his debt to England. It was the Anglo-Irish who were responsible for a series of ordinances, grouped under the general heading, *Decree for the Government of Ireland,* authorised by the English king and his council and promulgated in 1357. These edicts were aimed to reform administrative abuses; they recognised the right of the colonists to be ruled with their own consent and to have the status of English-born subjects. While a further royal ordinance of March 1360 banned the Gaelic Irish from holding any office in church or state or in the towns, the Anglo-Irish had already been assured that they were to be accorded the laws, rights and customs of true Englishmen.

Seen in this context, the Statute of Kilkenny should come as no great surprise, any more than it was to the Ireland of 1366. The view that the Statute of Kilkenny was the handiwork of an impulsive English prince, bent on coercing the country, is an illusion. Lionel of Clarence, second son of Edward III, came to the country late in 1361 as King's Lieutenant, to subdue the Gaelic Irish and to curb the Anglo-Irish. He was not without a vested interest since he was married to the Anglo-Irish Elizabeth de Burgo, heiress to the Earldom of Ulster and the Lordship of Connacht. A show of military force served, at least temporarily, to quieten the native Irish, but his more important tasks were to ensure good government in the colony and the loyalty of the Anglo Irish. It was with these objects in mind that Lionel presided over a Parliament at Kilkenny in February 1366 which is commonly regarded as a landmark in Irish history. The determination of Lionel and his council, backed by the representatives from the 'loyal' shires and towns, explains the firm policy enacted by parliament. The statute codified in thirty-five chapters much of what had already been enacted in previous Irish parliaments and, in some cases, in English parliaments. Undoubtedly, the most striking provisions were those which forbade the colonists to mix with the Gaelic Irish or to adopt their culture in any of its forms, be it by marriage, concubinage, fosterage, the use of brehon or marcher law, the support of Gaelic minstrels, rhymers or storytellers, or the use of Gaelic surnames. Any colonist who adopted the Gaelic language, assumed a Gaelic surname, or practised Gaelic games, such as hurling, or their habit of riding without saddle, was to be attainted and his lands forfeited until he returned to English ways of life. Other enactments were directed specifically against the Gaelic Irish, who were excluded from cathedrals, benefices and religious houses. The Gaelic Irish of the marcher or frontier lands were also prohibited from pasturing on the lands of the colonists or of their Gaelic allies.

Nationalist historians have made more than full capital of these enactments. Hayden and Moonan, who have been the staple diet of history teachers in secondary schools for almost two generations, described it as a 'malicious statute', whose purpose was to keep the island permanently divided into 'two hostile nations'.[11] Curtis rightly pointed out that the purpose of the statute was *not* to declare war upon the Gaelic race and culture but to prevent the colonists from going native and thereby losing their allegiance to the Crown. Richardson and Sayles, and later Otway-Ruthven, showed that there was little new in the statutes—some of them had been first enacted in 1297. More recently, Dr Geoffrey Hand has given proper perspective to the problem by placing emphasis on what he aptly terms 'the forgotten statutes of Kilkenny'.[12] He demonstrated that the enactments dealing with Gaelic Irish were a minority in the context of the whole series promulgated at Kilkenny; English lawbreakers, negligent and rapacious royal officials were likewise dealt with. When all the commentators—Curtis, Richardson and Sayles, Otway-Ruthven and, more recently, Hand—have had their say, we must return to the gritty fact that the purpose and spirit of the Statute of Kilkenny are summoned up in the preamble, which states in clear terms that the main problem for His Majesty's government in Ireland was the inroads made on the English colony by the Gaelic culture so that allegiance 'due to Our Lord the King and the English laws are put into subjection and decayed, and the Irish enemies exalted and raised up contrary to reason'.

The statute, with its detailed instructions on how the enactments were to be enforced and regularly reaffirmed, was solemnly promulgated. Lionel, weary from his effort but, no doubt, consoled that parliament under his guidance had made a firm and apparently practicable stand on principle, left Ireland in November 1366 but was dead within less than two years, in his thirtieth year. It is a quirk of fate that his mortal remains are in the care of Irish friars in the Augustinian priory at Clare, Suffolk, in England. Even before his untimely end in Italy the very statute he had so resolutely sponsored was, in effect, flouted at the highest level of government in Ireland. His successor was Gerald, third Earl of Desmond, known affectionately to the Gaelic Irish as *Gearóid Iarla*, who composed Gaelic verse with facility, but he lasted only two years as justiciar. He was replaced in 1369 by William of Windsor, a man who had the ability and the resolution to achieve the positive aspects of the Statute of Kilkenny, namely government which would be firm and just. If it were firm, it would rally the Anglo-Irish to a sense of their English heritage, if just, it would not unduly alienate the Gaelic Irish; if profitable, it would pay its own way (which administration in Ireland had not been doing). Windsor had come to Ireland, with Lionel of Clarence, as a soldier and knew what was involved in trying to govern the country. It was too much to expect that Ireland would, as in the thirteenth century, contribute to the war-effort in France but, at least, it must pay its way and not be a drag on English finances already sorely strained by the costly campaigns on the continent. But, in order to place Windsor in a position of strength, the English government had initially to back his enterprise to the tune of £20,000—a considerable sum in those days. After that, he must stand on his own financial legs. He had, therefore, to turn to the colonists for support and, since he could expect no adequate gifts, he had, of necessity, to use taxation. But the Anglo-Irish were not merely passive subjects and, to obtain their consent, he had to summon parliaments and great councils. It was Windsor's efforts to raise money through taxation which gave a new prominence to the House of Commons and accelerated the evolution of the Irish parliament.

William of Windsor was in his own day a sign of contradiction and is still a figure of controversy among historians. A contemporary chronicler, in the Annals of St Mary's Abbey, Dublin, described him as 'too grasping' because of the way he turned the financial screws on the colonists. Forty years ago, Maude Clarke, having made the first critical investigation of his career in Ireland, concluded that, since it was due to him that 'the Irish parliament acquired the shape, coherence and functions which it retained until the Reformation', it would be almost correct to style him 'the true founder of the Irish parliament'.[13] This has been challenged by Richardson and Sayles as an exaggerated view, and it has remained for Professor James Lydon in recent years to give a balanced statement on Windsor's career in Ireland and, in particular, his dealings with the Irish parliament.[14]

Within less than five years Windsor summoned seven parliaments and five great councils. His frank purpose in collecting together the barons, the bishops, prelates, knights of the shires and representatives of the towns and of the lower clergy, was to extract money from them. It suited all parties to stress that, where taxation was concerned, the representatives of the commons must be consulted. It meant that the nobility need not bear more than their due share of the burden; it gave the commons an opportunity to express their importance. When Windsor called a council of barons in 1371 to raise a subsidy, his request was cut short with the reply that such a financial grant required the Commons present in a full session of parliament.

It was accepted that the representatives of the commons had full power to act for their respective shires, towns, boroughs and (in the case of the lower clergy) the dioceses. The English government attempted to take advantage of this procedure in 1376 when it found that the Irish parliament refused a subsidy. The royal agent, Nicholas Dagworthy, produced a royal decree commanding that Ireland should send sixty representatives— two proctors from each diocese, two knights from each county and two representatives from each city and borough—to consult with the king and his council in England. Obviously, it was intended that these delegates would be intimidated or awed into submission in the presence of the king.

The Anglo-Irish had a twofold answer. Firstly, the Irish parliament stated the all-important principle that it was under no obligation to send representatives to England. Secondly, though it did in fact send representatives, it omitted to give them full power to act on their behalf; this was a clear demonstration that ultimate power was to rest with the local communities which sent the representatives. Here, indeed, a democratic principle was expressed, no matter how limited may have been the franchise. The delegates went to England and agreed to a subsidy, but they also managed to secure the removal of a number of the chief English officials in Ireland. Even William of Windsor was superseded in office later in 1376 by the Earl of Kildare. The Anglo-Irish, through the medium of parliament, had taken their stand and made an effective protest.

The fourteenth century was a time of the most significant developments for the Irish parliament; it was during the tensions and disputes of this period that several features emerged which eventually distinguished the Irish from the English parliament. Two have already been referred to in passing—great councils and clerical proctors—and it would be well at this point to explain their distinctive roles.

It may seem to confuse the whole picture if we state that in Ireland a great council was in many ways as powerful as a parliament and could be as representative. How then, it may be asked, did it differ from a parliament?

Parliament and the great council have been described by Richardson and Sayles as twin institutions. Were they identical twins? Both parliament and the great council stemmed from the same source—the king's consultors and advisors who formed the inner or royal council. In England, parliament acquired two functions as its exclusive activities, taxation and legislation, but in Ireland these powers also remained within the competence of the great council. However, parliament had a higher status than a great council, as indicated by the period of summons which must be forty days for a parliament, but could be less for a great council. Yet the forty days' requirement could be (and often was) a drawback in a country like Ireland where recurrent crises demanded the rapid assembly of the royal officials with other representatives to deal with a grave or desperate situation. Hence one reason for the extensive use of the great council in Ireland by the justiciar or the king's lieutenant; occasionally, but not frequently, it was an alternative to parliament. It was during the period 1400–50 that the competence of the great council to pass legislation and grant taxes was fully recognised.

Another feature of the Irish parliament—clerical proctors—merits attention, for their eventual recognition as a separate entity meant that the Irish parliament had three 'Houses', of Lords, Commons, and lower clergy.[15]

In both England and Ireland bishops and certain abbots sat as spiritual peers, a powerful group if need be, in the House of Lords. In Ireland clerical proctors, the representatives of the lower clergy, participated directly in the civil legislature. Furthermore, at least by the fifteenth century, they sat as a separate house, a privilege which their fellow-clerics in England did not enjoy. It was not special reverence in Ireland for holy orders which dictated the difference. The Irish clergy literally paid for their privilege; the proctors were summoned apparently in order to obtain consent of the lower clergy to taxation. They were called (perhaps for the first time) to the Parliament of 1371, and thereafter became a normal part of the Irish parliaments.

The privilege of a separate 'House' was only gradually acquired and, unlike the knights of the shire, the number of clerical proctors was neither fixed nor uniform. Proctors came from dioceses and cathedral chapters, but not all dioceses and chapters were represented—the political state of the country goes far to explain the discrepancies. The maximum number of dioceses represented appears to have been eighteen, but Armagh sent only one proctor, while Dublin had four representatives—two for the diocesan clergy and a further pair for the cathedrals of Christ Church and St Patrick's. Unrest in the country undoubtedly affected the attendance; in 1420–21 only twenty-seven proctors were in attendance, and the same number in 1450.

How active were the proctors? Understandably, their interests, and consequently their participation in parliamentary affairs, were limited. Their consent was certainly sought for taxation, and they appear to have joined in matters of general interest on various occasions, but this activity was intermittent. The precise constitutional position of the clerical proctors was never clarified, but their participation in parliamentary affairs was undoubtedly accepted. It was only when their persistent opposition to the ecclesiastical legislation of the Reformation Parliament of 1536–37 proved a grave embarrassment to royal policy that the government adopted the highly questionable solution of abolishing the clerical proctors, by reference to the absence of any such separate house in the English parliament. There was no opposition to Henry VIII's legislation from either

Lords or Commons in the Irish parliament. Let it be remembered to the credit of the clerical proctors that they went out with a bang, not with a whimper, on this their last performance as a body.

During the twenty years from 1374 to 1394 English control over Irish affairs steadily disimproved. It is unnecessary to recite the chopping and changing of justiciars between 1376 and 1394 —now an Anglo-Irish lord such as Kildare (1376) or Ormond (1376–77), then an English peer, such as Edmund Mortimer, Earl of March (1379–81), of royal blood and with a legitimate claim to the Lordships of Trim and Laoighis as well as the Earldom of Ulster, then a highly-placed royal favourite such as Robert de Vere, Earl of Oxford (1385–87). It was to little effect. England had its own fierce distractions at home and on the continent, the colonists in Ireland were retreating dispiritedly, the Gaelic Irish advancing apparently inexorably. As the area in Ireland controlled by the royal government diminished, so did the power of the parliament. Between those years (1374 and 1394) parliaments and great councils met, the parliaments with diminishing membership, the great councils with increasing unreality. Then, in October 1394, the great change came with the arrival in Ireland of King Richard II.

A fleet of some five hundred ships sailed into Waterford to land the greatest army ever seen in Ireland : at least eight thousand men—knights, men-at-arms, archers and all the paraphernalia of war. The very size and efficiency of the army intimidated and flattered the Gaelic Irish; the Anglo-Irish exulted that the king himself had finally come. The logic of Richard's policy was simple. He would secure the submission of all his subjects, Anglo-Irish and Gaelic. His writ would run throughout the country. The 'land of peace' would be extended to cover the whole island, the hitherto unconquered territory would be divided into counties, given its sheriffs and royal officials; parliament and great councils would be as fully established as in England. The rule of law, of civility, of loyalty would prevail. But to ensure that this would come to pass the country must first acknowledge the authority of the king. This he achieved by his impressive demonstration of military force. The Gaelic princes, even Art MacMurrough Kavanagh, submitted fully. Only Turlough O'Donnell and his ally, Maguire, remained uncommitted, and it was their geographic isolation rather than any nationalist factor which kept them from paying court to Richard II.

It is significant that when Turlough O'Connor Don submitted he took an oath which obliged him to be faithful in all things, to attend King Richard and his heirs and their parliament and council, whenever they should summon him. The climax of these submissions took place in Christ Church Cathedral, Dublin, on 25 March 1395 when the four Irish kings, O'Connor of Connacht, O'Neill of Tyrone, O'Brien of Thomond and MacMurrough of Leinster were knighted, and entertained to a royal banquet in Dublin Castle. The interpreter between Richard and the Gaelic kings was James, Earl of Ormond, who was equally fluent in Norman-French and Irish.

All was settled in theory and on parchment. The Gaelic Irish would be welcome to the benefits of English law and to participate in the Irish parliament; but parliament for all the people of Ireland could not operate until English law and custom ran throughout the land. That was the rub. Richard left Ireland, and he also left the Gaelic princes unchanged in heart and in their way of life. Nevertheless, his considerable achievement would probably have been crowned with success if royal sheriffs had then been established in the territories of the four provinces of Ireland. But his manifold political distractions in England and his growing financial embarrassment gave Ireland a minor place in his preoccupations. When he returned, an indignant monarch, in 1398, he had a reduced army and a restricted purse. Art MacMurrough Kavanagh played a large part in toppling Richard from his English throne.

When William of Windsor withdrew from Ireland in 1376, the decline of the Irish parliament had begun in earnest. It became more and more an instrument of the occasional English justiciar or, more commonly, of the powerful Anglo-Irish lords. The power of the commons declined as fewer and fewer representatives attended from shires and towns. A desperate lack of financial resources seems to have been the main immediate problem of the government. If it were not possible to collect taxes effectively, there would also be little point in calling parliament to grant the taxes. There could be no future for parliament in Ireland until the country was conquered.

4

A Century of Decline

ART COSGROVE

THROUGHOUT the fifteenth century, parliament in Ireland was, almost exclusively, an Anglo-Irish body. The attempt by Richard II in 1395 to include leading Irish chieftains in the assembly came to nothing, for, although a number of chieftains had then promised that they would come to the king's parliament or council whenever they were required, there is no evidence that any Irish chieftain was ever summoned or ever attended parliament during this period. The only representatives of the Irish nation who might be required to attend were ecclesiastics, in particular Irish bishops and abbots who were entitled to be summoned as peers of parliament. That they occasionally obeyed such citations can be inferred from the complaint of the English parliament in 1416 that some Irish bishops brought with them to parliament Irish servants who discovered the secrets of the English and reported them to the king's Irish enemies. This fear that the presence of Irish ecclesiastics, or indeed of any Irish, would weaken the security of the colony was naturally prevalent among the colonists themselves. As Archbishop Fleming of Armagh explained in 1409, it was not customary to issue a summons to the Dean and Chapter of Armagh to attend parliament; for they were pure Irish (*meri Hibernici*) living among the Irish and it was not fitting that the king's council should reveal its secrets to them. Clearly, a parliament which had as one of its functions the discussion of measures against the 'Irish enemies' would not welcome the presence at its meetings of these who were thought to be closely associated with the enemy. And the unreality of Richard II's plan to include the Irish chieftains in the assembly was made clear by parliament's request to the King in 1421 that he should ask the Pope to launch a crusade against the Irish enemies on the grounds that their leaders had broken their oaths of allegiance made to the Crown in 1395 and had not forfeited to the papacy the large sums of money which they had promised if they failed to keep faith. On occasion Irishmen might be obtruded into parliament—one of the accusations made against the Earl of Ormond in the 1440s was that he had illegally made Irishmen knights of the shire—but in law and for the most part in fact, parliamentary representation was confined to those who had been granted the rights of English law and who were prepared to obey that law. Thus were excluded not only the great majority of the Irish but also those who were classed as 'English rebels', men who, despite their English ancestry, now refused to recognise the Crown's authority in Ireland. Essentially, therefore, parliament was a colonial assembly which drew its representatives only from those areas of the country where the authority of the Dublin administration was still acknowledged, and in the fifteenth century the extent of those areas was gradually dwindling. Summonses were still issued to numerous dioceses, counties and towns as well as to the lay and ecclesiastical peers, but as the colony was driven back upon itself it is doubtful whether the majority of these were obeyed. In the Parliament of 1420 eleven counties and liberties and ten towns were represented, all of them in the provinces of Leinster and Munster. But the representation from the latter province seems to have fallen off in the course of the century. Certainly it cannot have been easy for representatives from Limerick to make their way to parliament if, as was complained in 1450, the city was so surrounded by Irish enemies and English rebels that supplies had to be brought in by sea. And in the Parliament of 1463–64 (held, untypically, at Waterford) it was stated that such a long time had elapsed since the county of Cork was represented that the sheriff was unable to ascertain how much expenses should be paid to the two knights for the shire. In the second half of the century it seems likely that only the four counties of the Pale (Dublin, Kildare, Louth and Meath) and their boroughs sent representatives with any regularity to parliament, along with the two burgesses from Waterford, a city noted in the fifteenth century for its loyalty to the Crown.

In Ireland, unlike England, parliament also included representatives or proctors of the diocesan clergy. In 1420 the thirteen dioceses which sent representatives cover an area roughly similar that of the counties represented. Again, Ulster and Connacht lay outside the ambit of parliament, and only the clergy in the southern part of the Armagh diocese *inter Anglicos* sent a proctor. As with the counties and towns, it seems likely that the number of representatives decreased as the century wore on.

Scarcity of evidence makes any estimate of the numbers attending parliament hazardous. But the upper house, composed of spiritual and temporal peers along with the chief officers of the administration, can hardly ever have numbered much more than thirty, and may at times have been only half that number. The two lower houses of knights and burgesses, on the one hand, and clerical proctors on the other, while they may have comprised over seventy representatives at the beginning of the century, probably had little more than thirty in attendance at a later date. The comparative importance of the houses should not, however, be gauged merely by the numbers in attendance. Parliament was the instrument of the administration rather than a check upon it, and power lay with the upper house and more particularly therein with the members of the chief governor's council. It was necessary to gain the assent of knights, burgesses and clerical proctors to taxation, but in other matters their role was a clearly subordinate one. For parliament was in essence an extension of the council of advisors surrounding the chief governor, a fact which is underlined by the application of the term 'great council' to assemblies which in the fifteenth century differed little in composition or function from those styled 'parliaments'.

Only rarely did these assemblies meet outside of Leinster. Travelling in Ireland was a dangerous business and to move outside the Pale was to risk one's property and, indeed, one's life; Dublin was the normal venue, with Drogheda a second choice, and in the earlier part of the century occasional visits were made to Trim, Naas, Castledermot and Kilkenny. But as the assembly came more and more to represent only the Pale area there was an increased unwillingness to journey too far from the safety of the Leinster coastal strip, and in 1478 it was decided that, in view of the perils of the road and the danger to life and property, parliament should be summoned in future only to the city of Dublin or the town of Drogheda.

The legislation of parliament naturally reflects the views of a colony now diminishing in extent and under increasing pressure from the attacks of Irish enemies who penetrated, on occasions, to the outskirts of Dublin itself. The determination to maintain English culture and habits was displayed by the re-enactments of the Statute of Kilkenny. A statute of 1447 even attempted to enforce conformity in the matter of wearing moustaches by ordaining that anyone who wished to be accounted an Englishman should have no hair upon his upper lip 'so that the said lip be once at least shaven within two weeks, or of equal growth with the nether lip'. The Parliament of 1465 repeated this injunction that Irishmen dwelling within the four Pale counties should shave like Englishmen, and also ordered them to take English surnames like Chester, White, Smith or Cook.

But whatever the success of such measures in maintaining the English character of the Pale area, they can have had little relevance to outlying areas which were forced by economic circumstances to have contact with those Irish enemies or English rebels so often condemned by statute. In 1463 parliament recognised the plight of many of the Munster towns by rescinding the prohibition on trade with the Irish, since it was reported that the livelihood of these towns depended upon such trade. Concessions of this nature may only have served to increase the frequently expressed fear of the colonists that they might be entirely overwhelmed. The Parliament of 1455 had granted the not inconsiderable sum of 200 marks to six emissaries to seek aid from England on the grounds that the land was 'likely to be finally destroyed unless the most speedy remedy be had out of England for the reformation thereof'.

The remedy sought, then as always, was support from England to bolster up the defences of the colony. Ireland had long ceased to be able to pay for its own defence, and as the area of the colony declined, so too did its taxable capacity. The knights, burgesses and clerical proctors were unwilling or unable to pay taxes more than once a year, and by the later fifteenth century it was recognised that a normal parliamentary subsidy would bring in, at most, 700 marks (£466), a sum which, even by fifteenth-century standards, was totally inadequate to the colony's needs. Increasingly, those on the border areas of the colony had to make their own arrangements, and often taxation was levied on particular localities to buy off Irish enemies by means of yearly tributes or 'black rents', payments which further decreased their capacity to pay taxes to the Dublin administration. Alternatively, the colonists might pin their faith on private armies for their own defence, but these armies often proved as great a menace as the Irish enemies, for they were quartered and fed by the inhabitants of the countryside under the system of 'coign and livery', whereby armies simply took what was necessary for their support without payment or with empty promises of future reimbursement. Attempts to stop the payment of 'black rents' met with little success, and reliance on local self-help together with the standardisation of the amount of the parliamentary subsidy served to undermine the importance of parliament's fiscal functions. The bargaining power of the two lower houses was thus decreased and with it the opportunity of the elected representatives of the commons and the clergy to influence the policy of the administration. For if the commons did not control taxation, they had little hope of extending the role they played inside parliament.

Repetition of parliamentary legislation is a pointer to its ineffectiveness, as in the case of the numerous condemnations of such evils as coign and livery. To much of the country parliament's decrees were irrelevant since there was no system whereby they could be enforced. Yet the importance of parliament in the life of the colony should not be underestimated. It remained the focal point of the colony's endeavours to rescue order out of increasing chaos. Not only did it provide a meeting-place for the colonial representatives wherein they might coordinate their activities against the Irish enemies, but it also remained the supreme forum for the resolution of disputes in accordance with the dictates of law rather than of *force majeure*. As the local and subordinate courts of law decayed, much parliamentary business was concerned with the settlement of private quarrels, which, in more settled circumstances, would have fallen within the jurisdiction of the lower courts. Whatever happened in fact, it remained true that only parliament could give legal sanction to that fact.

That such legal sanction was not without significance is

clear from a statute passed by the Parliament of 1478 which, in effect, legalised the marriage between Con O'Neill and Eleanor FitzGerald despite the prohibition of such unions by the Statute of Kilkenny. The very fact that it was thought necessary to grant Con O'Neill the rights of an English subject and to safeguard the property of Eleanor FitzGerald is a clear pointer to the view that parliamentary ratification still carried some weight. For there remained always the possibility that parliamentary legislation might be enforced—as it was so dramatically in 1468, when the statute of attainder against the Earl of Desmond led to his execution at Drogheda by an English chief governor, Sir John Tiptoft. Parliament was and remained the supreme law-making body inside Ireland, and, as such, its decrees could not be ignored even by the most powerful or independent-minded colonist.

It is true, of course, that the Irish parliament was a subordinate one. If Ireland was 'England's first colony', then the Irish parliament provided England with her first colonial legislature. That much of the legislation passed in Ireland was of trifling or ephemeral significance was due in part to the fact that English legislation applied to Ireland without the need for re-enactment here. There had been occasional disputes about the application of such legislation to Ireland, but on the whole it was still accepted that the English parliament had power to legislate for Ireland.

In 1460 this view was directly challenged by the Irish parliament's declaration that Ireland was bound only by those laws which were accepted and passed by her own legislature. This claim may have had slim precedent to support it, but it reflected the wide divergence of opinion then prevalent between the majority of the Anglo-Irish colonists and the English administration. The latter, under the weak Lancastrian King Henry VI, had convicted Richard, Duke of York, of treason and stripped him of all his offices. The Duke sought refuge in Ireland, the lieutenancy of which he had held since 1447, and received a warm welcome from the great majority of the colonists, who, ever since Richard's first visit to Ireland in 1449, had been strongly Yorkist in sympathy. In one sense, therefore, the 1460 declaration can be seen merely as a measure to protect the Duke by its refusal to accept that the legislation convicting him of treason and stripping him of all his offices, including the lieutenancy of Ireland, was applicable in Ireland. From Richard's point of view it was a natural stratagem which gave the necessary legal sanction to his continued tenure of the lieutenancy and which, by extension, entitled him to the loyalty and support of the colonists at a time when the tide of battle had turned against him in England.

However, to see the declaration solely as a Yorkist manoeuvre in the struggle commonly known as the Wars of the Roses may be to underrate its significance. The declaration that 'the land of Ireland is and at all times has been corporate of itself . . . freed of the burden of any special law of the realm of England' may have had little historical justification, but it can be be seen as representing a certain impatience, if not dissatisfaction, among the Anglo-Irish aristocracy with the relationship between the London and Dublin administrations. This was to some extent caused by the natural antagonisms that spring up between two bureaucracies whose areas of competence are not as clearly defined as they might be; the subordinate administration in Dublin felt on occasions that its authority was being undermined by ill-founded complaints made to London concerning its conduct. The attempt made in 1460 to invalidate all writs summoning people to answer charges outside Ireland, unless they were channelled through the Dublin administration, can be viewed simply as a device to protect the Duke of York against such a writ; but there is little doubt that it also reflects a certain annoyance on the part of the Dublin administration with royal instructions to Ireland which by-passed or ignored the administrative procedures established in Dublin.

It is probable, too, that the declaration owed something to the normal feeling of 'separateness' which grows up among colonists divorced from their motherland. Three hundred years in Ireland had not made the colonists indistinguishable from the Irish, but it had clearly distinguished them from the English. Even those who remained loyal and still participated in the governing institutions of the colony must have felt that there was a less sympathetic understanding of their problems in England than they would have wished. Differences in dialect or accent would have enforced a sense of regionalism, and while such differences existed inside England, too, in the fifteenth century, there was no regional parliament to give expression to them. This is not to attribute to the colonists such anachronistic aspirations as 'Home Rule' or a desire for UDI. But administrative friction, a sense of regionalism and an independent-minded aristocracy all contributed to the creation of a climate of opinion in which the predicament of the Duke of York met with a ready and sympathetic response. How far the colonists would have gone, in their support for the Yorkist cause, to separate themselves from the jurisdiction of the English administration was never really put to the test, for the victory of the Yorkist cause in England in 1461 ended the possibility of a head-on clash between a Lancastrian England and a Yorkist Ireland.

Nevertheless, the legislation of 1460 remained on the statute-book and, despite the orders of Edward IV to the contrary, it was not to be finally repealed until Poynings' Parliament in 1494–95.

The 1460 episode had demonstrated clearly the danger that an Irish parliament might enact legislation at variance with or completely opposed to the wishes of an English king. The dynastic quarrel in England had raised the additional possibility that an Irish parliament might refuse to recognise the monarch sanctioned by its English counterpart. A quarter of a century of almost uninterrupted Yorkist rule postponed the confrontation of this issue, but even Yorkist kings found it difficult on occasion to control an administration which, under the headship of deputies like the Earl of Desmond and, later, the Earls of Kildare, tended to pursue a policy of its own making. In this situation, particularly under Garret Mór FitzGerald, the eighth Earl of Kildare, parliament could be seen more as an instrument of the deputy rather than of the king.

In 1485, for example, when Henry Tudor was preparing to invade England in his attempt to wrest the crown from Richard III, Kildare had parliament pass a statute designed to secure his position whatever the outcome of the forthcoming struggle. For should Richard III lose his throne, Kildare's appointment as Lord Deputy would lapse and his exercise of authority over the country would lack any legal basis. Parliament was therefore persuaded to enact legislation which would empower

Kildare to continue as chief governor in the eventuality of a change of king. When Richard III lost the Battle of Bosworth, Kildare retained his position and was later confirmed in it by the new king, Henry VII.

Once more, a Lancastrian occupied the English throne—and once more the Yorkist cause was taken up by many of the Anglo-Irish, who were not prepared to recognise that this 'son of a Welshman' was either a legitimate or a permanent incumbent of the monarchical office. Hence, in 1487, they welcomed the arrival in Ireland of Lambert Simnel, who claimed that he was Edward, son of the Duke of Clarence, and thus the legitimate Yorkist heir to the throne. Simnel was crowned king as Edward VI in Christ Church Cathedral and an Irish great council recognised him as the true King of England and Lord of Ireland. Once more, an Irish parliamentary assembly was in disagreement with its English counterpart and, though Simnel's ill-fated bid for the throne ended with his defeat and capture at the Battle of Stoke in June 1487, there could be no disguising the facts that an assembly summoned by the king's representative had supported a treasonable conspiracy against the king and that Kildare's influence over the legislature was more immediate and more powerful than that of Henry VII.

For the moment, the Tudor king was not in a strong enough position to take stern measures against Kildare and his supporters in Ireland; but the appearance of a second pretender, Perkin Warbeck, in Ireland in 1491 underlined the danger of Ireland becoming a base for rebellion against him, and Kildare was finally dismissed from office in 1492. The disorder that followed the dismissal clearly showed that this in itself presented no solution to the problem posed by an overmighty lord in Ireland. As in England, Henry had to find a means of suppressing the magnates' abuse of their power, while preserving the power itself. What distinguished the Earl of Kildare from other magnates was not simply that he was Anglo-Irish, but the fact that he controlled a separate parliament which could be used, as in 1487, to give a clothing of legality to essentially treasonable activities. It is in this context that we should view the legislation passed by Sir Edward Poynings who was finally despatched to this country in 1494 to 'put Ireland in order'.

c

The parliament summoned by Poynings to Drogheda stated that Ireland was bound by legislation passed in England, thus rejecting the claim of 1460, and also revoked any pretended privilege whereby people in Ireland might disobey writs summoning them to answer charges in England. Then, in the act which was to be known to history as Poynings' Law, it was laid down that, in future, parliament could meet in Ireland only with the king's licence, and that any legislation proposed for such a parliament must first be inspected and approved by the king and council in England. Hitherto, the king had been presented with legislation which was already a *fait accompli*, and, if he disapproved of it, he had to secure its repeal. But prevention is better than cure, and the new act ensured that all proposals for legislation would in future undergo the scrutiny of the king's advisors in England, and that only such proposals as they found satisfactory would actually pass into law.

The act was to influence Irish parliamentary history for the next three centuries, but, at the time, its main aim was to prevent the passage of legislation in Ireland hostile to the royal interests. In effect, it removed parliament from the control of a great magnate like Kildare and made it, in fact, what it always was in theory—the instrument of the Crown; it also meant that, if Kildare or any other Anglo-Irish magnate who was placed in charge of the Irish administration were to rebel against the king in future, at least there would be no assembly which could grant legitimacy to that action. Kildare's acceptance of the act was followed by his restoration to power in 1496, and his loyalty to the Tudor dynasty until his death in 1513 is a testimony to the success of Poynings' Law in achieving its immediate objective—the prevention of parliamentary support for Yorkist conspiracies inside Ireland.

By 1495, then, the Irish parliament was a body which represented essentially only the four counties of the Pale, the area around which Poynings' Parliament had ordered the construction of a ditch to increase security. It was an assembly which could meet only with the express approval of the king and which could accept or reject only those proposals for legislation sanctioned by the king. In this sense, it did not, at the time, differ radically from the English parliament, where legislation was greatly influenced by the king's presence. It was his absence from Ireland that necessitated a preview of proposed legislation. Like the English parliament, it was an instrument of royal government, not a popular assembly, but, despite its truncated power, it also maintained within it the same seeds of development as its English counterpart, and its very existence as a separate institution was to have far-reaching consequences in future Irish history.

The Beginnings of Modern Ireland

BRENDAN BRADSHAW, SM

Introduction

One great advantage of examining the Irish parliamentary tradition in the sixteenth century is that it provides us with a much needed new perspective. We have, perhaps, tended to over-emphasise the familiar landmarks of that apocalyptic age : the defeat of the FitzGeralds of Kildare; the abortive Geraldine League; the Reformation; the plantations; the Desmond Rebellion; the Nine Years' War; Kinsale; the Flight of the Earls. We remember the heroes, wildly romantic figures, each acting out in his life an epic and a tragedy : Silken Thomas; James FitzMaurice FitzGerald; Fiach MacHugh O'Byrne; Red Hugh O'Donnell; the great O'Neills—Con, Shane, and Hugh, the last and greatest of them all. 'We tell them in song and in story, The deeds of our heroes of old.'

The deeds of the heroes that I shall consider here have never been told in song and seldom in story, despite the fact that their influence on the course of Irish history in the sixteenth century was no less profound than that of the heroes I have already mentioned, and, in my opinion, more constructive. Perhaps this is because of the epic quality of our nationalist historical tradition and the Celts' natural delight in the saga, neither of which finds congenial material in the lives of upper-middle-class politicians whose careers were more or less successful and prosperous and who, most incongruously for Irish heroes, died in their beds.

The main reason for the neglect is, however, the fact that the history of sixteenth-century Ireland—what really happened and why—has not yet been fully worked out by the scholars. With the history of parliament there is the added, though not unique, problem of scarcity of documentary evidence. The story can be pieced together only incompletely and by an immense output of time and labour, sifting through archival collections for the occasional nugget. It is rather like rummaging through the scattered pieces of a highly complicated jigsaw for the ones that fit together. We need not doubt that this particular game is worth the effort, for here we are working not on some isolated aspect of the jigsaw of sixteenth-century Ireland but on the broad background contours which give the scene in the foreground its perspective.[1]

Poynings' Law

My obvious starting point is Poynings' Law. It comes right at the beginning of the Tudor period, in 1494. Scholars regard it as marking a watershed in Irish history, a point of transition between medieval and modern; and it became a flashpoint in the history of the Irish parliament for another three hundred years.

The old school of nationalist historians viewed Poynings' Law as the precursor of the nineteenth century Act of Union. They poured vituperation on both as tyrannous oppression. Inevitably there was a reaction against this. More recent scholars stressed that the law originated as a result of the exploitation of the Irish parliament by dynastic pretenders, that at that stage the later constitutional union was not foreseen, and that the act in fact rescued the Irish parliament from shipwreck in the stormy seas of Anglo-Irish political life and set it full sail into a phase of new development. I find this latter interpretation more contrived than the former.

It is not enough to say that Poynings' Law was formulated to deal with a passing dynastic threat without advertence to its more fundamental implications. It is clear from the total historical context of the parliament at which it was enacted that it was addressed to basic constitutional and parliamentary problems which the activities of Yorkist pretenders simply highlighted. It formed part of a whole body of reforming legislation which in turn was part of a general political and administrative programme, the first attempt by a Tudor monarch to reform government in Ireland.

Essentially Poynings' Law provided that a parliament could not be validly held in Ireland without the consent of the king, formally granted under the Great Seal of England, both to the convening of parliament and to the projected legislation. The subordination of the Irish parliament to the Great Seal of

England is significant. It asserts a constitutional relationship between the two countries which was to be increasingly questioned in Ireland in the Tudor period and which, in the last Tudor parliament, was specifically rejected. This constitutional relationship was to emerge as the most fundamental issue in the parliamentary politics of the period.

In terms of the reformation of parliament itself the effects of Poynings' Law were immediate, lasting, and drastic. It must be made clear that what was involved was not simply an alteration of the procedure by which the Irish parliament was called and passed its legislation. The effect of the law was to constitute a new partner in the legislature, the Irish council. According to Poynings' Law, it was for the Lord Deputy and the Irish council to decide what bills were to be submitted to the Irish parliament and to obtain approval for them under the English Great Seal before submitting them to parliament. In this way the role of formally initiating legislation was exercised by the Irish council on behalf of the Crown, leaving parliament itself only with a function of veto, though it also exercised a power of amendment with dubious legality.[2]

The practical consequences of Poynings' Law are highlighted by comparing the operation of parliament before and in the immediate aftermath of the act, up to the Reformation Parliament of 1536. The first striking feature is the abrupt reduction in the number of Parliaments. In the thirty-three years from the accession of Edward IV to 1494 parliament sat in every year save two or perhaps three. By contrast, in the forty-one years from then to the Reformation Parliament of 1536 only eight Parliaments were held. The convening of the Irish parliament was now a matter for the personal decision of the king. Henry VII had little use for parliament as a device of regular government, so he convened the Irish one only when he needed a parliamentary sanction for the renewal of the financial subsidy, a policy which Henry VIII maintained for thirty of the thirty-eight years of his reign.

Apart from the regressive implications of this, politically and constitutionally, so far as Irish institutions of government were concerned, it also created a judicial difficulty. The judicial function of parliament in England had already hived off almost completely at this stage, establishing itself outside parliament as a regular court of justice. In Ireland, on the contrary, parliament continued to be resorted to as a court, and in fact its judicial role developed enormously in the fifteenth century.[3] However, after Poynings' Law it could no longer be effective in this capacity because it was not convened with the necessary frequency. There may indeed have been a deliberate policy to force Irish litigants to use the English courts, complementing, in the judicial sphere, the centralising policy which Poynings endeavoured to implement in the administrative and legislative spheres. Intended or not, Poynings' Law had the effect of curbing parliament in Ireland as a judiciary as much as it curbed it as a legislature.

In its legislative aspect one further consequence of the law needs to be noted. This was a dramatic change in the volume and content of legislation. There was less of it now and it dealt less than hitherto with matters that were 'with rare exceptions ephemeral and vague, unimportant, designed to solve an immediate problem and not to inaugurate a new policy'.[4] More is the pity. This was overwhelmingly the kind of legislation parliament in England continued to produce because it continued to reflect the preoccupations not only of the government but of the members of parliament and to cater for their needs. In Ireland, however, it was unfortunately almost impossible to get anything as far as parliament after Poynings' Law except public government legislation.

In fact, apart from authorising the renewal of the subsidy to Crown revenue at the expiry of the period stipulated in the previous renewal, parliament served very little function and might well have become ossified. It was saved by two developments. The first of these was the English Reformation, the marital and dynastic crisis which culminated in the assertion of Henry VIII's supreme jurisdiction over the Church in his dominions. In the accomplishment of this constitutional revolution the legislative role of parliament assumed a new importance and this had a resuscitating effect on the Irish parliament. The second saving factor was the emergence in Ireland of a succession of very able parliamentarians.

Henry VIII's Irish Reformation Parliament, 1536–37
The Reformation Parliament of 1536–37 is of particular

interest in the history of the Irish parliamentary tradition. Obviously, this is partly because it marks the point of time at which the Church of Rome was first outlawed and the Church of Ireland legally established. It is important for another reason also. At this parliament dissent, which was to become so marked a characteristic of the Irish parliamentary tradition, is clearly discernible for the first time in the modern era.

It seems obvious to associate the two and to assume that the opposition was directed against the Reformation legislation. We owe it to historical accuracy to state that the association is not warranted by the evidence. The Irish parliament passed Henry VIII's Reformation legislation without a murmur of opposition apart from the voice of the proctors of the lower clergy, and this was ignored. It was not that the parliament was against the Pope, or for the schism of Henry VIII. Nor was it that the members were browbeaten into passing measures of which they strongly disapproved—the later sessions showed that not even the king could bully the Commons. It was simply that at this stage they were not very committed one way or the other. To insist that they were is to project on to them the attitudes of a later era, of Trent and the Counter-Reformation, when the papacy was no longer regarded merely as an administrative institution but also as a rallying point for orthodoxy. In 1536 the Irish parliament was prepared to humour the King in what seemed to be just another quarrel with the papacy about jurisdiction, just as their fathers had humoured his father at Poynings' Parliament when they legislated against the papacy asserting control over ecclesiastical appointments.[5] It is of importance to note that religious sectarianism did not become a characteristic of the Irish parliamentary tradition with the coming of the Reformation.

If the king and the Irish parliament were not at loggerheads over religion in 1536 what was the cause of the storm? Parliament might have summed it up in two words, extortion and expropriation. At the second session, after the Reformation legislation and an act attainting the leaders of the Kildare rebellion were safely passed, the government presented tax and customs bills and a bill for the suppression of certain monasteries. This was a major tactical blunder. Not only did they jangle simultaneously the sensitive nerves of money, privilege and property, but at the same time they struck at two of the most influential groups in parliament, the merchants of the towns and the landed gentry and professional lawyers of the Pale.

I should emphasise that parliamentary opposition at this stage must not be envisaged in terms of a modern opposition party. The situation was much more fluid. A member now supported, now opposed the government for reasons which were dictated by his own interests or by those of his locality or his patron. Nevertheless, one can see in the combination of the ports and the Pale an alliance that was to challenge the government, if not invariably, at least consistently for the rest of the Tudor period. The leadership of opposition, now as later, was taken by the representatives of the Pale, the area surrounding Dublin in Kildare, Meath and Louth. The other significant interest represented in the Commons was that of the Earl of Ormond, who himself, of course, sat in the Upper House. In 1536–37, as ever, his influence was exercised on behalf of the Crown, except where its interests clashed with his own.

Within this context I want to draw attention to a feature that was to be characteristic for the rest of the period—the emergence of a spokesman for the local community who was also in the service of the Crown and who acted as a bridge between the two. In 1536 it was Patrick Barnewall. He is typical of a succession of outstanding Anglo-Irish parliamentary leaders in the Tudor period; men of substance and ability, lawyers by training, government administrators by profession, young and ambitious for their own futures and the future of the community for which they spoke. They professed loyalty to the Crown but did not take this to oblige subservience. Their outlook was secular. That does not mean that they were religiously indifferent, still less anti-religious. It means that they preferred to keep religion in the private sector and to expend their considerable talents in public affairs that were more narrowly political.

The significance of the parliamentary opposition of 1536–37 is not only that it was manifested but that it was successful. It was possible to persuade the Crown either to withdraw or to amend substantially four priority measures : tax and customs bills, a bill for devaluing the coinage, and a bill for administrative reform. The possibility of negotiating with the Crown in parliament meant that parliament could continue to fulfil an important governmental function and that the concept of constitutional dissent could retain credibility.

The amendment of two of the ecclesiastical acts should also be mentioned, though it is not clear whether this was on the initiative of parliament or the Irish executive. In either case, it indicates that practical expressions of Ireland's constitutional subservience to England, of which Poynings' Law was one, were now resisted in Ireland. In devising the new arrangements by which the juridical machinery of the Church in Ireland would operate, the English Chancellor proposed that the ultimate juridical authority should reside in England. He based this on the principle that England was 'the chief part of the Crown and Ireland a member appended to it'. He formulated proposals for the issue of ecclesiastical faculties and for the hearing of spiritual appeals on this basis. Both were amended in Ireland to provide an additional arrangement whereby all these functions could be administered in Ireland without recourse to the Archbishop of Canterbury or the English Lord Chancellor.

It is also necessary to consider the act 'that the proctors be no members of parliament' which passed at the last session. The proctors of the lower clergy had earned the ire of the government for alone opposing the Reformation legislation at the first session and for maintaining a policy of non-cooperation throughout the other sessions. When the crunch came the Commons were glad no doubt to see the end of a rival lower assembly, and the spiritual Lords, who might have saved them by using their majority in the Upper House, sheepishly, if one might be permitted the pun, bleated their ayes when called upon by the Crown. I must simply underline the expulsion of the proctors as a further modification in the constitution of the Irish parliament, extol their integrity in single-mindedly and single-handedly resisting legislation which touched not their pockets but their consciences—and pass on.[6]

If there is a watershed in Irish Tudor history it is to be found in the period of this parliament. Twice before in Tudor times an English Lord Deputy, Poynings in 1494–95 and Surrey in 1521–22, had presided over parliament in Ireland. Both marked the inauguration of a reformation of government in

Ireland. Both proved abortive. The third attempt, of which the Parliament of 1536–37 formed part, was to be sustained. Henceforth English jurisdiction in Ireland was a palpable reality.

The enactment of the ecclesiastical Reformation and the attainder of the FitzGeralds of Kildare, even if neither proved permanent, presaged the passing of the late medieval order in Ireland. This is not to say that here we sound the crack of doom. If the medieval edifice was crumbling, the Parliament of 1536–37 reveals a new leadership emerging and a community with the vitality and the tenacity to build anew out of the ruins. This was the challenge that was taken up in the Parliament of 1541–43.

The St Leger/Cusack Parliament, 1541–43

If I had to name the most significant event of sixteenth-century Ireland, I can think of none of greater consequence for the course of national history than the Parliament of 1541–43. Though it was conceived originally as a sequel to the Reformation Parliament, an opportunity to complete that Parliament's unfinished business, it immediately began to take a radically new course. Events in the meanwhile had paved the way. A second military crisis, precipitated by the Geraldine League, had come rumbling in the wake of the Kildare rebellion, like a second eruption from the same volcano. The experience for the Pale community was traumatic but salutary. It was clear that a new political situation had been created outside the area of the Crown's jurisdiction and that the policy towards the Gaelic Irish enshrined in the Statutes of Kilkenny and reiterated at Poynings' Parliament was no longer adequate. This realisation coincided with the arrival in Ireland of a new head of government bent on solving the problems of the lordship by conciliation, and the appearance at his elbow of an outstanding Anglo-Irish administrator. The Lord Deputy was Sir Anthony St Leger. The Anglo-Irish politician was Sir Thomas Cusack, head of an influential family of the Pale. These two men provided the impulse for the Anglo-Irish community to rid itself of its medieval constitution and the political attitudes there enshrined and to take in hand the task of fashioning a new constitution and a new political strategy appropriate to the new age. The basis was laid at the Parliament of 1541–43, over which St Leger presided as representative of the Crown and at which Cusack acted as Speaker of the Commons. The focal act of this parliament was the declaration of Henry VIII to be King of Ireland.

To explain in any satisfactory way the implications of the act 'that the king and his successors be kings of Ireland' would require a paper to itself. Here I can only state very baldly what was involved. But first let me make the point that this was not the brainchild of Henry VIII. Contrary to what is usually supposed, he was unenthusiastic when it was mooted, procrastinated when it was presented to him for his approval, and was enraged when he discovered too late what he had committed himself to.[7]

What difference did the act of kingship make? In a nutshell, it abrogated the constitutional arrangement enshrined in the Statutes of Kilkenny. The Statutes in effect formally accepted the state of jurisdictional partition between those of English and Irish race in Ireland. Thenceforward only those in the English areas came within the framework of the English constitution, were entitled to its privileges and were subject to its laws. But in taking the title of King, Henry had contracted an obligation to the whole of Ireland as his kingdom, and to all its inhabitants as his subjects. He was pledged, in effect, to the political unification of Ireland under the jurisdiction of the Crown. Henry denied none of this. What rankled was that the Irish council had allowed, indeed encouraged him, to make such a commitment without, he complained, adequate advertence to its implications.

After the act had been passed with great pomp and circumstance in June 1541 St Leger sent Cusack to London with a sheaf of parliamentary bills and proposals for a major political initiative which, it was argued, the King must undertake as a result of assuming the title of King of Ireland. The purpose of Cusack's mission was to sell a political strategy to the King and his council. The only way, he urged, that the King could make his claim to the kingdom of Ireland a reality was the way of conciliation. A conquest by force was a practical impossibility in a land he reckoned to be as great as England and Wales together, but the Irish would be found ready to accept the status of subjects provided they could experience its benefits rather than be burdened with its responsibilities. In particular, the confidence of the Irish chiefs had to be won. This could only be done by giving them security in their possessions and being moderate in demands for revenues from their lands. These were pills that stuck in Henry's gullet. The plan got a very cold reception. But eventually, as a result of much persuasion on the part of Cusack and the Irish council, it got guarded approval as a temporary expedient. What was proposed as a final solution was approved in the cynical spirit of renaissance statecraft, as a temporary expedient of 'sober ways, politic drifts and amiable persuasions'.

The long-term significance of the episode has not been grasped because the conciliatory programme of the 1540s has not been studied in the context of the act for the kingship of Ireland with which it originated. These together gave rise to two allied strands of constitutional thought in the Anglo-Irish community. One centred on the idea of breaking the medieval deadlock between the English and Irish communities in Ireland by extending the status and privileges of the subject to the Irish universally. The other concerned the new status of Ireland as a kingdom. This concept enabled the Anglo-Irish to consider their constitutional status in quite a new light. They began to regard themselves more as subjects of the kingdom of Ireland than as subjects of the Crown of England. There was a shift of focus from Crown to kingdom. The fusion of these two strands produced a veritable explosion in Anglo-Irish constitutional thought. A new ideology of nationhood emerged, and a new goal of political endeavour was proposed: the achievement of a united Ireland as a sovereign constitutional state. From 1541 onwards the political activities of the Anglo-Irish in parliament, in government administration, and in the community at large, must be seen in this context.

Just as parliament proved an apt instrument in effecting the revolutionary constitutional changes in England in 1527–34 so the sponsors of the new Irish constitution of the 1540s looked to parliament as the chief instrument of its designs. However, the use made of parliament differed in the two countries. Firstly whereas in England parliaments legislative function was the instrument of change, in Ireland its deliberative and judicial functions were seen as more important. As a deliberative body it acted as a centripetal and unifying device, a medium through which independent leaders could be associated with one another and with the central administration in the task of government. For this reason St Leger worked very hard at getting independent chiefs to come to parliament and at involving them as much as possible in its operation. Secondly, parliament enabled the executive to implement its policy of securing peace and good order by the administration of justice rather than by force of arms. Primarily, the king's council in parliament provided a court of sufficient status to arbitrate in the disputes of Irish and Anglo-Irish lords.[8]

The result of the efforts of the Irish executive to implement its constitutional policy through parliament was that for the first time it was possible to regard the meeting of parliament in Ireland as a national event. It was made in some sense nationally representative. It arbitrated as the highest national court, trying the complaints of Irish and Anglo-Irish alike. It deliberated upon matters of national policy. As well as all of this, the Parliament of 1541–43 managed to produce one of the greatest bodies of legislation of any Tudor parliament apart from Poynings'. It did so, moreover, while observing, faithfully on the whole, the stipulations of Poynings' Law, and with remarkably little evidence of opposition. The key to this parliament's efficiency is the dominance of Anglo-Irish political leaders both in parliament and in the Irish council. Anglo-Irish administrators under the tutelage of St Leger had regained a strong position in the council. It was possible for these to achieve a sustained consensus among all the members of the legislature, including the council. This consensus was not repeated at any of the remaining four Tudor parliaments. The first two were to be marked by an atmosphere of sinister mystery, the others by explosive confrontation between the Crown and the locality. For that reason historians tend to present the Parliament of 1541–43, if they think of it at all, as a tiny light in a naughty world. It was a great deal more than that. It marks the origins of Irish political nationalism. It was a truly epoch-making event.

Mary's Parliament, 1557–58

When peers and commons assembled in June 1557 parliament had not met for fourteen years. The history of the St Leger/Cusack plan, like the history of the men themselves meanwhile, had been a chequered one. St Leger and Cusack were finally eclipsed under Mary in 1556. The new head of government was Lord Fitzwalter, soon to become Earl of Sussex. His coming signalised the end of sixteen years of flirtation with the conciliatory constitutional policy and the espousal of the policy of conquest and colonisation. This marriage may have waxed hot and cold. But it was lasting, and was cursed with abundant children of wrath. In the history of the invasions of Ireland 1556 is as significant a date as 1169.[9]

The supporters of the constitutional policy of the 1540s had hopes of a different kind of parliament than the one Mary gave them. A set of proposals for a parliament submitted in England in the period was obviously framed in the context of specifically Irish problems and from a standpoint that was clearly that of the St Leger/Cusack plan. The same methods were to be used to ensure a parliament that would be nationally representative, that would join local leaders in deliberations, and that would make arrangements, with their cooperation, for a system of government tailored to local conditions and assimilated to the central jurisdiction of the Crown. The actuality was a parliament that assembled briefly in Dublin to push through a programme of legislation legitimising Mary's claim as Queen, repealing the Reformation legislation and asserting the Crown's right to the lands of the Irish in Leix and Offaly.

It cannot yet be said, in view of the rudimentary nature of the investigations so far, if the dissent of the local community manifested itself in explicit parliamentary opposition. I can only point to circumstantial evidence. Parliament met in an atmosphere seething with resentment against the English troops brought by Sussex. Whatever explicit opposition there may have been in parliament, there was considerable stalling and backsliding by Anglo-Irish professional administrators to prevent obnoxious legislation getting as far as parliament at all. Sussex felt obliged to take stern action against at least one dissenting lawyer and was advised by the Queen 'to spare none others that hereafter shall contempn authority for that we must and will have it maintained as you wisely have considered'.[10]

The best that can be said about Mary is that she did not understand, have sympathy with, or care very much about the Irish political community, delegating at every opportunity 'the whole order thereof' to Sussex's 'good discretion'. In this she was perhaps not untypical of the aristocratic Counter-Reformation tradition in England that hearkened back to her.

Before leaving this parliament, I should draw attention to the way the constitutional change effected by the 'act for the king's title' of 1541 was first reflected in its legislation. Hitherto legislation reflected the state of jurisdictional partition actually existing under the Statutes of Kilkenny; it was phrased so as to legislate only for the king's faithful subjects, inhabiting the loyal areas. In 1557, however, it was assumed, irrespective of the actual situation, that all the inhabitants of Ireland were under the Crown's jurisdiction.

Elizabeth's Irish Reformation Parliament, 1560

Elizabeth's Reformation Parliament, which met briefly in 1560, did practically nothing except to legislate a new ecclesiastical settlement, the third to be enacted by parliament in twenty-five years. What made this one different was that it proved final. Despite what I have already said about the desire of Anglo-Irish politicians to avoid embroilment with religious issues, I would not want to suggest that the attitude of the local community to the ecclesiastical legislation in 1560 was as casual as it had been in 1536. In the intervening quarter of a century people had got a taste of what Reformation meant, not simply in terms of the replacement of one jurisdictional head, the Pope, by another, the King, but, what affected them more deeply, in terms of liturgy and doctrine. Few relished it.

Given sufficient attention, I am satisfied that the mystery surrounding Elizabeth's Reformation Parliament can be penetrated, to the extent, at least, of revealing the reluctance of the members to enact the religious measures. I suspect, on the basis of a cursory examination, that the ecclesiastical legislation was not presented in the Upper House at all, where it had little hope of succeeding, and that it scraped through the Commons as a result of the government increasing support for itself by placing New English colonisers in newly created shire seats.[11]

The passing of the Elizabethan religious measures raises serious doubts about the Irish parliament as a constitutional and representative assembly. English parliamentary historians defend the devices resorted to by government in the Tudor period to ensure the passage of government legislation. They call it parliamentary management, and maintain that the evolution of such methods to ensure that government legislation got through prevented parliament from becoming a useless and even destructive instrument. These arguments are less impressive in the Irish context. The number of New English members who sat in the Commons in 1560 is a case in point. Parliament was now being manipulated to legislate on behalf of a minority of the community represented in parliament and against the interests and wishes of the majority. Increasingly the Irish parliament was to become a minority assembly and its claims to be representative and constitutional correspondingly discredited.

The Anglo-Irish members tried to arrest this trend at the next Parliament. They demanded adherence to the residence qualification enjoined on candidates. In line with English practice, their claim was disallowed. But the comparison was invidious. The tie of the parliamentary representative to the locality had always been stronger in Ireland than in England, and the demand for it had been reiterated as late as the Parliament of 1541–43. In any event, there was an obvious difference between an English country gentleman taking the seat of a rotten borough in the English parliament and the same man being foisted on the Irish Commons at the expense of the representation of the dominant local political groups. The political consequences of this became evident in the Parliament of 1569–71.

Sidney's Parliament, 1569–71

In this parliament one can see, at least embryonically, a colonial government party confronting an Irish national party. Just as the Crown was hoisting English newcomers into seats under its patronage, local interests, particularly the Pale party, invariably the most aggressive and forward, looked for support to the Gaelic Irish, now trickling into parliament as a result of the extension of the shire system.

It was on the basis of such a division that the three major

issues of the Parliament were fought: the bills for the suspension of Poynings' Law, for the imposition of a wine custom, and for the abolition of coign and livery. Two of these, the two in which the opposition was completely successful, were directly related to the national political question. The row over the Poynings' Law bill was inspired, on the one hand by a desire to recover the legislative autonomy of parliament, and on the other by a determination to secure it against arbitrary action by the Crown when Poynings' Law procedure was removed. The real issue in the coign and livery bill was whether the military force should be provided substantially by local magnates and therefore controlled by them, or whether it should take the form of a standing army recruited mainly in England, under the direct control of the Lord Deputy, but provisioned by Irish taxes.

I accept the traditional view, though it has recently been questioned, that the opposition at this parliament must be seen in the context of the evolution of a 'national' or 'patriot' parliamentary party. Members and groups retained their freedom of action, of course, and continued to be influenced to a considerable extent by narrow self-interest. But the nature of the opposition reveals an increasing alienation between the local community and the Crown. To this extent the traditional interpretation is correct in seeing in the opposition an incipient nationalism. It fails, however, to go far enough. The ramifications of the nationalist position involved wider issues than those represented by merely local bodies of opinion; the emerging patriotism crossed the bounds between government and opposition. The tension basically arose over specifically *national* policy. The clash between conciliation and conquest runs through the whole of Sidney's Parliament. It is evident, for instance, in the contrast of tone and message between the act for the attainder of Shane O'Neill, clearly drafted from the Anglo-Irish perspective, and the jingoistic tirade with which Sidney concluded the parliament.

In his concluding address Sidney's main concern was to defend a militarist policy and to stress the need for a standing army to forward it. Where the framers of O'Neill's attainder felt the conquest was completed, Sidney insisted that it had hardly begun. The most ominous feature of his speech was its avowed racialism, so stridently asserted as to indicate that he was addressing himself deliberately to the problem of averting a rapprochement between Irish and Anglo-Irish. He reminded the Anglo-Irish of their origin from 'our [English] ancestors' and warned that the Irish were to the common enemy, 'a sort of barbarous people, odious to God and man, that lap your blood as greedily as ours'.[12]

This speech and the presence of John Hooker in parliament remind us that a new phase in Irish history was well under way. Hooker was a lawyer from Exeter. He had been commissioned by an English courtier, Sir Peter Carew, with the encouragement of the government, to revive ancestral titles to vast tracts of land in Ireland. His claims threatened not only the Kavanaghs in Leinster and the MacCarthys in Cork, but also the Chivers family in the Pale. Henceforth the conquest of Ireland is to be seen as part of a European movement of colonial expansion. The conquistadores, whether Spanish, or Dutch, or English, embarked upon the adventure in a common frame of mind: aggressive, predatory, totalitarian, discriminatory.

Paradoxically, however, the same European phenomenon which imbued the Crown policy of conquest with an ideology of colonialism endowed the Anglo-Irish conciliatory policy with an ideology of nationalism. The advent of the new colonialists in Ireland was marked by the transformation of the earlier colonists into Irish nationalists. This development had a unique result: while political nationalism elsewhere tended to express itself in racialist, totalitarian attitudes, the logic of their situation led the Anglo-Irish to adopt a liberal constitutional position. The quiet revolution in ideology and attitude taking place even in the most loyal of the Anglo-Irish community is evident in the *Description of Ireland* written in the 1570s by Richard Stanyhurst, the son of the Speaker in Sidney's Parliament. When he insists he is an Irishmen, not just an Englishman born in Ireland, when he defends the worthiness of the island and all its inhabitants, whether wild Irish or ancient English, when he castigates those who are ashamed of their country, and speaks of Ireland as his native country, he is articulating his sense of national identity in the language of ideological nationalism. Within the Anglo-Irish community the conciliatory policy, the proposal to grant the native Irish a place within the community on acceptable terms, was now subsumed in a national policy and underpinned by a national ideology. At this point political nationalism must be considered a specific element of the Irish parliamentary tradition.[13]

Perrot's Parliament, 1585–86

The trends discernible in Sidney's Parliament took definite direction in the last Tudor Parliament which met under Lord Deputy Perrot in 1585–86. It is clear from the use of the terms in parliamentary legislation that by now 'English' and 'Irish' connoted a national rather than an ethnic description. As this suggests, the political alignments of Crown and new colonialists against Anglo-Irish and native Irish had become more clear cut. The chasm between government and local community had gaped wider so that the presence of Anglo-Irish within the government now failed to bridge the gap. This was ominous.

Despite the opposition at Sidney's Parliament, a considerable body of legislation had been enacted. This underlines the fact that parliamentary opposition was not necessarily a negative and destructive force. One of the functions of parliament was to provide a means of reconciling the conflicting interests on which the government of the community impinged. Not all government measures were opposed and not all opposition was directed against government measures. One does not assume in the sixteenth century, as one might perhaps today, that the function of the opposition was to frustrate the government's purposes as far as possible. Parliamentary procedure should more correctly be seen as providing the means for establishing dialogue between conflicting interests, with the possibility of reaching an acceptable compromise by way of an amendment. More sophisticated procedures had been evolved to ensure the orderly examination of proposals in three stages, and the practice of voting by poll rather than by acclamation had established itself. When, therefore, intransigence, firstly over a government proposal to suspend Poynings' Law and then over a cess bill, brought Perrot's Parliament to a standstill, it was a hollow victory for the opposition because it represented a defeat for the parliamentary method. Ultimately it was for the Crown to convene parliament and it would do so only for considerations of utility or necessity. Where need did not constrain and where parliamentary opposition diminished utility, parliament was in danger of going by default. In fact, it was not until twenty-seven years after this largely abortive parliament that another was convened.

But the most interesting feature of the parliament for our topic is the concluding speech of the Speaker, Justice Walsh. Here we are provided with a comprehensive and lucid statement of Anglo-Irish political nationalism set in a constitutional framework.

Before discussing the contents, it is instructive to consider the style. Elegant, structured, erudite, it is evidence of a quality of parliamentary practice in sharp contrast to the rude rusticity suggested by John Hooker. Walsh's background should also be borne in mind. Like his predecessor, Stanyhurst, he had been elected to the office of Speaker as the government nominee against an opposition candidate put forward by members from the Pale. He had already begun a career in government and had ties with the loyalist Earl of Ormond. He therefore represented the most loyal and moderate element of the Anglo-Irish community.

Underlying Walsh's lengthy discourse there were three basic concerns. Firstly, he wanted to situate the operation of government within a constitutional framework. He drew out the constitutional principles which underlay the machinery of government and the built-in safeguards it provided, if they were respected, against the assumption of arbitrary power by any one of the three political estates, the Crown, the Lords, or the Commons. Having shown how autocratic government was repugnant to the constitution, his second concern was to show how it ruled out racial discrimination also. He emphasised that the basis of privilege was one's constitutional status as a subject and that therefore there could be no discrimination as between subject and subject. Finally, he expressed this principle of non-discrimination most emphatically by developing the idea of Ireland as one body politic. Her Majesty was 'head of this body politic and in that respect allied to all'. Therefore the representative of the Crown in Ireland ought 'to accept in the same sort of us, without any differences or distinctions of persons'. His use of the notion of Ireland as a body politic is most significant. The assertion of Ireland's political autonomy runs through the whole discourse; but the use of the constitutional concept of the body linked directly to the head is the clearest reflection of the constitutional principle on which Poynings' Law was based, and which had been reiterated throughout the Tudor period, namely that Ireland's constitutional link to the Crown was indirect, as an appendage, joined and subordinated to the kingdom of England.[14]

The recalling of these principles on the one hand served to explain to Lord Deputy Perrot that the thwarting of his legislative programme in parliament was a normal hazard of constitutional government. On the other hand it was a reproach to his methods which were tending increasingly to be autocratic and harsh. It served also as a refutation of the constitutional theory propounded by New English colonialists like John Hooker who chafed at the constitutional stone-walling of the Anglo-Irish and sought to circumvent it by appeal to the Crown prerogative. Finally, and most importantly, it provided the only realistic basis for binding the racial communities of Ireland into a unified state with justice and peace.

This truly great parliamentary speech brings down the curtain on the Irish Tudor parliaments. One succinct phrase of Walsh drew attention to the political crux which the play had thrown up and left unresolved. 'Better', he said, quoting Scipio Africanus, 'to save one citizen than to overthrow a thousand enemies.' The object of government was to preserve not to destroy. This had been the watchword of the constitutionalists since 1541. But with the arrival of Sussex in 1556 that spirit had ceased to inform the policies of the Crown. The consequences were to prove dire.

Considered purely in terms of the evolution of parliament also the phase gave cause for foreboding. The Crown's zeal for efficient management had overborne its respect for law and constitutional government in two important respects. Poynings' Law had seriously vitiated parliament's legislative function and the manipulation of parliamentary membership in favour of the new colonialists had vitiated its representative character. The government might have legitimately desired a bridle. It provided itself with a halter.

Yet the tone of Walsh had been quietly optimistic. Despite the grim background of rebellion preceding the parliament, he caught the mood of the loyal Anglo-Irish community as a whole. The Renaissance had blossomed late among them bringing with it sophistication, culture, and a measure of affluence. Hope wells up easily in such breasts. The laments of contemporary Irish chroniclers would have sounded strange to their ears. So indeed would the laments of later historians.

Considered in the full sweep of Irish national history there is no need for the *olagón*. The pall of gloom obscures the fact that the sixteenth-century parliamentary tradition generated the most dynamic, and in its own way revolutionary, idea to emerge in the history of modern Ireland. Historians have not grasped this because they have missed the significance of the so-called liberal Henrician policy of the 1540s. This, as we have seen, was not Henry's policy at all, but a strategy devised in Ireland to give flesh to the bare bones of the new constitution enshrined in the act of 1541 which gave Ireland the status of a kingdom. It is here that modern Irish political nationalism has its source.

I want to emphasise that the movement originated within the framework of a parliamentary tradition. It was sponsored by men committed to finding a solution to political problems by constitutional means. They were men who succeeded in transcending their own cultural traditions and the burden of their past. This does not mean that they ignored history and tradition. They were too realistic as politicians to do that. But they refused to be dominated by them. They might have accepted the inveterate hostility of the two racial communities as the decree of an inexorable historical process. But they dared to transform it by working for the establishment of a constitutional government in a unified Ireland. They aspired to establish a united land of peace and prosperity, of constitutional rights and impartial justice. That aspiration still challenges us today. Was it a pipe-dream—or political vision?

6

The Irish Parliament in the Early Seventeenth Century

HUGH KEARNEY

To make sense of Irish history in almost any period involves placing Ireland in a wider perspective than these islands. Students of the Irish Bronze Age who looked no further than the Boyne Valley would not make much of New Grange. The same applies, I think, to the subject of this essay. The Irish parliament in the early seventeenth century sounds a very restricted topic, and if I confined my remarks to analysing the proceedings of an assembly which met for a few weeks in 1613–15, 1634–35 and 1640–41, I cannot believe that much illumination would result. What is needed, I think, is to set the history of this institution against as wide a background as possible, considering its European character as well as characteristics peculiar to Ireland.

All over Western Europe, during this period, there were local representative assemblies, summoned at irregular intervals to discuss the remedy of local grievances in return for grants of financial aid. There were many such 'estates', as they were called, in France and Germany, as well as in societies with a strong traditional culture, such as in Catalonia and Ireland.[1] But of whom were these assemblies representative? At the period in question, nearly all of them were dominated by the local aristocracy of landowners. In theory the assembly might consist of three estates of Church, Lords and Commons; in practice the landlords held the whip-hand. The bishops who sat as representatives of the Church normally belonged to prominent local families, the burgesses who represented the towns either deferred to their betters, or in some cases were themselves younger sons of gentry families. In short, the assemblies of Western Europe represented what later came to be called the landed interest.

Before the plantation of Ulster in 1610 the Irish parliament, or the Dublin parliament, as it is perhaps more sensible to call it, was an assembly called to discuss the affairs of the greater and lesser landlords in parts of Ireland controlled by the English Crown. There were two houses in parliament, the House of Lords and the House of Commons, the difference between them being that the greater landlords, such as the Earl of Ormond sat in one and the minor gentry in the other. This was a difference which was apt to break down in practice. We assume today that the 'Upper House' (so-called) was the weaker of the two, but this does not seem to have been the case in the early seventeenth century. It is understandable that the greater landowners should have been regarded as the patrons of lesser men and as the spokesmen for their interests because they were persons less likely to be intimidated by the government.

It is obvious that an assembly of this kind, though called a parliament, was very different from the assemblies which we call parliaments today. The exercise of political power was confined to a limited group, access to which depended upon the possession of a landed estate. Politics were gentry politics, a state of affairs which, during the Puritan Revolution in England, was to be bitterly criticised by such radical groups as the Levellers. The Irish parliament, like similar assemblies in Western Europe, was an aristocratic not a democratic body. Its members assumed that society was ordered on hierarchical principles, according to which every man had his place and politics were best conducted by the landowner. There is no reason to think that Gaelic society in sixteenth-century Ulster was conducted on less aristocratic lines.

An institution which met at intervals varying between ten and twenty years was obviously an odd kind of institution. What was the point of summoning it? The answer lies, in part, I think, in the attitudes of successive governments in England. Parliament was summoned at what appeared to be crucial moments as a means of initiating new departures. From this point of view, parliament was a monarchical institution, an instrument of government. The meeting of parliament set the scene for complex and intricate political manoeuvres by which the government tried to get new policies accepted with as little concession as possible to established interests. The government, or 'court party' as we may term it, enjoyed the advantage of being in power; but there was always opposition, and the anti-government party, or 'country party', was never without weapons. In particular, the government depended upon financial grants by parliament if it was to make ends meet. There was also the ultimate threat of revolt, not so much in the hope of defeating the Crown, as to create a military bargaining position from which to reach eventual compromise. But this was exceptional. Parliament was the normal mechanism for solving political problems.

The Irish parliament, then, was an assembly in which court and country played the game of politics. It was a game in which both sides had important cards to play. In the absence of a bureaucratic administration, the Crown depended upon the support or acquiescence of the landlords if its policy was not to remain a dead letter. Conversely, the landlords' legal and political powers rested upon the support of the Crown.

The Parliament which met in 1613 was arguably the most important in Irish history before 1782 for a number of reasons.[2] First, it was the first to draw its members from all thirty-two counties. In the parliaments of the mid-sixteenth century, the House of Lords numbered about 40 peers, ecclesiastical as well as lay, and the House of Commons about 100 members. In 1613 the Crown created about 40 new parliamentary boroughs, which brought membership of the Commons to a new total of 233 members. In theory the Crown was extending the right of parliamentary representation to parts of Ireland which had hitherto been excluded, but in practice the new boroughs were 'rotten boroughs' without inhabitants and their representatives were members of the royal administration in Dublin. The critics of the government described the new boroughs as 'consisting of some few beggarly cottages' in order that 'by the wills of a few selected for that purpose, under the names of burgesses, extreme penal laws should be imposed on your subjects'. The Crown was attempting a constitutional revolution by creating seats for a court party.

These changes in the 1613–15 Parliament reflected a new religious and political situation in Ireland. The Reformation had made surprisingly little headway in Ireland, despite the efforts of the administration. Its influence was confined in large measure to government circles, though the foundation of

Trinity College, Dublin, in 1591 marked the beginnings of an attempt to educate a Protestant clergy which could spread light into the dark corners of the realm. In general, however, the penal laws against the English Catholics did not apply in Ireland and such penalties as did exist were more honoured in the breach than in the observance. The aftermath of Kinsale in 1601, however, of the Flight of the Earls in 1607 and of the Ulster Plantation in 1610 led to a new phenomenon—the appearance of a growing Protestant community in Ulster. The Reformation ceased to be a small-scale affair of the elite and became numerically significant. The Ulster Plantation thus marked a shift in the religious balance within Ireland, and the Crown proposed to press this home in the 1613–15 Parliament by introducing stiffer penal laws against Jesuits and secular priests and those who harboured them. A religious as well as a constitutional revolution was being attempted.

Connected with all this there was a social shift of immense significance. Ulster was the last great bastion of Gaelic society. The Flight of the Earls marked the end of Gaelic political power and the Plantation of Ulster witnessed a successful attack upon the social foundations of the Gaelic world. Sir John Davies, Attorney-General for the Crown, saw the imposition of English common law and the destruction of brehon law as a necessary condition of civilisation. He accepted an axiomatic that 'improving' agriculture was a superior way of life to that based upon cattle. To us the situation is not so simple. The colonisation of the Lagan valley by land-hungry settlers from the Scottish lowlands brought about the downfall of a way of life that had existed since neolithic times. Sir John Davies, however, was willing to see it depart without regret, and his plans for the 1613–15 Parliament included legislation to make illegal 'barbarous' customs, as they seemed to him, of Gaelic society. Anglicisation and civilisation were to go hand in hand.[3]

The importance of the 1613–15 Parliament thus lay in its being the instrument of an attempted constitutional religious and cultural revolution. The creation of a court party in the new parliament was not an end in itself but a means of easing the passage of new measures towards the statute book. This party included among its members, senior officials in the Dublin administration, such as Sir William Parsons, the Surveyor-General, as well as William Temple, the Puritan Provost of Trinity College. Ranged against the court party were the Catholic gentry of the country party, led in the Lords by such peers as Lords Gormanston, Slane, Trimleston, Louth and Dunsany, and in the Lower House by Sir John Everard, former Justice of the King's Bench, who had resigned in 1607 rather than take the Oath of Supremacy. The attitude of the country party was complex. In some ways they were like a modern opposition in that their aim was to regain power under the constitution. They were in agreement with the court party on some major points, such as the attainder of O'Neill and O'Donnell. Their main point of conflict with the court party lay in the extension of English penal laws to Ireland and in the exclusion of Catholics from the administration by a religious test. The country party felt that their loyalty to the English Crown had been amply demonstrated during the Anglo-Spanish war, when they had refused to join with Hugh O'Neill in what he claimed was a religious crusade. So long as O'Neill was a threat to England, the country party was wooed by the Crown. After Kinsale, however, they found that their political power was much weaker. Loyalty was no longer enough. The court party demanded religious conformity.

But the country party was not entirely without influence. The Catholic gentry, approximately two thousand in number, still held the best land in Ireland and Catholic merchants were dominant in trade. Economic power was not to be despised, as was seen in 1605 when pressure exerted by the Catholic gentry at Whitehall compelled the Dublin administration to draw back from a more actively intolerant policy. Though placed at a numerical disadvantage in the new parliament, the country party had the economic power to prevent the court from putting its legislation into effect. In modern political terms, they were a 'veto group'.

The political and religious importance of the 1613–15 Parliament for the future was realised fully by the country party. They pressed the government hard before the parliament met, and as soon as it did meet they contested the election for the Speakership. Their own candidate was Sir John Everard; the court party's candidate, backed by seventy office-holders, was

Sir John Davies.[4] On 18 May 1613, Sir James Gough of Waterford, seconded by Sir Christopher Nugent of Westmeath, proposed Everard as Speaker but refused to take part in a contested election. Indeed, Sir Walter Butler of Tipperary placed Everard in the Speaker's chair, where he was held down by Sir Daniel O'Brien of Clare and Sir William Burke of Galway. The court party elected Davies who was placed in Everard's lap by tellers. Everard was ejected, whereupon the country party withdrew from parliament. This list of names gives us most of the leadership of the country party in the Commons. Parliament was prorogued and did not meet again for over a year. During this interval, a bitter legal battle went on about the status of the newly created boroughs. At the end of this the government gave ground by withdrawing its anti-Catholic bills and by conceding that some of the new borough members should not sit. It is worth remembering also that in England itself the Crown had run into opposition which made the Addled Parliament of 1614 a resounding flop. The Irish country party had won a victory, along with its English counterpart.

It is clear from all this, however, that the role of the Irish parliament itself was only part of the political story. In a sense the government was trying to produce a drama on the parliamentary stage; the opposition refused to play the part allotted to it and chose to work by direct appeal to Whitehall. The historian is tempted to conclude that the parliamentary story is much less significant than what went on behind the scenes. Indeed, the three sessions of the 1613–15 Parliament lasted only for one week, six weeks and four weeks respectively. The parliamentary odds were weighted so heavily against the country party that it was in their interest to reduce direct parliamentary confrontation to a minimum.

The result of these years of political crisis was compromise. The Crown received its subsidies, and the opposition was successful in preventing an extension of the penal laws. However, the recusancy fines for non-attendance at church remained, along with the insistence that Catholic lawyers should be required to take the Oath of Supremacy.

There was a good deal in all these comings and goings which conformed to the general European pattern, particularly to the conflict in France which culminated in the rebellion known as the Fronde. Ireland does not provide an exact parallel to France, but it is not unreasonable to see Elizabeth's Irish wars as the equivalent of the French wars of religion. Following this parallel, Hugh O'Neill may be regarded the Irish counterpart of the *noblesse de l'épée*, the nobility of the sword, who looked upon themselves as the natural leaders of their people. This traditional type of aristocrat, rooted in the code of honour, the duel and the military virtues, was under pressure in the late sixteenth and early seventeenth century from the so-called *noblesse de la robe*, the nobility of the gown, with its base in the royal bureaucracy and office-holding. It was to this type that Sir John Everard and many of the country party belonged.

There was as little common ground between the aristocratic O'Neill and the lawyer Everard as between the Sword and Robe in France. Ulster stood for a scale of values opposed to that of the Pale, and O'Neill got no support there in the 1590s, despite his appeal on religious grounds. Kinsale, in fact, was a victory for the Irish Robe as much as for Elizabeth, and in the natural course of events they expected to serve under the Crown and to enjoy the perquisites of power. In fact, however, the religious issue was used by a new generation of bureaucrats to exclude them from office. The parallel with France may be reinforced if we recall that Richelieu followed James I's example in doubling the membership of local *parlements* and creating at one stroke a built-in court majority to support his policies. Without straining matters too far, similar patterns may be seen in Spain, where Philip III favoured Castilians in the Catalan administration at the expense of the native Catalans. In other words, the political conflict of 1613 was between two sections of Ireland's equivalent of the *noblesse de la robe*.

It was nearly twenty years before the Irish parliament met again, during which time the uneasy balance of power between 'court' and 'country' remained much the same. What change there was, however, favoured the country party. The reason lay in the opening of the crisis in Germany which came later to be called the Thirty Years' War. England was caught up in it through the Palatinate, ruled by James I's son-in-law, and James chose diplomacy rather than war as a means of helping the Protestant cause. As a quid pro quo, toleration increased for Irish Catholics during the 1620s. By 1625–26, after the accession of Charles I, England found herself at war with Spain and France. Then, as later, England's difficulties were Ireland's opportunity and the country party pressed for further concessions in documents known as 'Matters of Grace and Bounty' of 1626 and the 'Graces' of 1628.

The 'Matters of Grace and Bounty' and the 'Graces' dealt with such grievances as the exclusion of loyal subjects from the administration, the exclusion of Catholic lawyers from practice, the activities of the Court of Wards and the insecurity of land titles in Connacht. Office-holding under the Crown and the possession of land—these were the subjects of the documents presented to the Crown, and they were the standard basis of similar lists of grievances presented in other countries. The linking of the two was not accidental. To hold Crown office was to be put in the way of acquiring landed estates. Indeed, the point of office was not in the salary, but the perquisites, which could be large. The exclusion of Catholics from the practice of law cut them off at one remove from office-holding and this exclusion left them exposed to land-hungry officials.

This was the whole point of the complaints raised against the Court of Wards and Liveries. At first sight many of the 'Graces' appear to be concerned with antiquarian niceties involving the Court of Wards.[5] In practice, however, the Court was an administrative device for attacking the Catholic gentry at their weakest point—their land. The Court of Wards had been in existence in England since the days of Thomas Cromwell, but it was not seriously active in Ireland until the 1620s. The object of the Court was to raise money from the gentry by requiring them to fulfil the letter of outmoded law, to raise what was in effect the equivalent of a land tax. In Ireland, it was also being used to prevent Catholic heirs from succeeding to their father's estates. The Court of Wards is significant from our point of view in that it demonstrates the importance of possessing office and the penalty of being excluded from it. Here lay the attraction of being a member of the 'nobility of the robe'.

Professor Hugh Trevor-Roper's distinction between 'court' gentry and 'mere' gentry is illuminating here. The holding of office implied something more than administrative power, like the higher civil service today. It meant access to the perquisites of office and in particular the opportunity of acquiring large estates for a negligible cash outlay. Few office-holders were more successful than Richard Boyle, the monument to whose success is Lismore Castle, dominating the Blackwater. To be excluded from office meant that the odds were weighted against the survival of a landed family.[6]

The country party granted the Crown £40,000 a year for three years on the understanding that a parliament would be called to confirm the 'Graces'. The sum involved is an indication of the economic strength of the Catholic gentry. Their leaders, Richard de Burgh, Earl of Clanricarde and Richard Nugent, Earl of Westmeath, seem to have played their cards well in the negotiations with Whitehall. They could hardly have expected that the new Lord Deputy appointed in 1631 was to be one of the most powerful personalities in English history, Thomas Wentworth. Wentworth, better known perhaps by his later title, Earl of Strafford, was to dominate Irish politics until his fall from power in December 1640.[7]

Strafford had been a member of the English parliamentary opposition during the 1620s. He joined Charles I's government in 1628 but he was never really trusted by the king. His acceptance of the Lord Deputyship of Ireland was therefore a political gamble which he intended to pull off at almost any cost. His enemies expected him to fail as so many of his predecessors had done; he himself was determined to succeed. The country party thus found themselves facing a poacher turned gamekeeper, a member of the English country party who had turned to the court. Strafford was the English equivalent of one of Richelieu's *intendants*, a Crown servant who came to govern, free of local ties, with all the benefits and drawbacks of being a newcomer.

The next two Irish Parliaments, summoned in 1634 and 1640, were to a large measure Strafford's parliaments, and his methods of handling them recall those adopted by Elizabeth and James I in England. Strafford was never afraid to bully and threaten when diplomacy failed.

It was the country party, however, that originally took the initiative in pressing for a parliament. The hard bargaining had already been done behind the scenes and Strafford had indicated his intention of making concessions (i.e. accepting the Graces) in return for additional cash grants.[8] What the country party failed to realise was that Strafford had a 'Grand Design' for Ireland. One of his friends, Sir Edward Stanhope, compared earlier Deputies to 'mere Galenists to the miserable and distempered body of that nation', implying that they had not found a permanent cure for the diseased Irish commonwealth. Strafford's radical cure was to set up an absolute government which would override the conflicting interests of Ireland. He proposed to set the government upon a sound financial footing, not as an end in itself, but in order to provide himself and his successors with freedom of action above the hurly-burly of politics. Revenue was to be raised by confirming defective titles, by the extension of the Court of Wards and Liveries to include Protestant landowners and by the reacquisition of Crown land. He also saw the reclaiming of the Church of Ireland from Puritanism as a prime objective.

To what extent may it be said that the pattern of Irish politics had changed by the time of Strafford's Parliaments? At first it seemed as if the old country party of Catholic gentry had developed an understanding with the new Lord Deputy which might lead to their return to power. At least they were closer to the court in 1634 than they had been in 1613. The greatest change, however, was the creation of a new country party led by planters like Richard Boyle, Earl of Cork. Strafford's policy of toleration for the Catholics, allied to his association with Archbishop Laud brought about a rift at the highest political level with many of the Protestant planters. When Strafford summoned parliament in 1634 it looked as if his parliamentary majority might rest upon an alliance with the old country party. So it turned out for the first session of this parliament. Strafford played his cards so cleverly that he was able to persuade his new allies to vote subsidies before their grievances had been redressed.

The second session of Strafford's 1634–35 Parliament, however, was an explosive affair. The old country party felt that they had been tricked when Strafford announced that only a small number of the Graces would be incorporated in legislation. On some crucial issues, such as the freedom of Catholic lawyers to practise and the inheritance of land by Catholic

D

gentry without religious tests, Strafford was willing to allow considerable latitude though no legal guarantee. On two points which the old country party regarded as essential, namely the confirmation of land titles and the plantation of Connacht, Strafford took the opposite point of view. The result was a storm in the House of Commons which led to a defeat for the court by nine votes. Strafford dealt with the opposition by imprisoning its leaders, first Sir Edward FitzHarris, member for Limerick and a prominent landed proprietor, and then Geoffrey Barron, member for Clonmel. For two weeks, apparently, the Lord Deputy lost control of the House and could only restore it by arbitrary measures. Freedom of speech obviously went by the board.

Those who were most bitter in their complaints against Strafford were members of the Puritan party, now excluded from power. Strafford and his ecclesiastical associate, Bishop Bramhall, urged a crusade against those who had illegally acquired church lands. They reformed, according to their own lights, the Puritans' seminary, Trinity College, Dublin. When troubles in Scotland arose in 1637, Strafford imposed a religious test upon the new Scottish settlers in Ulster, and armed the Catholics in a standing army. Those who dared to oppose him were quickly brought to heel. Strafford's pressure upon the new colonists created enough discontent to keep a second opposition party in being. We can thus talk of two country parties, the old and the new, the Catholic and the Puritan.

This was the situation in 1640 when Strafford was forced to summon his second parliament to raise money for the king. By doing so he hoped to equip an army which would bring the Scottish Covenanters under control. So long as Strafford remained in Ireland to conduct affairs personally, all went smoothly. Parliament voted four subsidies for the king without demur. But he left for England at the end of March, leaving his deputy Christopher Wandesforde to manage the second session of parliament in June. By then Charles I was losing ground against the Scottish Covenanters and the opposition groups in Ireland began to flex their muscles. Their first step was to increase the representation of the Catholic country party by allowing seven boroughs to return members; these were the boroughs which Strafford had formerly prevented from returning members in accordance with a plan he had outlined to the King in 1635.

From then on there was an open alliance between the two opposition parties, Catholic and Puritan, against Wandesforde's court party. It was an odd alliance, since the only thing which they had in common was hostility to Strafford. In religion, the two parties were further from each other than they were from Strafford. The difference between the two was also revealed in their London contacts, the Catholics working with friends at court, the Puritans with Pym and the opposition. Both groups, in fact, had different aims in view. The Catholic country party led by Patrick Darcy, the Galway lawyer and associate of Clanricarde, pressed for the reversal of the Plantation of Connacht and for security of land titles, the two 'Graces' which Strafford had refused to countenance in 1634.[9] For their part, the Puritan country party objected to the setting up of a Court of High Commission to enforce religious uniformity, and to the arbitrary action of the Lord Deputy, not least his intolerant policy towards the Protestant settlers of Ulster. He was also associated in their minds with a fine imposed by Star Chamber upon the London companies which had failed to fulfil the terms of their plantation undertakings in Londonderry.

Much of the interest of the history of the Irish parliament during the early seventeenth century derives from the tensions which were felt by the Catholic gentry. Clearly they were not seeking independence from the Crown: Patrick Darcy said, 'England is our mother.' Their primary objective in 1634 was to obtain the extension to Ireland of one of James I's statutes providing security of land titles. As their knighthoods suggest, they saw themselves as part of the English social and political structure. The 1641 rising in Cavan was made by the 'gentry and commonalty' and the Confederation of Kilkenny drew up a list of 'all persons of rank and quality'.[10] On the other hand, they had no wish to see all English statutes extended on principle to Ireland, least of all the penal laws. Like other colonists, they wished to retain control of their own destinies under the protection of the mother country. Control of their own destinies was no doubt a legitimate aim, but it was made difficult to achieve by losing, first, control of the Church, secondly, control of the administration, and, thirdly, control of parliament.

Despite all this, the country party waged a not unsuccessful defensive battle. They knew people in high places in Whitehall, they controlled local administration in their own parts of Ireland, and in time of military crisis their opinions could not be ignored. The English connection was still the only alternative for them. Their alliance with the Ulster Irish after the 1641 rising was as surprising a combination as the alliance between Robe and Sword in the French Fronde of 1648. Indeed, if the country party were the equivalent of the *noblesse de la robe*, Owen Roe O'Neill was the Gaelic counterpart of Condé and the *noblesse de l'épée.* To some extent the Irish Fronde and the French Fronde of 1648 took a similar course. The tensions between Robe and Sword in France were paralleled by the internal conflict between the Confederation of Kilkenny and Owen Roe. The Irish Robe made peace with Ormond in 1646 much as the French Robe came to terms with Mazarin in 1649. Only the climax was different. The Irish Robe went on to Hell or to Connacht, the French Robe to Heaven and to Versailles.

Although we are studying the Irish parliament purely in its seventeenth-century context, we may also recognise features which are analogous to the parliaments of our own day. If there was not a party system, there were certainly parties in the sense that the assembly was composed of groups of men who decided upon particular policies and courses of action. The decision to elect Sir John Everard as Speaker in 1613 and then to withdraw from the House of Commons must have been planned beforehand. Strafford in his speech to the 1634–35 Parliament warned the members against meeting in private, which was almost an admission that such party discussions were normal.

What is missing from my account of the Irish parliament during these years is a sense of constitutional doctrine or of political thought. The Irish parliament saw itself in the image of the English parliament, which in turn saw itself as the 'High Court of Parliament', a royal court stretching back to time immemorial. The defenders of the Crown policies argued that parliament was a royal court, founded by royal decision and hence unable to resist the royal will. The opponents of the Crown believed that parliament went back to before the Norman Conquest. The Irish parliamentary opposition were denied the chance of taking this latter position. It was absolutely clear that the Irish parliament was a creation of the English Crown after the Norman Conquest of Ireland. Upon what theoretical grounds, then, could opposition rest? Not upon the Rights of Man, liberty, equality and fraternity, for such principles if they had been known, would have destroyed the basis of aristocratic society. The only firm basis of opposition was on the ground that the king's subjects were being denied their rights. The country party tried to be more English than the English themselves. This was the gist of the treatise which the opposition lawyer Patrick Darcy wrote in 1640. It was concerned not with the Rights of Man, but with the rights of Englishmen in Ireland. What could be more galling to such men than James I's reference to their custom of ploughing by the tail, Strafford's reference to Ireland as a conquered country, and the Puritan Parliament's confiscation of the land of 'Irish Papists' in 1642? Students of social psychology may recognise in the political dilemma of the country party the familiar symptoms of an 'identity crisis'. But that is another story.

The Confederation of Kilkenny

DONAL F. CREGAN, CM

THOMAS CARLYLE once described the decade of the Confederation of Kilkenny as 'confused and confusing' and, though the historical vision of the Eminent Victorian was sometimes distorted and occasionally blurred, in this case we must allow the aptness of his remark. The use of the term 'Confederation of Kilkenny' is itself somewhat confusing: sometimes it refers specifically to the Confederate governmental system, but it is also employed in a wider sense to denote those events which occurred between the rising of 1641 and the Cromwellian settlement. This was, of course, a momentous period in Irish history, a period of warring factions, of prolonged negotiations and of broken treaties. It is the decade of Owen Roe O'Neill and Ormond, of Inchiquin, Rinuccini, Cromwell—and the name of Cromwell suggests that thereafter Ireland was never to be quite the same again.

The Irish imbroglio involved royalists, parliamentarians and Scots as well as Confederates, and there were different shades of opinion, even within these parties. Seen in a broad perspective, the war in Ireland is merely an important episode in the events which convulsed these islands during the 1640s, and to which historians have referred as 'the War of the Three Kingdoms'. In the still wider European context, the Confederate period must be placed against the background of rivalry between France and the Habsburgs, especially the Spanish branch, which was then reaching a climax in the closing years of the Thirty Years' War. Indeed, there are few periods in which Irish politics have been so much a part of the main stream of European history. In this respect it is significant that both France and Spain maintained resident agents at the Confederate capital in Kilkenny, while the Confederation, in turn, employed representatives at most of the Catholic European courts. In recent years early seventeenth-century European history has received remarkable attention from historians, and the theory of a 'general crisis of the seventeenth century' is one of the most fashionable historical theses of our day. But while there is general agreement as to the existence of the crisis, its nature has eluded an agreed interpretation. In its Irish context, certainly, the period is notoriously complicated by the discord and warfare between, and even within, the multiplicity of parties, by the civil war in Britain into which the Irish struggle was partially subsumed, by the effects of a war abroad which was European in magnitude, and, finally, by a mysterious 'general crisis'.

The Confederation of Kilkenny was formally established on 24 October 1642, when the first General Assembly of the Confederate Catholics of Ireland met at Kilkenny in the house of Robert Shee, a member of one of the most illustrious families of the city who, by one of the minor coincidences of history, was great-grandson of Hugh O'Neill, the great Earl of Tyrone. This inaugural meeting was the culmination of at least a year's preparation. It is possible, indeed, that the first thinking on Confederate organisational structures had been done by Irish exiles abroad, but what is certain is that plans for a central executive occupied the attention of the Irish leaders, especially the lawyers and clergy, from the beginning of the rising. At a very early stage an oath of association was being administered by the clergy and an hierarchical system of government was adumbrated. Before March 1642 a document which foreshadowed the main features of Confederate government, 'most exactlie and accuratelie penned and considered of by some learned in the lawes and otherwise'[1], was being circulated in the Pale. Curiously enough it emanated from Connacht.

It was from Ulster, however, and by the clergy, that the movement for a systematic organisation of Confederate activities was definitely launched. The initial impulse came from a provincial synod of the province of Armagh, which met at Kells on 24 March 1642, and, more especially, from a national synod which was convened at Kilkenny in the following May. At the conclusion of the national synod the clergy were joined at Kilkenny by a number of nobility and gentry, mainly from Leinster, and during the months of May and June the fundamental structures of Confederate government were decided on and a provisional executive or Supreme Council was set up. But it was during the four-week session of the first General Assembly, which sat from 24 October to 21 November, that the Confederate governmental system was officially established; and the creation of a detailed machinery of government with the appropriate administrative personnel was the most important work of that month.

Confederate government was democratic in system, if aristocratic in personnel. The two chief organs of government were the General Assemblies and the Supreme Councils. In all respects, except in name, the General Assemblies were clearly modelled on parliament. In the first place, the Assemblies, like parliament, were convened by means of writs issued to all the Lords spiritual and temporal (in this case the Lords spiritual denoted the Catholic bishops) as well as to the counties and boroughs which had a right to return members to parliament. Secondly, the county and borough franchise was presumably similar to that required for parliamentary election which was governed by an act of 1542. At the same time this act, following an earlier English one of 1430, limited the county franchise to freeholders of forty shillings and upwards a year. The members of the corporate cities and towns were elected by their own burgesses, according to their respective charters. Thus, in the matter of franchise and constituencies, the Confederates anticipated by nearly three centuries the parliamentary procedure adopted by the First and Second Dáil whose members were elected on a British franchise in British parliamentary constituencies. Thirdly, the legislative structure followed parliamentary practice, with one important deviation. Parliament was bicameral, with a House of Commons and a House of Lords, whereas in the General Assemblies the Lords, spiritual and temporal, and the Commons or county and borough representatives all sat, debated and voted as one house. The full complement of members, Lords and Commons, was about three hundred persons.

There was a fourth and most important respect in which the General Assemblies resembled parliament. Many of the members of the General Assemblies had been actual members of the Parliament of 1634–35 or the Parliament which met in 1640 or of both. On 22 June 1642 alone, more than forty Catholic members were expelled from the Irish House of Commons, then sitting at Dublin, and most of these were elected members of the General Assembly. These were augmented by the Catholic lay peers from the same parliament and by other members from this or the previous parliament. Two prominent Confederates, Viscount Mountgarret and Sir Daniel O'Brien of Carrigaholt, Co. Clare had even sat in the Parliament of 1613–15, nearly thirty years before. Thus a considerable number of the members of the General Assemblies had personal experience of parliamentary procedure and practice, while many others belonged to families which had been accustomed to provide members to parliament and to this extent they had themselves been brought up in the parliamentary tradition.

Yet it is important to emphasise that the General Assemblies made no claim to be the legitimate parliament of Ireland. On the contrary, they proclaimed in the most solemn form that they were not a meeting of parliament, the calling and dissolving of which they declared to be an 'inseparable incident to your Imperial Crown'.[2] Their General Assembly, they said, was 'only a general meeting to consult of an order for their own affairs, until his majesty's wisdom has settled the present troubles'.[3] The clearest testimony of their respect for parliamentary tradition was their horrified rejection of the notion that they might have arrogated to themselves the prerogatives of king or parliament. It was for this reason that they were careful to avoid some of the details of parliamentary procedure. For instance the official who presided over the assemblies was termed 'Chairman', not 'Speaker', and during the sessions he was always addressed by name, never as 'Mr Speaker' nor even as 'Mr Chairman'.

I have identified nine General Assemblies, or sessions of Assemblies, held between the formal establishment of the Confederation in October 1642 and its dissolution on 17 January 1649. Each was called for an *ad hoc* purpose. They were convened by the Supreme Council when a major issue arose on which deliberations and decisions of a General Assembly were thought necessary. Most, in fact, were convened to discuss important issues of war or peace. Actually the Assemblies met at fairly regular but increasing intervals which ranged from about six months to nearly a year. The early Assemblies generally lasted about five to six weeks but the later sessions tended to become longer and the ninth Assembly lasted between four and five months. All the Assemblies with the exception of the third, which met at Waterford, were held in Kilkenny.

The other main organ of Confederate government was the Supreme Council which, as its name implies, was the central executive to govern the country during the crisis of the 1640s. I have been able to establish that the number of Supreme Councils which administered Confederate affairs was ten. This does not include the provisional Supreme Council called in June 1642 before the formal establishment of the Confederation. The Supreme Council was composed of twenty-four members elected by the General Assembly and was equally drawn from each of the four provinces. Twelve members known as 'residents' (three from each province) were required to remain at the seat of government. The others might, on occasion, retire to their homes or be employed on missions abroad. All members of the Supreme Council were to have equal votes and a two-thirds majority was required to carry a motion. Nine members were necessary to constitute a quorum, of whom seven at least should concur for the validity of an act. The President and Secretary were elected from among the twelve 'residents'. Viscount Mountgarret, a grand-uncle of Ormond was chosen as President and Mountgarret's gifted son-in-law, Richard Bellings, a lawyer, filled the office of Secretary of most of the Supreme Councils. In case of the President's absence or death the other resident members were empowered to elect a temporary President from among the remaining twenty-three members of the Council. He was to hold office until the meeting of the next General Assembly. Though not explicitly stated, the same arrangement presumably held in respect of the Secretary. Indeed the Secretary of the Supreme Council was the most important individual in the Confederate governmental system since through his hands all business to and from the Council was channelled.

During the recess of the Assembly the Supreme Council combined the functions of an executive, legislative and judicial body and was the supreme authority in all matters, civil and military. It is possible to see in this original combination of judicial, executive and legislative power the persistence of an earlier parliamentary tradition whereby medieval Irish parliaments exercised certain judicial functions. In August 1644, however, a judiciary, separate from the Supreme Council, was set up to bring the division between the executive and judicial powers into line with contemporary practice. In the new arrangement Patrick Darcy, who had hitherto been Lord Chancellor as well as member of the Supreme Council, was replaced as Chancellor by Bishop John Bourke of Clonfert who resigned his seat on the Supreme Council. His resignation was perhaps intended to emphasise the fact that the two powers, executive and judicial, were now separated. It is significant also that the right of declaring war was expressly excluded from the powers of the Supreme Council and was reserved to the General Assembly. This again underlines the Confederates' respect for the prerogatives of parliament for, in contemporary England, king and council required the assent of parliament before committing the country to war. Finally, it may be noted that the clergy sometimes held a clerical 'congregation' while the Assembly was in session. This was obviously a matter of convenience but it was also simply an imitation of the old tradition whereby parliament and clerical 'convocation' met simultaneously. It would seem, then, that just as the General Assembly organised itself in a parliamentary fashion, while acknowledging that it was not parliament, the clergy sometimes, at any rate, met after the manner of convocation but under the name of congregation. These details suggest, among the Confederate Catholics, a strong sense of parliamentary tradition.

The creation of provincial and county councils was part of the elaborate framework of government envisaged at a very early date by the insurgent leaders. An order for the creation of such councils was issued during the May and June meetings at Kilkenny in 1642, but it was not until the inaugural session of the first General Assembly in the following October and November that a clear notion of the composition, functions and powers of the two lesser councils emerged. The provincial council occupied an intermediate position between the supreme and county councils. It was to consist of two members chosen from each county, and it would appear that each city or notable town in the province was also given representation. The provincial council was to elect its own president, to meet four times a year, and more often if necessary. The main function of the provincial council was to examine the judgements of county councils, to decide all lawsuits normally settled by the judges of assizes, to hear and determine all civil cases, to establish rents and possessions but not to meddle with other suits about land except cases of dower and jointure. From the decisions of the provincial council appeal might be made to the Supreme Council.

The lowest grade in the hierarchy of councils was the county council. It was to consist of one or two members from each barony to be elected by the entire county. Where there were no baronies the council was to consist of twelve members chosen by the county as a whole. In general the functions of the county council were similar to those of justices of the peace. It was, in addition, to name all the county officers except the high sheriff. Appeal from the decisions of the county council could be made to the provincial council or Supreme Council. This was a remarkable essay in local government, and because of its electoral franchise which, one may reasonably assume, was the same as that for the General Assemblies, it was a comparatively representative one.

In brief, then, the division of power within the Confederate governmental system was as follows: legislative power and, while it was in session, executive power, resided in the General Assembly. From the summer of 1644 there was also a separate judiciary. When the Assembly had been dissolved or while it was in recess—that is for most of the year—executive power, with the single major limitation of the right to declare war, was exercised by the Supreme Council. Provincial and county councils, within their respective areas, had the more limited powers already described. In the machinery of government elaborated by the first General Assembly of October-November 1642 there is no mention of subordinate assemblies to correspond with the subordinate councils and yet a number of scattered references indicate that occasional provincial meetings, described as assemblies, took place. These meetings appear to have been convened to settle particular issues rather than to have met on a regular basis. Apart from the main governmental structures, the elements of a civil and diplomatic service can be discerned, and the identity of many government officials is disclosed in Confederate documents.

The strength of the Confederation of Kilkenny ultimately depended on the support and involvement of the landed interest, that is the aristocracy and gentry. This was so not only because wealth in seventeenth-century Ireland depended mainly on the possession of land, but also because all the other groups —clergy, lawyers, professional soldiers, and wealthy merchants of the towns—were indirectly connected with land ownership. Even the civic families were buying themselves into the landed class. Most of the bishops, apart from the southern group, and many of the regular clergy were drawn from the landed aristocracy and gentry, while both the lawyers and professional soldiers were generally the younger sons of the same class and very often were owners in their own right of considerable estates. An examination of the composition of each of the Supreme Councils suggests that between one third and one half were peers and gentry who were exclusively landowners, that is to say they were not at the same time lawyers or professional soldiers or merchants. Indeed, many of the members of these three categories were in fact also landowners, though their holdings were more modest. The landed interest, therefore, directly or indirectly, was overwhelmingly predominant in Confederate government.

If the *strength* of the Confederation derived from the landed classes, the dominant *influence* in its affairs was exercised by the lawyers and bishops. The lawyers, who constituted about one third of the membership of the Supreme Councils, had been educated in the common law at one of the four Inns of Court in London. The Inns at that period were partly professional schools and partly academies for the learning of polite behaviour. For this reason they were described as 'the third university of the realm' and, in fact, their students usually came from a higher social stratum than the undergraduates of Oxford and Cambridge. Serious students at the Inns steeped themselves in the common law, were interested in politics and maintained close contact with the court; in addition they developed their literary skills, learned the polite accomplishments such as dancing, fencing and lute-playing. This was the educational background of some of the most influential members of the

Confederate government: of Richard Bellings, Secretary of the Supreme Council; of Patrick Darcy, Confederate Lord Chancellor; of Nicholas Plunkett and Sir Richard Blake, Chairmen of the General Assemblies; of Geoffrey Barron, their roving ambassador; and of the majority of the negotiators of the Cessation of 1643, the Ormond Peace of 1646, the Truce with Inchiquin of 1647 and the Second Ormond Peace of 1649. These were sophisticated men, well versed in the ways of the world as well as in the intricacies of the law.

The bishops, as Lords spiritual, sat by right in the General Assemblies and they usually constituted about one fifth of the members of the Supreme Councils. They had been educated in Catholic universities and seminaries abroad and had received their professional education in a period of great vitality in philosophy, theology, political theory and canon law. The main theological problems of the age—grace, free will, predestination—were characteristically western, that is to say they centred on man and his relationship with God. But in the area of political theory and ecclesiastical law the new controversies, which concerned such questions as the relationship of Church and State, the extent of papal power and the lawfulness of the deposition of tyrants, were of more practical significance in the education of future Irish bishops and ecclesiastics. Contact with this ferment of theological, philosophical and politico-ecclesiastical ideas obviously enlarged the intellectual outlook and horizons of Irish students, and the issues involved were part of the intellectual furniture of the Confederate bishops. These bishops, who between them had studied or lived in almost every Catholic intellectual centre in Europe, were cosmopolitan in outlook and impressively qualified by contemporary European academic standards. If we are to judge them by their exposure to and involvement in university education, by their first-hand knowledge of European countries, and by their language equipment (many of them had a knowledge of half a dozen languages), this was probably the most distinguished body of bishops ever to fill the Irish hierarchy. One may feel, however, that while their academic training and religious outlook matched the confident climate of Counter-Reformation Europe, they were less fitted to cope with contemporary Irish conditions.

Because of the ambience of their training and the dissimilar nature of their studies, the dominance of lawyers and bishops did not take the form of a single unifying influence in Confederate affairs. Their thought processes and the general climate of their minds were not congenial, and the existence of two jurisdictions within the country was always a latent source of friction. Their different educational backgrounds meant that the lawyers were oriented to the English court and the bishops to Rome, to Spain or to France; translated for the Irish context and in terms of public figures, the lawyers were oriented to the Lord Lieutenant Ormond, and the bishops to the nuncio Rinuccini, the twin poles around which, from 1645, Confederate affairs revolved. Indeed, although they never met, the clash of these two personalities greatly heightened the drama of the later stages of the Confederate movement.

When, in October 1645, Giovanni Battista Rinuccini, Prince Archbishop of Fermo in Italy, arrived as Apostolic Nuncio to Ireland a typical example of the Counter-Reformation churchman, at once spiritual and cultivated, had appeared on the Irish scene. Despite indifferent health he was austere in his mode of life, free from personal ambition and devoted with absolute singleness of purpose to the service of the Catholic Church. A man of strong and even masterful disposition, and not without a dash of Italian cynicism, he was a curious mixture of realism, shrewdness and naïveté. That, in spite of initial prejudice, he came to appreciate the sterling qualities of the taciturn and ageing 'General of Ulster', Owen Roe O'Neill, and quickly sensed the hidden but disruptive influence of Ormond among the Supreme Councillors is a tribute to his perspicacity. On the other hand, errors of judgement lost him the united support of the hierarchy and exacerbated the already existing divisions within the Confederate ranks. The primary objective of Rinuccini's nunciature was, of course, spiritual—to preside over the restoration of the Catholic Church in Ireland—but this could not be done without some involvement in temporal affairs. Whether he exceeded papal instructions and concerned himself more than was necessary in Confederate politics is a matter of legitimate debate. But perhaps the main criticism which may be made of his years in Ireland was not his involvement in affairs temporal which were inextricably mixed with things spiritual, but that he used spiritual sanctions unwisely in an age when they were becoming less appropriate and were no longer entirely effective.

Since James Butler, twelfth Earl, first Marquis and later first Duke of Ormond lived to become something of the 'grand old man' of Irish politics (he died in 1688) it is well to bear in mind that all during the Confederate period he was only in his thirties. At the outbreak of the rising he was merely on the threshold of a half century of public life and, as yet, neither friend nor foe had taken his measure. The fact that he was an unknown quantity constituted his real strength in negotiation. Nearly all his relatives and many of his friends were among the Confederates, and it was as difficult for them in the 1640s to resist crediting him with some sympathy for their religion as it was in later controversies to avoid blaming him for not being pro-Catholic, rather than realising that he had never been so.

In general, Ormond's personality was more impressive than his abilities. There was an eighteenth-century polish to his manner and bearing which was suave, courteous and dignified. Even by contemporary standards, however, he was excessively conscious of his rank and honour; for this reason, perhaps, he had many admirers but few friends. He displayed little originality of mind and less military capacity. As a diplomat, however, he was patient, subtle, infinitely cautious, but lacking in initiative. Though born a Catholic he never showed the slightest leaning towards the faith of his ancestors and indeed seems to have viewed it with some distaste. Self-interest, however, rather than religious intolerance was probably the key to his dealings with the Confederacy. That he needed to be spurred on by the English king and council to implement the powers granted him to conclude a treaty with the Confederates seems to reflect the caution of a man who was afraid to commit himself too deeply in the eyes of parliament. He had much to lose and he was determined to preserve his heritage. But where his own interests were not concerned he was generally fair and moderate. His ambition in old age was, as he put it, 'to stand well in the chronicle', but to what extent he has succeeded from the viewpoint of the twentieth-century chronicler is a very open question indeed.

Because the affairs of the Confederates were conducted against a background of continuous, if desultory, warfare it is sometimes assumed that the Confederate Catholics were exponents of the theory of physical force and that the Confederate movement was revolutionary in its aims. Nothing could be further from the truth. If one carefully examines the course of the war to see who was fighting whom, it will be found that the Confederates were engaged in intermittent warfare against the king's forces for periods which totalled considerably less than three years. Secondly, not only were they not always at war with the royalists, but for two-thirds of the period they were engaged in peace negotiations with them. In contrast, they were at war with parliament and the Scots during the entire period, so that in fact for most of the decade king and Confederation were faced by a common enemy. Catholics and royalists, however, did not join forces against this common enemy until after the dissolution of the Confederation. By this time Charles I was dead, Rinuccini had departed, Cromwell had arrived and departed, and Owen Roe lay dying. Furthermore, from the very beginning of the rising of 1641 the insurgents drew a distinction between His Majesty's Dublin government and the king himself and even produced a supposedly royal commission to legalise their insurrection. When the lords of the Pale met the Ulster insurgents in December 1641 at the carefully rehearsed piece of drama at the Hill of Crofty, they agreed to join forces with the Ulster Irish on the assurance that the insurgents had taken up arms not only for religious reasons but also in defence of the king's prerogative against his recalcitrant English and Scottish subjects. The Confederate oath of association embodied an oath of allegiance to the Crown, and every single approach to the king or his representatives with a view to initiating peace negotiations was based on the clearly expressed assumption that the Confederates were 'His Majesty's loyal subjects' who had been 'necessitated' to take up arms against 'the puritan faction'.

This protestation of loyalty must be viewed against the background of seventeenth-century political thought and in particular against the background of events in England. In March 1642 the English parliament had passed an act setting aside two and a half million acres of Irish land to be sold for one million pounds to English adventurers who would come into possession of the land at the end of the Irish war. Then in August 1642 civil war between king and parliament broke out in England. There was no doubt where Irish Catholic sympathies lay. The king, by the exercise of his royal prerogative, had at least connived at the practice of Catholicism whereas Puritan parliament was its implacable foe. But the Confederates' hostility to the English parliament was more than a piece of political opportunism. The operation of Poynings' Law had been a long-standing grievance, especially among the Anglo-Irish, and agitation among the Confederates for Irish parliamentary independence was a 'carry-over' and development of policies pursued by the 'Old English' and other opposition members in the Parliament of 1640–41. Indeed, it was the future Confederate, Patrick Darcy, who as member of the Irish Parliament of 1640–41, had drawn up the historic *Argument* setting out the proper relationship between the Irish and English parliaments, common law and the king, and had expounded the *Argument* in a conference with members of the House of Lords in June 1641.[4]

That it was riven by faction is the best-known fact about the Confederation of Kilkenny and its divisions, as I have suggested, were personified in Rinuccini and Ormond. If so many things divided the Confederates we may end by asking what united them. They were, of course, Confederate *Catholics*: as such, they took the oath to assure liberty of conscience. They demanded the right freely to practise their religion, to educate their children according to the tenets of that religion, to prepare themselves for and to practise their professions, to achieve public office and—most important for a majority of the Confederates—to retain or regain their lands and property. They eventually differed in their views as to how far they should press their demands: whether, for example, they should insist on the retention of the churches. They especially differed as to how these aims might be achieved: whether they were to be left to the exercise of the king's prerogative or to be guaranteed by law in an independent parliament. But the common factor uniting all Confederates was the demand for the end of religious discrimination and the recognition of their right publicly to practise the Catholic religion. They conceived themselves, in varying degrees, as loyal subjects and in their oath of association, as we have seen, they enshrined a protestation of allegiance to the king. Finally, they saw themselves as a separate

Irish nation entitled to a parliament independent of that of England and they were prepared to give conditional allegiance to the English Crown. In a broad sense, therefore, their programme is fairly represented in their motto: *Pro Deo, pro Rege, pro Patria Unanimis*: For God, King and Country, United. To this extent they were seventeenth-century Home Rulers.

The Patriot Parliament of 1689

BRIAN FARRELL

THE choice of the Patriot Parliament of 1689 as a focal point for a consideration of late seventeenth-century Ireland might seem eccentric. This was, after all, the age of Sarsfield, of the Siege of Derry, of the Williamite invasion, of the Battle of the Boyne, of the Siege and Treaty of Limerick. Beside these stirring and momentous events, the short-lived assembly in Dublin, with its doubtful legality, its curious composition and ineffective legislation, might seem of transient importance. It might be regarded as a forgotten episode in Irish political development. Its enemies intended that it should be so : they destroyed the records of the parliament. Yet it survived to contribute a lively and significant chapter to the Irish parliamentary tradition.

The name 'Patriot Parliament' is taken from the title of Davis's well-known work on the subject. It is Davis's major historical work, and if the title is a misnomer the fault lies with his editor, Charles Gavan Duffy.[1] In fairness, it must be acknowledged that it does represent the propaganda purposes to which the history of this parliament was put. For this parliament was invoked not only by Davis and Young Ireland, and by Wolfe Tone before them, as evidence of a separate Irish nation. It has also been claimed as a forerunner of Grattan's Parliament. Like that more famous assembly, its reputation owes much to its place in national mythology; like Grattan's Parliament, its real significance is exaggerated.

The Patriot Parliament of 1689 was a failure and a symbol of failure. The first Irish parliament to sit for twenty-three years, it attempted to roll back the tide of the later English conquest and settlement. It asserted the independence, not of the Irish, but of the Old English interest in Ireland; it defined that independance in terms of freedom from submission not to the Crown but to the parliament and courts of England. It failed with the failure of the Jacobite cause.

The later seventeenth century saw parliament in decline in both Britain and Ireland. The restoration of the Stuart monarchy in 1660 put innovation at a discount. There was a desire to return to the old way of doing things after the upheaval of the Cromwellian revolution. In Ireland, as in England, the transition back to monarchy created some problems of adjustment; it provoked singularly little heart-searching or serious intellectual justification. Ireland seemed as ready as England to accept Charles II back from his travels. Cromwellians dissatisfied with Oliver's ineffective successor, loyal royalists both Protestant and Catholic, the newly established English settlers and hopeful Catholic Irish were at first ready to welcome the Restoration. Henry Jones, Bishop of Clogher (who had been Cromwell's Scoutmaster-General), preached a thanksgiving sermon for what he called 'this great work of God'.[2] A Catholic author, writing about the troubles of twenty years earlier argued that to restore the Catholics and 'conserve the English Interest in that Kingdom' (i.e. Ireland) were not 'things incompatible'. The Irish had always, he said, been in favour of 'the King's Interest or Authority, in which only and properly the English Interest is involved'.

A prophetic hint of future trouble lay in the sophistry. The English interest in Ireland was no longer a simple matter of royal allegiance, for that was now overlaid by the landed interests of English settlers—some secure for decades, others with new titles—and by the development of an Irish economy so often hindered by laws favouring English trading interests. The difference of conditions between the two kingdoms was such that the methods by which the Restoration might succeed in the one would doom it in the other. Thus in Ireland the change in land ownership in the previous twenty years had been very considerable and the problem was dealt with very sketchily by the Act of Settlement of 1662 and the Act of Explanation of 1665. In effect, Catholics received back about a third of their 1641 holdings and few Cromwellians were displaced. The land compromise in Ireland appeared to repudiate Charles II's original declaration promising restoration to loyal Catholics without disturbance to their Cromwellian supplanters. Catholics were disappointed that they received so little; Cromwellians objected to giving up any part of their new possessions. To satisfy all, a radical settlement would have been necessary, but this would have contradicted (and militated against) the restraint shown in England.

There was also a marked difference in the English and Irish responses to the religious settlement. The English people were not sorry to see their higher clergy returning from their travels considerably more anti-papist and less 'high' in liturgy and doctrine than in the days of Archbishop Laud's Anglicanism. In Ireland, however, the return of Primate Bramhall and his bishops was not welcomed by those, whether Catholic or Presbyterian, who did not conform to the Established Church, which thereafter remained a small island in a hostile religious sea— serving about one tenth of the population, dependent on state support and with an undistinguished (and frequently absentee) clergy. The situation required a policy of at least tacit toleration, originally even supported by the Church of Ireland Primate. In a coronation sermon preached in Dublin in 1661 Bramhall was careful to press for unity.[3] However, this hint of a new policy of comprehension for all under the Crown rapidly hardened into a doctrine of unquestioning and complete obedience.

Something of this emphasis can be seen less than a month later in a sermon by Charles II's eloquent advocate, Jeremy Taylor. Preaching at the opening of parliament, his argument for the obedience of subjects was largely based on the plea of utility and on the divine nature of authority.[4] Rather surprisingly, he quoted St Teresa of Avila's dictum: *in omnibus falli possum, in obedientia non possum.* Much of the sermon followed the line then current in England: kingly authority is God-like; man is a little lower than the angels, but we are much lower than the king; without full obedience 'you cannot have a Village prosperous or a Ship arrive safe in harbour.' But in an obvious reference to the special conditions in Ireland he also argued that though the conscience of the prince should direct the state, nevertheless 'the Superior is tied by the laws of Christian Charity so far to bend in the ministration of his Laws, as to pity the invincible ignorance and Weakness of his abused people.'

Jeremy Taylor spelled out his attitude on religious policy that same year in a set of *Rules and Advices to the Clergy.*[5] He still insisted that passive obedience was not enough and that secular government was instituted for man's salvation. Yet he admonished his clergy that their zeal for converting 'Papists or Sectaries' should not lead Protestants to stir up 'violencies against them' but rather should 'leave them if they be incurable to the wise and merciful disposition of the Laws'.

As the Restoration became established more firmly in England, it became less necessary to make exceptions for conditions in Ireland. The trend is evident in the treatment of the Irish parliament. Initially, Charles II required a parliament and Ormond as Lord Lieutenant convened one in order to secure the legislation necessary to provide the Restoration settlement. There was, of course, difficulty over the land settlement but no difficulty in establishing allegiance to the Crown and—even more important—providing the money for royal government: the parliament voted twenty subsidies, although voting money was one thing and collecting it another. By August 1666 Ormond had secured all he needed from a parliament now enmeshed in a procedural wrangle between Lords and Commons, and itself becoming a financial burden. The parliament was dissolved and while Charles II reigned no other Irish parliament was called.

But over the next quarter of a century the demand for a new parliament was frequently repeated. It came from two main groups: from those intent on securing their own advantage in a reorganisation of the land settlement, and from merchants seeking protection for the Irish cattle and woollen trades against legislation from England. For most of Charles's reign religious dissenters, whether Catholic or Presbyterian, saw little protection or improvement in their position coming from any Dublin parliament.

There was only one thing likely to force the King to summon an Irish parliament—the chronic need for money. Ormond, who had been removed from the Lord Lieutenancy in 1668, returned to office nine years later with a governmental financial crisis on his hands. He proposed a new parliament as a ready means of raising money and recognised that part of the price to be paid would be a new attempt to rectify the land settlement. The scheme was agreed and in 1678 Heads of Bills were sent to London (as required by Poynings' Law). However, the eruption of the Popish Plot cancelled all plans and Charles II died in 1685 without summoning his second Irish parliament.

The accession of his brother, James II, triggered off a new demand for parliament in Ireland. This time the main promoters of the idea were almost exclusively Catholic and they hoped to trade on the sectarian sympathies of their royal co-religionist. They spoke essentially not as representatives of the great Catholic mass of the Irish population but as a landed interest still intent on securing a reversal of the land settlement changes of the previous half century. It was a radical rather than a revolutionary demand. Yet the parliament they eventually secured was seen then, and presented subsequently, as a revolutionary body, the first truly independent Irish parliament. This was the Patriot Parliament of 1689.

James II never did summon an Irish parliament while he retained power in England. When he landed in Ireland, having been driven out of England and encouraged by Louis of France, it might have been expected that the Stuart king and his advisers would, as a matter of urgent priority, attend to military needs in the North—to end the Protestant revolt and secure the area against the threatened invasion by Williamite forces. Instead, he was compelled in the interests of his supporters in Ireland to summon a parliament in Dublin. Already, even without the crisis created by the Glorious Revolution, James II was considering an Irish parliament. Preparations had been made to draft revised versions of the Acts of Settlement and Explanation. In Ireland his new Catholic Lord Deputy, Richard Talbot, Earl of Tyrconnell, had been busy reorganising the corporations of towns up and down the country and replacing Protestants with Catholics in order to pack the House of Commons. So, from the outset, the Patriot Parliament, like its Caroline predecessor and its Williamite successors, was to be a largely sectarian body. In this case, however, it was to be a Catholic body, not for a Catholic people but for a Catholic landed interest.

There were some Protestants in the House of Commons—six out of a total of 230 members attending. The proportion is small, especially when it is noted that two were representatives of Dublin University. On the other hand, another seventy seats in the Commons were not filled. There were no representatives from the scene of the fighting in Derry, Fermanagh and Donegal, the Protestant strongholds into which co-religionists from many other counties—Sligo, Down, Armagh and Antrim —had flocked. Others had fled the country in a refugee movement that began as soon as Tyrconnell was appointed Lord Deputy early in 1687. In view of the temper of the time, the religion of the king and the doubtful legality of the parliament, many Protestants would have been reluctant to contest any election. There was a stronger and more vigorous representation of the Protestant interest in the House of Lords. At least four —according to some accounts, six—Protestant bishops sat as Lords spiritual. The Catholic bishops had no right to sit. Anthony Dopping, Bishop of Meath and brother-in-law of William Molyneux, became virtual leader of the Opposition in the parliament and spoke strongly against a number of measures. There were also five Protestant lay lords sitting in 1689, two of whom, the Earls of Granard and of Longford, joined with the Bishop of Meath to form a vocal and vigorous opposition.

Discussing the composition of the House of Commons, Thomas Davis pointed to 'a sort of Sept representation': the members included O'Neills from Antrim, Tyrone and Armagh; O'Reillys from Cavan; MacCarthys, O'Briens and O'Donovans from Cork and Clare; O'Tooles, O'Byrnes and Eustaces from Wicklow. He notes, in the same way, the scattering of old Gaelic names in the House of Lords. The inference is that the 1689 Parliament marked some continuance of the old Gaelic political order. In fact, both houses were far more representative of the 'Old English' or Anglo-Norman Catholic interest in Ireland than of the Gaelic Irish. These two groups may have shared religion; there was no question of sharing either land or political power. The 1689 Parliament, like its seventeenth-century predecessors and eighteenth-century successors, was closed to the Gaelic Catholic majority. They remained dispossessed and underprivileged. What is marked in the marriage of family and place names is that same stress on localism which has been a feature of the Irish representative tradition right down to our own time.

The constitutional status of this parliament has often been questioned. The Williamites argued that James II had abdicated the English throne and thus forfeited any right to rule in Ireland. They claimed that the parliament was also illegal because of the technical failure to comply with Poynings' Law by sending proposed bills to England to be certified there. On the other hand, it could be argued that James could still claim a legitimate authority in England, that the two kingdoms were separate political entities, and that Poynings' Law was not intended to apply when the king and his council were available in Ireland to scrutinise Heads of Bills. Moreover, there was throughout the seventeenth century a long history of objections by Irish constitutional lawyers to the provisions of Poynings' Law and to the claim of the English parliament to legislate for Ireland.

In fact, before the session began, James and his council examined the proposed legislation in some detail. There was pressure to repeal Poynings' Law *in toto*. This was, of course, a challenge not only to English control but to royal authority. James resisted the effort then and again later in the actual session; when a repeal bill was attempted a spokesman reported the king's insistence on maintaining his royal right to approve proposed legislation before it was introduced into parliament.[6] The incident underlines the continuing commitment of the Stuarts, even when in a tight corner, to the claims of he royal prerogative. However, James could not block a bill declaring 'that the Parliament of England cannot bind Ireland'. This specified the grounds for Irish legislative independence: that the two kingdoms were distinct, that there was no Irish representation in the English parliament, and that only an Irish legislative was entitled to make laws for Ireland. This so-called Declaratory Act also prohibited appeals from Irish court decisions to the English House of Lords.

It is largely on the basis of this Declaratory Act—foreshadowing as it does the claims for legislative and judicial independence later asserted by Molyneux, Swift, Lucas and Grattan—that the 1689 Parliament was invoked by Davis. However, in a careful historical reconstruction he could point to other parts of the legislative programme as being in accord with later Irish aspirations. There was, for example, an 'Act for Liberty of Conscience, and Repealing such Acts or Clauses in any Act of Parliament, which are Inconsistent with the Same'.

Such a degree of religious toleration was, as Lecky noted, 'in advance of the age . . . although, no doubt, mainly due to motives of policy'. The act as passed was a compromise between the Catholic parliament's impulse to repeal the old Acts of Supremacy and Uniformity and the English king's political need to preserve the Established Church and, with it, the Reformation Settlement. This act was indeed invoked in a later royal proclamation to prevent Catholics seizing Protestant places of worship. Another series of acts regulating tithes could be seen as meeting a major Catholic grievance and as depriving Protestant clergymen of their incomes, although their really distinctive feature was the emphasis on religious co-existence. The spoliated clergy, as Lecky noted, were not reduced to the category of criminals, but were guaranteed full liberty of professing, practising and teaching their religion. There was provision for a reduction in the higher scale of tithes in Ulster and for Catholics to pay tithes to their own clergy. Whatever the motives inspiring the religious legislation of the parliament, it can in fairness be claimed as enshrining a degree of toleration that would not be witnessed in Irish, English, or indeed other European, assemblies for another century. It was not a nonsectarian, secular policy but a multi-sectarian recognition of religious difference.

Apart from its assertion of Irish legislative independence and religious liberty, the parliament has been praised for promoting Irish trade, industry and agriculture. There were acts for the recovery of waste lands, for the improvement of trade, shipping and navigation, for the establishment of free schools in the main ports to teach mathematics and navigation, and an act which anticipated the famous protectionist dictum of Dean Swift by prohibiting the importation of British coal. However, a careful examination of the legislation shows that it committed Ireland less to a 'Sinn Féin' economic policy than to a continuing close relationship with and dependence on trade with England. In commercial as well as religious matters James II put his English interests before any demands in Ireland. The French ambassador, the Comte d'Avaux, who was a member of the king's council, recorded that efforts to transfer the woollen export monopoly from England to France and to secure Irish citizenship for French subjects gained some support in the

Commons but perished in a dispute between the Lords and the Commons. It is hinted in his reports, and elsewhere, that much of the opposition to legislation expressed by the Protestant peers was sponsored and supported by James himself.[7] Clearly it was in the King's long-term interest to moderate the demands being made in Dublin if he was to preserve any realistic expectation of regaining his English throne. Even in the limited role of king in Ireland, toleration rather than exclusion was the sensible policy. But two acts of the 1689 Parliament rendered all such calculations nugatory: one was the Act for Repealing the Acts of Settlement, and Explanation; the other was the Act for the Attainder of Divers Rebels, and for the Preserving the Interest of Loyal Subjects. The two went hand-in-hand.

Repeal of the Restoration land settlement was a major but contentious priority. It cut across sectarian and other interests. James himself favoured the status quo: politically it was the more acceptable policy in England, and economically it protected the large Irish estates he had secured for himself under the Act of Settlement. Moreover, among his major Catholic supporters there were many (including Tyrconnell and several of his senior judges) who had secured new land titles either by grant or purchase that would now be in question. An early attempt to repeal the whole land settlement was carried with acclamation in the Commons; a less ambitious proposal put forward in the Lords. The dispute between the landed interests in the two houses brought a vigorous opposition speech from Bishop Dopping. He argued that any large interference with land titles would be unjust and inconvenient; to carry such proposals in the middle of a civil war and with invasion imminent was against 'the good of the King, who is the Vital Head of this great Body . . . because every Man's Eye and Heart will be more on his own Concerns, than on his Majestie's Business'.[8] James agreed but when the Commons threatened to withold money he was forced to give a reluctant royal assent.

It is easy to understand James's reluctance to rake over fifty years of contested Irish land titles. Shortly after the parliament adjourned he issued a proclamation postponing any court of claims. The proclamation picked up Dopping's argument: the land question was deferred 'because some may neglect the public safety of the kingdom upon pretence of attending their private concerns'.[9] The same message is echoed down the corridors of time in the action taken by the First Dáil to prevent unauthorised seizure of land in the West. There can be little doubt, however, that subsequent action could not wipe out the effect of this piece of legislation on James's support not only among Protestants but also among recent Catholic purchasers. On the other hand, throughout the seventeenth century every major political change in Ireland had been accompanied by a new division of land and a series of appeals. It was customary for kings to reward their followers; natural for established interests to protect their possessions. Far more than religion, land was *the* political issue in Stuart Ireland.

Even more damaging to the king's political ambitions and to the parliament's reputation was the Act of Attainder. It listed several categories of persons—and named over two thousand of them—who were to be regarded as traitors. The measure has often been condemned as discriminatory and vindictive. Certainly it gave little opportunity for those accused under its provisions to make a case. But in this, as in other matters, legislative motives were mixed. Vengeance was one thing; the rich rewards of forfeited lands another. The act specified that the guilty 'shall suffer such pain of death, penalties and forfeitures respectively, as in cases of high treason are accustomed'. The Act of Attainder can be seen, then, as a necessary appendix to the land legislation since it would provide a large land-bank that could be used to satisfy new claimants. One noticeable provision of the Act of Attainder was that a deadline was placed on the royal right of pardon—a limitation that emphasised the extent to which the 1689 Parliament became progressively more independent of the king's will. A similar provision was introduced by the Protestant parliament in 1697. Clearly, irrespective of religion, dominant Irish political groups wanted to curtail royal interference with policy, especially when it impinged on land. The point reinforces a more general characteristic of the 1689 Parliament, often obscured by polemical writing. The Patriot Parliament was novel in late seventeenth-century Ireland as a Catholic interlude in the early phase of Protestant ascendancy; it was unique in its relationship with a dispossessed English king. It remained, however, essentially an institution of its own time, a mirror-image of other Irish parliaments. The charges by contemporary opponents that it was unjust, unrepresentative, discriminatory and oppressive are no more accurate than the claims of later defenders that it was more representative, equitable, advanced and freedom-loving.

Certainly, had James II won the war, the legislation passed in 1689 would have reshaped the internal balance of power in Ireland in the eighteenth century. A Catholic 'Old English' landed oligarchy would have replaced the Protestant Ascendancy. An Irish parliament could have asserted independence of English parliamentary control. Had its economic legislation been upheld, 'the worst measures of commercial repression in the eighteenth century would have been impossible.' But the royal interest would have remained dominant. This would have been enough to guarantee a continuance of English political and economic control. It is true that the practice of Catholicism in Ireland would have been legalised, although probably subject to royal control. The condition of the great mass of the people would scarcely have been affected in any material way, although their sense of shared identity and community might well have been fractured by anglicised church leaders. Later Irish parliaments would no doubt have been much more securely controlled by the patronage, power and interest of kings entrenched in England itself.

The independence asserted in 1689 was not a function of advanced nationalist or liberal views in the parliament but a reflection of the political weaknesses of a king 'on the run'. Given the same opportunity, any other Irish parliament might have behaved in a similar, fundamentally selfish way—securing maximum possession, advantage and liberty for the small and privileged group it represented. In the event, the opportunity did not arise. James was defeated. The 1689 Parliament was condemned as an illegal assembly, its acts declared invalid and its records destroyed. It passed from the world of political reality into the world of political myth. Initially, it became part of a sectarian demonology—a popish conspiracy to destroy the liberties, possessions and lives of Protestants. This simplistic Protestant case, and with it some valuable information on the parliament itself, was forcefully presented by William King, later Bishop of Derry and Archbishop of Dublin, in his book *The State of the Protestants of Ireland*. Published in 1691 as a justification of the switch of allegiance from James to William, it struggles hard to fit the argument into the traditional doctrine of obedience by putting the case that a king who plans the destruction of his people has no claim to sovereignty over them and that in such circumstances it is lawful for another prince to interfere on behalf of oppressed people. It is an interesting original exposition of the ambiguity of the loyalist position. The theoretical argument is, however, only a small part of this long historical account of how James II set out to destroy the Protestants of Ireland. The parliament is presented as a central part of the plot.

Later the 1689 Parliament was pressed into service in another cause. Its short-lived and unreal assertion of legislative independence, though not its policies of religious toleration, became a model for Protestant patriots in the eighteenth century. It was incorporated into the more advanced popular nationalism of Young Ireland in the nineteenth century in the ringing words of Davis's peroration :

It boldly announced our national independence, in words which Molyneux shouted on to Swift, and Swift to Lucas, and Lucas to Flood, and Flood and Grattan redoubling the cry, Dungannon church rang, and Ireland was again a nation.

The Case of Ireland Stated

J. G. SIMMS

AFTER the defeat of the Catholic Jacobites by the Protestant Williamites in the war that ended with the Treaty of Limerick in 1691, a new phase opened in the Irish parliamentary tradition. The series of parliaments that came after the war represented what has been called 'the Protestant nation', in contrast to the Catholic nation that was the predominant element in the Patriot Parliament of 1689. But the Protestant parliaments were faced with the same problems—Poynings' Law and the application of English acts of parliament to Ireland. Poynings' Law gave final drafting power to the executive in England, the king's ministers and the rest of his Privy Council; it did not concern the English parliament. That parliament was at the heart of the second problem, the growing practice of passing laws in England for the regulation of Irish affairs. There were Protestants who reacted to both these situations in exactly the same way as the Catholics of the Patriot Parliament had done, though for a long time Protestants discreetly ignored the parallel; it would have been distasteful and imprudent to acknowledge the support of Catholic Jacobites in the effort to win constitutional rights for a Protestant parliament. These two problems continued to be a cause of occasional friction for the next ninety years, until the inauguration of 'Grattan's Parliament'.

To begin with, the English executive appeared to Protestants to represent more of a threat than the English parliament. In the war against France, which went on for several years after the war in Ireland had finished, William III had Catholic allies, the Holy Roman Emperor and others, who pressed him to give fair treatment to Catholics in Ireland and, in particular, to observe the Treaty of Limerick. In that treaty King William had undertaken to do his best to get the terms ratified by the Irish parliament and to recommend to that parliament that

Catholics should be given such further security as 'may preserve them from any disturbance upon the account of their said religion'. Protestants, who had felt themselves humiliated and harried during the Jacobite regime and whose estates had been the subject of confiscatory legislation, were in no mood for granting concessions to Catholics and did not relish the prospect of ratifying the Treaty of Limerick, to say nothing of giving additional security to Catholics.

In comparison with what was regarded as the pro-Catholic policy of the English executive, one act of the English parliament was reassuring to Irish Protestants. Within a few weeks of the Treaty of Limerick that parliament had passed a law appointing new oaths for Ireland and requiring members of both Houses, the Commons and the Lords, to take an oath and make a declaration that no Catholic could possibly agree to. The declaration, which already applied to the English parliament and continued to do so until 1829, was particularly offensive: it repudiated transubstantiation and referred to the invocation of the Virgin and the celebration of the Mass as idolatrous and superstitious. For the first time there was a law —and it was an English law—that effectively barred Catholics from either House of the Irish parliament. It remained an integral part of the constitution of that parliament until the Act of Union of 1800.[1]

The first of the Protestant parliaments met in the autumn of 1692. The great majority of the 300 members of the House of Commons were landowners. As men of property they naturally agreed with John Locke's opinion that the preservation of property is the end of government. Their estates had been acquired in a series of confiscations from Catholics, and their chief aim was to ward off any possibility of a Catholic attempt to get them back. They were a minority in a countryside that, apart from Ulster, was overwhelmingly Catholic. They were afraid of the hazards to which the European war might expose them, and above all they were haunted by the spectre of a Stuart restoration. They wanted security and they thought that it was to be found in the suppression of Catholics in general and Catholic gentry in particular. They were disturbed by what they considered the partiality of the government towards Catholics and by the quantity of land already given back to

E

former owners under the Treaty of Limerick and special pardons. They expected the Treaty of Limerick to be put before parliament for ratification and they were in no mood to agree. Their feeling of insecurity and the bitterness engendered by civil war made them aggressive and intolerant.

The Parliament of 1692, after a short and stormy session, broke up without ever considering the Treaty of Limerick. The immediate point of contention was Poynings' Law; this was exemplified in the disputed right of the executive to draft a money-bill without previously consulting the Irish House of Commons. Most of the government's income was on a permanent basis, but the balance had to be found from additional taxes levied by passing supplemental money-bills from time to time. The government took the view that by Poynings' Law it was entitled to draw up money-bills, or any other bills, without prior consultation and that the Irish parliament must either accept or reject them; it had no right to make amendments or suggestions. The question was one of principle; in the eyes of the English government Ireland was a dependent kingdom. So two money-bills were sent over from London to open the parliamentary session.

The Irish House of Commons took exception to this procedure and resolved that they had the sole right to propose heads of money-bills, that is, the right to choose the ways in which they were to be taxed. The sanction that they possessed was the power of the purse. They were ready to contribute to the expenses of government if they were allowed to choose the means of raising money and if attention was paid to their grievances. They passed under protest a beer-duty bill, but they rejected the government bill for a tax on corn 'because it had not its rise in this house'. They also rejected a militia bill and a mutiny bill, and they began a detailed inquiry into government mismanagement. They set up a highly organised system of committees to investigate the details of finance and administration. Strong words were used about the corruption and incompetence of government officials. The Lord Lieutenant, Lord Sydney, reported to Whitehall that the House of Commons were like a company of madmen: 'They talk of freeing themselves from the yoke of England, of taking away Poynings' Law . . . and twenty other extravagant discourses have been amongst them.'² Less than a month after the session had begun he brought it to an end with a rebuke: their resolutions, he said, were contrary to Poynings' Law and encroached on the rights of the Crown of England. It was an extraordinary end to a parliament of Protestant colonists who had just been delivered by the King of England from the loss of their property and their privileged position. The rejection of the money-bill of 1692 was long remembered and quoted in later conflicts between parliament and the executive.

The tough line adopted by the Irish Commons in 1692 made the governments of William III and Anne extremely wary in their handling of later Irish parliaments. The government's right to send over a money-bill was preserved by the token repetition of the beer-duty bill after each general election. Otherwise the Commons was allowed to choose its own method of taxation. Its control over the executive was fortified with a resolution that no money should be voted until the Committee of Public Accounts had scrutinised the revenue and expenditure, and the executive was made accountable for every part of the administration.

The Commons was also able to turn the government away from its original policy of conciliating Catholics. The formidable accumulation of penal laws passed from 1695 onwards was the price paid to Protestant politicians for their agreement to vote the necessary taxation. The Treaty of Limerick was not brought forward again until 1697, and was then ratified in so mutilated a form as to be hardly recognisable. The guarantee for the practice of religion on which Catholics had pinned their hopes was not ratified at all. At the same time, the attempts made by Whig administrations in England to secure religious toleration for Protestant Dissenters in Ireland were regularly frustrated at this period. Relations between the Church of Ireland and the Scots Presbyterians in Ulster were very strained, and a majority in the Irish parliament, and in particular in the House of Lords, where the bishops were a large element, were determined to make no concessions to what was regarded as a threat to the Established Church. Such party politics as there were turned on this question of toleration for Presbyterians. Whigs were for it; Tories, or the 'Church Party', were against it.

While the Irish parliament at this period showed itself a match for the executive, it had a formidable challenge to meet from the English parliament. This took two forms: English legislation, and judgements on appeal in the English House of Lords overruling the Irish House of Lords. Both forms developed in the course of William III's reign and provided the occasion for a celebrated book with the title *The Case of Ireland's Being Bound by Acts of Parliament in England, Stated*. Its author was William Molyneux, who had since 1692 represented Dublin University in the Irish parliament. He belonged to a family that had been prominent in Irish affairs since the sixteenth century. He was an attractive and talented man, of considerable standing in the world of science, a founder of the Dublin Philosophical Society, a member of the Royal Society of London, and the author of several books. He had an admiration for John Locke, the philosopher, and they often corresponded. He had a particular regard for Locke's *Two Treatises of Government*, which taught that there was a compact between ruler and ruled and that government should be by consent of the governed. Locke, as a member of the English Board of Trade, was concerned about a campaign by English cloth-merchants to stop the growing export of Irish woollens to foreign countries. Bills for this purpose were introduced into the English Commons in 1697. Locke, who had corresponded on the subject with Molyneux, hoped that the Irish parliament would itself put a brake on woollen exports and encourage the linen trade, but it became clear that this would not satisfy the English merchants and that there was a threat of English legislation.[3] At the same time there was a clash of appellate jurisdiction between the English and Irish Houses of Lords in a suit between the Bishop of Derry and the London companies who formed the Irish Society.

These two situations were the background for Molyneux's book, which he wrote early in 1698. It had two themes: (1) the historical status of the Irish parliament; (2) representational government as a human right. For the first theme he could draw on the researches of his father-in-law, Sir William Domville, who had been Attorney-General of Ireland and had collected a number of legal precedents from medieval times to show that the Irish parliament was the sole instrument for passing statute law applicable to Ireland. Among the documents in Domville's possession was the medieval treatise on Irish parliamentary procedure, *Modus Tenendi Parliamenta in Hibernia.* This had been published in 1692 by Molyneux's brother-in-law, Anthony Dopping, Bishop of Meath, a fact which suggests that there was an interest in the Irish parliament as an ancient institution and that the Protestant colonists regarded themselves as heirs of an earlier tradition. For the wider theme, the rights of man, Molyneux drew heavily on Locke's ideas and incorporated several verbatim (and unacknowledged) quotations from Locke in his own book. At the outset he argued that the cause of Ireland, which he called 'my own poor country', was also the cause of mankind in general.

To find a basis for deciding the relationship between England and Ireland Molyneux went back to the Norman Conquest. He maintained that Ireland was not conquered by Henry II in any sense that would give the English parliament jurisdiction over it. On the contrary, the Irish kings had voluntarily submitted and in return Henry had made a compact with the Irish people that they should enjoy the same liberties as the people of England. In the seventeenth-century manner Molyneux takes us down the ages with a wealth of precedents to show that the English parliament never legislated for Ireland until 1641, except in isolated circumstances when representatives from Ireland were brought over to take part in the proceedings. He goes on to say that in recent years there had been a number of occasions on which the English parliament, in which Irishmen were not represented, had passed laws for Ireland. He was 'sorry to reflect that . . . when the subjects of England have more strenuously than ever asserted their own rights and the liberty of parliaments it has pleased them to bear harder on their poor neighbours'.[4] Molyneux argued that a large part of the people of Ireland were descendants of those who had assisted Henry II and later kings to conquer Ireland. But his reference to the Irish kings shows that he was taking his stand as a citizen of Ireland and not merely as an Englishman who had brought his civic rights across the sea with him.

He does not specifically exclude Catholics from the rights of citizenship. But his references to them are coloured by the recent struggle between Jacobites and Williamites. He refers with approval to the English act of 1691 that imposed on members of the Irish parliament the requirement of making a declaration against Catholic doctrines. He regarded it as a law 'highly in our favour', and argued that voluntary compliance with this English law did not give the English parliament the right to bind Ireland with other less favourable laws.

Molyneux took his argument on to a wider plane when he declared : 'That Ireland should be bound by acts of parliament made in England is against reason and the common rights of all mankind.' All men, he said, were by nature in a state of equality and so had the right to be freed from laws to which they had not consented. Legislation without consent would naturally lead to taxation without consent : 'To tax me without consent is little better, if at all, than downright robbing me.' His argument was based on the right to enjoy representation in the legislature and he claimed that if the parliament of England could bind Ireland, the people of Ireland ought to have their representatives in it : 'This, I believe, we should be willing enough to embrace, but this is an happiness we can hardly hope for.'[5] English politicians had no intention of admitting Ireland to the privilege of a union with them.

A practical point was made of the uncertainty and confusion created for the Irish citizen by the existence of two parallel parliaments, each claiming to legislate and adjudicate for Ireland. This conflict was particularly troublesome in the case of appeals to the House of Lords, and Molyneux argued that the English House had no jurisdiction in Irish cases. The Bishop of Derry's case produced an open rift between the two Houses of Lords. It was followed by other cases of the kind, one of which was to bring about the English Declaratory Act of 1720 —the 'Sixth of George I'—which flatly contradicted Molyneux's contention.

In the closing passage of his book Molyneux referred to the Irish system of representative government as 'this noble gothic constitution'—an epithet based on the notion of a golden age of Saxon democracy—and he pleaded for its preservation in an era of absolutism.

Reaction in England to Molyneux's book was uniformly hostile. A shower of pamphlets expressed opposition to it: *An*

Answer to Mr. Molyneux; A Vindication of the Parliament of England; The History and Reasons of the Dependency of Ireland. A committee of the English Commons examined the book in detail and reported the more objectionable passages to the House, which resolved *nem. con.* that the book was

of dangerous consequence to the crown and people of England by denying the authority of the king and parliament of England to bind the kingdom and people of Ireland and the subordination and dependence that Ireland hath, and ought to have, upon England, as being united and annexed to the imperial crown of this realm.[6]

The reasoning inferred that the authority of the imperial Crown of England was to be exercised through the imperial parliament.

The usual ritual of ordering the book to be burned by the common hangman was for some reason not included in the resolution, though it is often said that the book was burned. The Commons addressed the King on the danger of the book and made the point that Molyneux was not speaking for himself alone, that his 'bold and pernicious assertions' were in line with the general attitude of the Irish House of Commons. The King was asked to punish those who had been guilty of such conduct and to discourage anything that might lessen the dependence of Ireland upon England. William confined himself to ordering the Irish government to prevent anything of the sort occurring in future. Molyneux had raised a constitutional storm, and it is clear that politically conscious people in Ireland were afraid of the consequences of this rash challenge to the English parliament. Their fears were justified, as in the following year (1699) the English parliament passed the law preventing the export of Irish woollens to foreign parts, and what appeared to be a promising export trade was killed by the most celebrated instance of Ireland's being bound by English laws. But by that time poor Molyneux was dead, a victim at the age of forty-two to an incurable kidney disease. His book became the classic statement of the rights of the Irish parliament, and it reached its tenth edition in 1782, the year in which the English parliament at last yielded to Molyneux's contention.[7]

A modern historian has made a study of Molyneux as one of

a group of what she has called 'commonwealthmen', a band of radical thinkers, influenced by Locke, believing in natural rights, freedom of thought and expression, and government by consent. Molyneux is seen as a link in the chain that leads to the American revolution.[8] Another link in that chain was Robert Molesworth, Molyneux's contemporary and fellow member of parliament, who sat for the county of Dublin. Molesworth had won international notoriety for his attack on the absolutist military regime in Denmark. He shared Molyneux's admiration for the so-called gothic constitution, the legislature consisting of King, Lords and Commons working together, and the executive accountable to the whole body of the people.[9]

Towards the end of William's reign the English House of Commons asserted itself against the king by taking complete control of the estates confiscated from Irish Catholics, with scant regard for the vested interests that Protestants had acquired in them. This rivalled the killing of the export trade in woollens as a factor in building up the resentment felt by Protestants in Ireland over the domineering attitude of the English parliament. In the first of Anne's Irish parliaments the House of Commons complained to the Queen about the distressed condition of the country and the way in which the constitution 'hath of late been greatly shaken'. The Queen was asked either to restore her Irish subjects to a full enjoyment of their constitution or else to grant them 'a more firm and strict union' with her English subjects.[10] This suggests that the primary demand was for freedom from interference with the rights of the Irish parliament; if that failed, union was asked for as a second-best. The Queen's reply was chilly and gave no hope that either request would be granted. On other occasions, stimulated by the negotiations for union between England and Scotland, emphasis was laid on union for its own sake: the surrender of an independent Irish parliament in favour of representation within a wider and more powerful imperial parliament. The Irish Commons, congratulating the Queen on the Scottish union, inserted in their address the prayer that God might 'put it in your royal heart to add greater strength and lustre to your crown by a yet more comprehensive union'.[11] But the English government did not consider that Ireland presented the problem that had made the Scottish union necessary, and there was no move on its part to extend the union to Ireland. When the Irish House of Lords continued to press the point and to hope that the Queen 'will perfect this great work by bringing her kingdom of Ireland also into the union' the Lord Lieutenant replied that he had no directions from Her Majesty to say anything on the subject.[12]

Swift contrasted the treatment given to Scotland with that given to Ireland in an allegory which he wrote, but did not publish, at this time—*The Story of the Injured Lady, Being a True Picture of Scotch Perfidy, Irish Poverty, and English Partiality.* Ireland is the lady, ruined and cast off by a gentleman (who is England) in favour of a rival—an unattractive female 'with bad features and a worse complexion', inferior to the injured lady in appearance and fidelity.[13]

It was for long to be a grievance with Irish politicians and publicists that laws affecting Ireland should be passed by a parliament in which there was no Irish representation. But to what extent was the Irish parliament itself representative of those for whom it legislated? and in particular could it be said to represent Catholics, who were not able to sit in it? But although from 1692 Catholics could not be members they still for some years had the vote, which was not finally taken from them until 1728. In the counties all forty-shilling freeholders had the franchise, and during William's reign a good many Catholics were therefore entitled to it. In some boroughs the vote was given to freemen, who might include Catholics, and in a few to residents. Catholics used their votes to show preference for one Protestant candidate over another, and defeated candidates often complained about this. In 1704 voters were required to take the Oath of Abjuration, that is, to swear that Anne and not James Stuart was the rightful sovereign. It was against the principles of many Catholics to do so, but some did and were therefore allowed to vote 'as amply and fully as any Protestant'. In 1709 it was proposed to take away the vote from Catholics, but a majority of the Commons took the surprisingly liberal view that it was unreasonable for them to be bound by laws not made by their representatives; it was pointed out that the same reasoning applied as in the case of objections to Ireland being 'cramped by English acts of parliament'.[14]

The force of this logic seems to have weakened by 1728, when Catholics as such were deprived of the vote.

The Irish parliaments of the late seventeenth and early eighteenth centuries had a strong sense of the rights of citizens and the traditions of representative government, but these privileges were primarily claimed on behalf of the 'Protestant nation', and there was a diminishing regard for the claims of Catholics to share in them.

From Swift to Grattan

J. L. McCRACKEN

HISTORIANS have tended to pass lightly over the half century or so that separates Swift from Grattan. They are inclined to write it off as an uneventful period, lacking in dramatic events and colourful personalities. Parliamentary affairs have seemed to them particularly drab in contrast to the excitement aroused by Swift and the victories won by Grattan. But in fact we must look closely at the character and conduct of parliament in these years if we are to understand the place of the eighteenth century in the Irish parliamentary tradition.

The Irish parliament in the eighteenth century was the preserve of the Protestant landowning aristocracy which had emerged victorious from the Williamite War. Catholic peers received writs of summons to the House of Lords but they were prevented from taking their seats by being unable to subscribe to the Oath of Supremacy. Catholics were also excluded from membership of the House of Commons throughout the century and between 1728 and 1793 Catholics and those married to Catholics could not vote at parliamentary elections. Protestant Dissenters were not subjected to such harsh legal disabilities, but no Dissenters sat in the House of Lords and very few in the House of Commons. A sacramental test, imposed in 1704, barred them from the corporations of towns, in some of which they had been strongly represented. In any case, parliamentary elections in the boroughs were so much under the control of the landlords that the test can have made little difference to the Dissenters' political influence. What really prevented them from playing a greater role was their social and economic status. Most of them were tenant-farmers in the North and it was only as forty-shilling freeholders that they were able to take part in county elections. Even the minority of the population who conformed to the Established Church had very little influence on political affairs.

One reason for this was that public opinion had few opportunities of finding expression. From the accession of George I in 1714 until the passing of the Octennial Act in 1768 the life of a parliament only came to an end with the death of the king. One parliament lasted all through the reign of George I and its successor continued in existence for the thirty-three years of George II's reign. In addition, for most of the century there was no machinery by which a member of parliament could resign his seat. If he could not attend or did not wish to attend he simply stayed away, but he remained a member. In December 1743 the Corporation of Sligo petitioned the House of Commons for a writ to elect a new member on the grounds that one of the Sligo members, Francis Ormsby, had been prevented by ill-health from sitting in the House since 1731 and would be unlikely ever to be able to attend again. Although Ormsby himself backed up the request it was refused; Ormsby was given permission to absent himself and he remained a member till his death in 1751.

More serious still as a restriction on an expression of the electorate's will was the control over the election of members to the House of Commons exercised by the landed aristocracy. Each of the thirty-two counties returned two members. The election of these county members was regarded by the great landowners of the county as a matter of special concern to them. The vote in the counties was enjoyed by the forty-shilling freeholders. By putting pressure on the freeholders, by controlling the appointment of the sheriffs who acted as returning officers, by using bribery and patronage and, if need be, by creating fictitious freeholds, they could ensure the election of their candidates, though usually at a price. Such prestige attached to county membership that there was often bitter rivalry between leading families and a lavish outlay on election expenses. The Co. Antrim election of 1761 cost the three families involved over £2,500; John Foster's expenses in the Co. Louth election of 1768 amounted to over £1,900 and Sir Lucius O'Brien's in Co. Clare to over £2,000. Small wonder that Richard Levinge described a county election as 'one of the most troublesome and expensive hobby horses that any man ever kept for the amusement of his youth or old age'.

The control of the 117 boroughs that returned two members

each to the House of Commons was less troublesome. In most of the Irish boroughs only the members of the corporation or the members of the corporation and the freemen had the right to vote. If a political magnate was able to ensure that the thirteen—sometimes twelve—members of the corporation were his nominees and, in addition, in freemen boroughs, that only his supporters were admitted as freemen, he could return the two MPs for the borough. Sometimes, if two families were interested in a borough, they made a formal agreement to divide the representation between them. Richard Jackson and the Earl of Tyrone entered into an agreement of this sort about Coleraine in 1751 and there were similar compacts about Cavan, Dunleer, and Maryborough. The twelve potwalloping boroughs', in which the resident householders had the vote, and the six manor boroughs, in which the freeholders of the manor voted, had all very small electorates and were easily manipulated by aristocratic patrons. Even the eight sizeable towns that ranked as county boroughs with an electorate made up of the corporation, the freemen and the freeholders were subject to aristocratic influence. Only in Dublin and, to lesser extent, in Cork was the popular vote significant. Finally, in the university constituency where the vote was vested in the twenty-two fellows and seventy scholars the Provost controlled the return of the members for he had 'in the plenitude of his power, such a magazine of resources, as cannot fail to operate powerfully on the majority'.

The composition of the House of Commons reflected the electoral system on which it rested. Country gentlemen and relatives of the aristocracy made up the bulk of the members. The oligarchical character of the House is illustrated by the strong hereditary element in the membership. Parliamentary representation tended to be a family affair, with seats passing from father to son and with the exclusiveness of the ruling class being maintained by intermarriage. In George II's Parliament, for example, eighteen members of the Gore family sat, nine of them at the same time. Eleven of them were the sons, five the maternal grandsons and eight the sons-in-law of members. Henry Boyle, Speaker from 1733 to 1756, had four sons and a nephew in the House, and the Ponsonby family was represented by three brothers, their uncle and his son, and one of them had a son-in-law in the House.

But this parliament in which the Protestant Ascendancy was all-powerful was not an all-powerful body. There were two important limitations on its powers. The English parliament claimed the right to make laws binding Ireland. This right had been challenged in 1698 in a famous pamphlet by William Molyneux, *The Case of Ireland's Being Bound by Acts of Parliament in England, Stated*, and it had been contested by the Irish parliament, but in 1720 the English parliament asserted its claim in an act usually called the 'Sixth of George I'. The restrictions imposed by one of the Irish parliament's own acts were even more serious. Poynings' Law, passed in 1494, had originally been designed to curb the king's representative in Ireland. By the eighteenth century it was being used to restrain the Irish parliament itself. A parliament could not meet in Ireland until the Lord Lieutenant and the Irish Privy Council had sent over some draft bills to the king and the English Privy Council as a reason for summoning it, and when it did meet any bills it wished to pass had first to be submitted for approval in the same way. These proposals, or Heads of Bills as they were called, might be suppressed or altered by either the Irish or the English Privy Council, and if they were returned, the Irish parliament had no power to make any further alterations; they had either to be accepted as they stood or rejected. The effect was to give the government great influence over legislation.

Yet, in spite of its limited competence, the Irish parliament met more regularly and played a more important role in the constitution in the eighteenth century than ever before. After the revolution it began voting the extra money necessary to carry on the government for two years only; this ensured regular meetings. Apart from two intervals between 1692 and 1703 when there was no parliament, meetings were held at least every other year. When a proposal was made in 1729 that supplies should be granted for twenty-one years it was rejected as a government ruse to avoid summoning parliament so frequently. Actually the government's dependence on parliamentary grants increased as time went on partly because of the rising cost of administration and partly because the growth of a national debt made it necessary for parliament to provide for paying the interest. It is a measure of the increased importance of parliament that only in the eighteenth century was a permanent meeting place provided for it. Between 1729 and 1739 the stately parliament house which still adorns College Green was erected.

With parliament meeting at regular intervals, the problem of the relations between it and the government became more pressing. The problem was not peculiar to Ireland; parliamentary management was as much a feature of the English political scene as of the Irish, but in Ireland the situation was complicated by the fact that Ireland was a dependent kingdom with a government completely divorced from the Irish parliament. The king's representative and head of the executive was the Lord Lieutenant. Throughout the century the office was filled by a succession of great noblemen whose tenure of office depended on the fluctuations of English politics, not on the support of a majority in the Irish House of Commons. From early in the century until the inauguration of a new policy in 1767 with the appointment of Viscount Townshend as a resident Lord Lieutenant the holder of the office lived in Ireland only for the six months or so every two years when parliament was in session. Such brief and infrequent visits gave him little opportunity of familiarising himself with Irish affairs. He was satisfied if he got the money-bills through parliament and prevented hostile inquiries into the expenditure of the previous grant.

This was not lightly achieved. On his arrival the Lord Lieutenant had to build up a body of support from among the various groups owing allegiance to the leading political magnates. There were no parties in the English sense in the Irish House of Commons. The names 'Whig' and 'Tory' were used in the early part of the century but they had little meaning in a parliament where all the members were vitally interested in maintaining the Hanoverian succession. How formidable the task of parliamentary management was is shown by a letter written by the Lord Lieutenant's Under-Secretary in 1715.

We have made a good session of it but it was not without much application and industry. We were forced to meet every night with the chief of our friends to provide against the next day's battle, the rest of the day was spent either in the house or in running about to solicit the members and keep our forces together whom Broderick [leader of the Opposition] with as much diligence endeavoured to debauch . . . and had this work lasted for a week longer it would have killed us all.

There was nothing permanent about a government majority constructed in this laborious way; by the time the next session of parliament came round the work had to be done all over again. Nor was it particularly secure, even in the short term. Internal dissensions might tear it asunder or it might disintegrate in the face of popular opposition. Any government proposal which appeared to conflict with Irish interests was liable to arouse resentment among the Protestant ruling class and when this happened the Irish parliament was apt to flow with the popular tide. Such a sitution arose in 1722 when a patent was issued to a Wolverhampton ironmonger, William Wood, authorising him to coin halfpence and farthings for Ireland to the value of £100,800. The proposal evoked a storm of protest which was skilfully nurtured by Swift in his famous pamphlets called the *Drapier's Letters;* the Irish parliament joined in; the government's supporters deserted it; and the patent had to be withdrawn.

The crisis gave English politicians a severe jolt and led to changes in their method of managing Ireland. On the one hand they made a concession to the colonial nationalism which had expressed itself so vehemently during the Wood's Halfpence dispute; on the other they tried, by installing Englishmen in key positions, to ensure that they would be better informed about political opinion in Ireland, especially during the long absences of the Lord Lieutenant. Instead of the Lord Lieutenant and his secretaries assuming direct responsibility for the building up of a government party in the House of Commons every time parliament met, the task was entrusted to leading political figures in Ireland. In return for their services the Lord Lieutenant allowed them to dispense a considerable portion of the patronage vested in him. These political magnates came to be known as 'undertakers' because they undertook to carry the government's business through parliament. This arrangement suited the Lords Lieutenant because it relieved them of the troublesome negotiations involved in building up a body of government supporters, and it suited the political magnates because it both gratified their aspirations and enhanced their importance by giving them a measure of control over Irish affairs through the appointments to offices that they were able to make and the other favours that they were able to confer on their supporters.

The other side of the English government's policy was inaugurated by the appointment of Hugh Boulter, Bishop of Bristol, as Archbishop of Armagh and Primate in 1724. Boulter became the permanent watchdog of English interests in Ireland and the persistent advocate of the appointment of Englishmen to bishoprics and judgeships. It was important to the government to have Englishmen in these offices because of the political duties attached to them. The bishops were all members of the House of Lords and were, in the first half of the eighteenth century, more active and able members than the lay peers. Moreover, four of them had the control of parliamentary boroughs in their dioceses and returned two members each to the House of Commons. The judges advised the government in Dublin and acted as its ears and eyes when they were on circuit. Furthermore, during the absence of the Lord Lieutenant the country was ruled by Lords Justices and after 1724 it became the normal practice to appoint the Primate, the Lord Chancellor and the Speaker of the House of Commons to the commission. The first two were foremost amongst the English government's agents in Ireland; the third was one of the principal undertakers and was included because it was thought necessary 'to have one of this country in the government, in whom there may be a proper confidence placed by the country gentlemen'.

The arrangement with the undertakers smoothed the Lord Lieutenant's path but it did not create a foolproof system. There were limits to what the undertakers could achieve or were willing to attempt. Their control over the House of Commons was never absolute. They had to contend with a hard core of anti-government members, 'the standing sour opposition of the country', and with what Lord Townshend called 'the second interest', country gentlemen who tended to take an independent line. Moreover, the undertakers were not prepared to run counter to public opinion by backing a government bill that they knew to be unpopular. They had their own principles, or prejudices, too. Even so mundane a matter as a bill designed to prevent riots in the city of Dublin was defeated in the House of Commons, largely because the Primate and the Lord Chancellor were in favour of it 'for some people have a mind to shew them, that they shall govern but by the people of Ireland'. Nor did their existence entirely relieve the Lord Lieutenant of trouble and anxiety. He had to make arrangements for the parliamentary session and ensure that the undertakers faithfully discharged their undertaking. He had to distribute favours, resist excessive demands and decide on rival claims in the way that would give least offence and would bring most strength to the government; and he had to steer a path through the jealousies and conflicting ambitions which existed within the ranks of the undertakers.

The troubles which could arise from such internal divisions were dramatically revealed during the Lord Lieutenancy of the Duke of Dorset in the early 1750s. The Primate, George Stone, had personal political ambition. He was not content to watch over the 'English interest' as his predecessor Boulter had done; he aspired to building up a party of his own in the House of Commons. In alliance with the Ponsonby family he tried to oust the Speaker, Henry Boyle, from power. Boyle went into opposition and in 1753 secured the rejection of a money-bill. He and his principal supporters were dismissed from their offices but the clamour was so great that the English government took alarm, Dorset was recalled and the Opposition was bought off. Lords Lieutenant continued for some years after this crisis to work through undertakers but they were becoming increasingly exasperated with the unruly conduct of the factions and the excessiveness of their demands. Changed political circumstances in England and the death of the two old protagonists, Boyle and Stone, provided a favourable opportunity 'to put an end to the absurd system'. At a meeting of the English Privy Council in February 1765 it was decided to insist on the Lord Lieutenant living constantly in Ireland. It took some time to find a nobleman prepared to accept the office on these terms but eventually, with the appointment of Lord Townshend in 1767, the new policy was put into operation. Now that the Lord Lieutenant was permanently resident and Lords Justices no longer necessary, it was hoped that the Lord Lieutenant would be able to take back patronage into his own hands and to undertake the management of the House of Commons himself. The undertakers realising what was on foot went into violent opposition but Townshend overcame them by a wholesale distribution of rewards and punishments. With the undertakers dismissed, 'the gentlemen of the House of Commons were taught to look up to him, not only as the source, but as the dispenser of every gratification . . . Thus were the old undertakers given to understand that there was another way of doing business than through them.'

The Irish parliament in the middle decades of the eighteenth century owed its distinctive features to the peculiar circumstances under which it functioned. In many ways it resembled the British parliament. Like the parliament at Westminster it was designed to represent property, not persons; it had a similar structure; it followed a similar procedure; and it was managed by similar corrupt practices. But there were notable differences. As in England, the majority of the population were excluded from participation in political life but in Ireland they were excluded primarily on political and religious, not social and economic, grounds. They were also deprived of what English political theorists called virtual representation. This concept was defined by Edmund Burke in these words :

Virtual representation is that in which there is a communion of interest and a sympathy in feeling and desire between those who act in the name of any description of people and the people in whose names they act, though the trustees are not actually chosen by them.

Under the penal laws no such community of interest could exist between members of parliament and the Catholic majority. Furthermore, the Irish parliament was not the parliament of a sovereign, independent state; it was a subordinate body subject to restrictions imposed by England and without any control over the Lord Lieutenant and his ministers, who were appointed by and responsible to the English government. The fact that this subordinate parliament was dominated by a colonial oligarchy which was torn between its obvious dependence on England and its colonial nationalism made the problem of Anglo-Irish relations a persistent one throughout the century. The years when the undertakers held sway were years of political calm, of stagnation even, simply because a way had been evolved of reconciling local aspirations with English requirements. But from the time of the money-bill dispute in the 1750s a group known as the 'Patriots' were pressing with increasing vociferousness inside and outside parliament for a series of reforms designed to promote the interests of Ireland as a distinct kingdom. By associating themselves in some measure with the popular demands the undertakers hastened the day of their own downfall. Once they were disposed of, the way was clear for a direct confrontation between the Lord Lieutenant, representing the English government, and the Patriots, representing the aspirations of the colonial nationalists and who were soon to move from strength to strength under the leadership of Flood and Grattan.

Grattan's Parliament

JOSEPH LEE

AN autumnal haze envelops Grattan's Parliament in the popular imagination. Political independence, economic prosperity, architectural splendour, Dublin—'Augustan capital of a Gaelic nation'—one of the great cities of the world, the style, flair and panache of a glittering and gifted generation—these, I think, are the images evoked by 'Grattan's Parliament'.

Although in the nineteenth century an occasional dissentient voice like James Fintan Lalor's might dismiss the constitution of 1782 as 'absurd, worthless and less than worthless', Parnell represented the mainstream of thinking in his famous Cork speech of 1885 :

We cannot ask for less than the restitution of Grattan's Parliament with its important privileges and wide and far reaching constitutions. We cannot, under the British constitution, ask for more than the restitution of Grattan's Parliament, but no man has a right to fix the boundary to the march of a nation.

In other words, Grattan's Parliament had been a good thing, if not quite good enough. Arthur Griffith based the original Sinn Féin case for independence on the argument that Grattan's Parliament had never been legally dissolved, and when Bulmer Hobson and Denis McCullough began the revival of Ulster republicanism in the early twentieth century they established 'Dungannon Clubs' in memory of the movement which had brought Grattan's Parliament into being. For over a century after its dissolution the parliament in College Green remained both a symbol and a goal of national aspirations for the majority of Irishmen.

That Grattan's Parliament should have been generally esteemed raises intriguing questions about the political conceptions of later generations for, historically, Lalor came closer to the truth than Parnell. The very name, Grattan's Parliament, is itself misleading. It was not Grattan's Parliament in any significant sense. Grattan himself remained in virtually permanent opposition before actually withdrawing in despair from parliament in 1797. Real power did not lie with parliament but with the government, and no one has ever ventured to call the government of Ireland between 1782 and 1800 'Grattan's Government'.

For what were those 'important privileges' to which Parnell referred, and what use did Grattan's Parliament make of them? Basically, the English parliament renounced the right to legislate for Ireland, but the English Privy Council retained power to veto Irish legislation. If it did not in practice use this power, this was only because the necessity rarely arose. The Irish parliament remained subservient to English governments, which continued to appoint the Lord Lieutenant, who, in turn, appointed the chief officers of state and continued to manage parliament in the traditional manner, mustering majorities through control of patronage. 1782 merely marked a change in relations between the Irish parliament and the English parliament; it involved no change in relations between the Irish parliament and the Irish people. Grattan's Parliament refused to couple parliamentary reform with legislative independence, and decisively rejected the electoral reform plan brought from the Volunteer Convention by Henry Flood in 1783. Throughout its existence only sixty-four of 300 MPs were elected by the county constituencies. Most of the rest represented pocket boroughs, owned by a small coterie of families, whose vote was at the disposal of the highest bidder, almost invariably the government. About a hundred people controlled two-thirds of the seats in the House of Commons, and parliament, Commons or Lords, in this respect was little more than a gigantic relief scheme for the nobility and their relatives. Even the sixty-four 'independent country gentlemen' usually owed their rents to local landlord influence. MPs could be induced to desert the government only when its fall appeared imminent, as in the Regency Crisis of 1789, when it seemed that Grattan's friend, Charles James Fox, would succeed William Pitt as Prime Minister of England and that Grattan and his circle would be called upon to occupy the main offices and to control patronage. Swarms of MPs therefore deserted the government to protect their jobs, only to swarm back with equal alacrity once it became clear that Pitt would continue in office. The Act of Union itself might well not have been carried had there been any prospect of the Opposition coming to power in the foreseeable future in England, but as Fox had withdrawn from parliament in 1797, Pitt's position seemed impregnable, so that those who disliked the Union but preferred their purses saw no hope of combining principle with expediency. The manner in which the Union was carried did not represent any departure from the standard eighteenth-century practice; it conformed, if somewhat energetically, to the generally accepted 'corruption code', and very few MPs changed their minds for money. It seems ironic that legislative independence should be associated with a parliament which established closer links than ever before with English parties—Grattan in alliance with Fox's Whigs, the dominant Beresfords in alliance with Pitt's Tories. The close relationship forged between Irish and English parties continued until the rise of the Home Rule Party a century later destroyed the Liberal Party in Ireland, and lasted even longer in the relationship between Unionist and Tory Parties. The existence of such a relationship helps explain why Irish MPs, with their similar social status and educational background, integrated so smoothly with their English colleagues in Westminster after transferring from College Green.

Perhaps the single most important reason for the popular reputation enjoyed by Grattan's Parliament is the widespread conviction that it successfully fostered economic development. 'No country in history,' wrote Eóin Mac Néill, 'not even modern Japan, ever made such rapid progress in material prosperity as Ireland' between 1783 and 1798. Even today it seems to be widely believed that the Irish economy stagnated—because of English discrimination, of course—for a century before 1782, that it then boomed, thanks to the wise legislation of Grattan's Parliament, until 1800, when the Act of Union brought economic disaster in its wake. This exclusively political interpretation—prosperity under a native government, poverty under alien rule—cannot survive scrutiny.

All that really happened was that Ireland rode the crest of a price rise from about the middle of the eighteenth century until 1814, and that Grattan's Parliament has been extravagantly praised, in fact, for having the good fortune to exist

concurrently with a phenomenon for which it was not responsible. The boom in the largest single export sector, linen, between 1783 and 1795 has sometimes been attributed to parliament, but when we place the linen industry in a broader context,
it becomes apparent that war, not legislation, exerted the
decisive influence on its fortunes. Linen proved particularly
vulnerable to the dislocation of international trade caused by
war, not only because it relied largely on export markets but
because it imported flax seed from America and better quality
flax from Belgium or Russia. The Seven Years' War ended in
1763 and linen exports boomed for the next decade. Trade
suffered from an over-production crisis in the world slump of
1773, but would probably have recovered sooner but for the
outbreak of the American War of Independence. The boom
that followed the end of the American War in 1783 was all the
stronger for having been artificially delayed, and Grattan's Parliament earned quite undeserved tributes for having revived a
languishing linen trade. Indeed, far from parliamentary initiative having stimulated recovery, it was precisely in 1782 itself
that the linen drapers of the North decided to build linen halls
in Belfast and Newry, shaking off the shackles of the government Linen Board in Dublin, which had proved more a hin-
drance than a help in the preceding decades.

Perhaps no measure of Grattan's Parliament so captured the
imagination of both contemporaries and posterity as Foster's
Corn Law subsidising grain exports. Lecky's judgement struck a
sympathetic chord in the popular heart: 'Foster's Corn Law of
1784 . . . is one of the capital acts in Irish history. In a few
years it changed the face of the land and made Ireland to a
great extent an arable instead of a pastoral country.' There is
very little truth in this familiar assertion. The expansion of
tillage acreage was not remotely as spectacular as Lecky
assumed. At most, five per cent more of the country was under
grain in 1800 than in 1784. But by no stretch of the imagination
can all of this be attributed to Foster's Corn Law. Tillage
acreage increased gradually from about 1760 as English population growth began to outstrip grain supply, turning England
into a grain importer. The 1770s, not the 1780s, marked
the transition of Ireland from a grain-importing to a grain-
exporting country. Foster's Corn Law did not reverse

an existing trend; at the very most it slightly accentuated it.

The most portentous economic development during the period was the increase in population from about four to five million. This, too, marked a continuation of a trend that had set in at least a generation earlier, and it continued for another two generations. Grattan's Parliament had nothing to do with it. It has sometimes been argued, it is true, that the enfranchisement of the forty-shilling freeholders in 1793 accelerated population growth by inducing landlords to subdivide, but no correlation existed between the rate of enfranchisement and the rate of population growth in different counties. Rising population did stimulate the economy at this stage, for Ireland was still a relatively thinly populated country with roughly the same population as today. It was not until about 1810 that population growth began to outrun resources and became a depressant instead of a stimulus to the economy. It was the good fortune of Grattan's Parliament to coexist with a favourable population situation, and to cease to exist before a positive trend became, willy nilly, a disastrous one.

Parliament subsidised a number of firms, but, as these made little attempt to modernise their methods, the subsidies were largely squandered. Ironically, just at the moment when the industrial revolution was gathering momentum in England, Irish manufacturers were being subsidised to remain in the old groove. The channel of commerce was changing and, instead of changing with the stream, Irish manufacturers sat in the old watercourse, subsidised by a solicitous parliament, and argued that it had no right to change direction. It was precisely in the decades of Grattan's Parliament that the technological gap between Ireland and England began to widen ominously, a trend which merely continued under the Union, on which it has so frequently been blamed.

The conviction that prosperity results automatically from self-government must bear not a little of the responsibility for the pathetic performance of the Irish economy during the first thirty-five years of independence. Only James Connolly seriously challenged the assumption that Grattan's Parliament was primarily responsible for the late eighteenth-century prosperity. Although Connolly wrongly attributed the economic progress to the industrial revolution, he rightly realised that policy was not responsible. Even his negative insight so disturbed national-ists that they hastened to repudiate it, welcoming George O'Brien's orthodox statement in his *Economic History of Ireland in the Eighteenth Century*. The *Freeman's Journal* noted in its review of O'Brien's book in 1918 that 'Mr O'Brien estab-lishes conclusively his point as against James Connolly that the advance made after 1780 was due, not to the effect of the industrial revolution, but to the amelioritive measures intro-duced by Grattan's Parliament.' The mentality that indepen-dence must bring prosperity and that the economy could be made to dance to any political tune persisted disastrously long in Irish thought.

The most important economic developments, then, occurred independently of parliament. Many of the most important pol-itical initiatives also occurred outside, if not independently of, parliament. Mild though the proposals of the Volunteer Con-vention of 1783 were, parliament indignantly rejected them. The Convention demanded that a general election be held every three instead of every eight years, that constituencies of less than two hundred voters should be abolished, that no life pensioner should sit unless re-elected, and that the vote should be extended to all Protestant £10 freeholders. All Catholics and poorer Protestants were still excluded from this scheme. The Volunteers, in other words, had no concept of a new constitution, merely wishing to purge the existing constitution of its abuses. Nevertheless, parliament felt its prerogatives out-raged. 'Good God!' exclaimed Sir Hercules Langrishe, suc-cintly formulating the creed of conservatives throughout the ages, 'Is the mind of man never to be satisfied?' Yelverton, the most prominent lawyer in parliament, claimed that the real question was 'whether this house or the Convention are the representatives of the people'. That was indeed the question, and the short answer was that neither represented the people in a twentieth-century sense, because both spoke for Protestants only. But the Convention was, probably, more representative of the Protestant community than was Grattan's Parliament, which represented merely a minority of a minority. Parliament con-tinued to reject, with monotonous regularity, all reform pro-posals until 1793, when William Pitt decided, in view of the outbreak of the French War, that an extension of the franchise was necessary to conciliate the increasingly militant Catholics, and compelled parliament to enfranchise the forty-shilling free-holders, Catholic as well as Protestant. This raised the number of voters from perhaps 50,000 to 150,000 in ten years, and it is surely ironic that the major reform measure of Grattan's Parliament should have been passed only at the insistence of the English Prime Minister.

Although the United Irishmen have hardly any direct relevance to a discussion of Grattan's Parliament, it is highly significant that Wolfe Tone and his associates embraced the goal of a representative parliament. The United Irish Society was itself fairly democratically organised, the executive Directory emerging from a local electoral process, and the reform plan which the United Irishmen proposed in 1794 envisaged far more radical reform than the Volunteer scheme—300 equal constituencies, universal male suffrage over the age of twenty-one, annual elections, payment of MPs and no property qualifications for MPs. The United Irishmen, however, represented only a small minority of Irishmen—perhaps as small a minority as parliament itself—and even they, particularly the Protestant members, balked at the secret ballot, fearful of landlords losing their entire influence over their tenantry. Their programme, nevertheless, indicated a commitment to a far more representative parliamentarianism than the Volunteers contemplated. Their thinking reflected the influence of American and French, as distinct from British, theory, and, in some respects, the history emerging from a local electoral process, and the reform history of waiting for Westminster to catch up with the principles of representation enunciated by the extra-parliamentary opposition in the 1790s. It was also to remain for long a fundamental tenet of Irish republicanism, firmly grounded on the doctrines of the United Irishmen, that 'an impartial and adequate representation of the Irish nation in parliament' constituted the ultimate goal. The distinction between physical-force and moral-force nationalists in the nineteenth century referred primarily to tactical means rather than institutional ends.

Less spectacular, but far more significant, was the rise of representative leadership within the Catholic community. This leadership emerged with the election of a new Catholic Committee in 1790, and was strengthened in 1791 by the rejection of the motion reflecting the views of the Catholic gentry and some bishops :

That grateful for former concessions we do not presume to point out the measure or extent to which such repeal [of the Penal Laws] should be carried, but leave the same to the wisdom and benevolence of the legislature, fully confiding in their wisdom and benevolence, that it will be as extensive as the circumstances of the times, and the general welfare of the Empire shall, in their consideration, render prudent and expedient.

In effect, the gentry and the bishops—the Catholic upper class—wished to prevent the Catholic middle and lower classes from entering politics. Their defeat, reaffirmed in the internal struggle on the Catholic Committee over the Veto question between 1808 and 1811, marks in some significant ways the most important development of the period. It proved decisive for the fortunes of the embryonic Irish democracy that the Catholic upper class was tamed before the Protestant Ascendancy was tackled. The Catholic Convention which met in December 1792 was probably the most representative group that had ever gathered in Ireland, and by suppressing it under the Conventions Act in the following year, Grattan's Parliament proclaimed itself to be merely the armed conspiracy of a minority against the majority.

But parliament did, indirectly, unintentionally but effectively, leave its mark on the Catholic Convention. For the Convention automatically assumed a parliamentary mould. Like parliament, it consisted of 300 delegates. It was deeply influenced by the form of the assembly it was itself attempting to influence. Professor P. J. O'Farrell has vigorously argued that there was nothing intrinsically Irish about the Catholic Convention 'in the sense of being traditional, or springing from any Irish sources : historically, until the eighteenth century, Irish claims against British oppression had been based on Irish laws or customs, or canon law and religious principle. By the end of the eighteenth century they were attempting to work through laws and principles professed by their rulers.' Although true up to a point, this, I think, partly misses the real significance of the Catholic Convention. The classes represented at the Convention were not, by and large, transferring their allegiance from an ancient indigenous political tradition to a modern, alien one.

They had no political tradition before the eighteenth century. They were not reconstituting, but creating, a political tradition. They were, it is true, working through the laws of their rulers, but not through their principles, for the Convention, by its mere existence, was reforming the representation of Catholics within the Catholic community in a manner in which Grattan's Parliament, at that stage, refused to contemplate for the Protestant community.

The real tragedy of Grattan's Parliament was not that it may have been somewhat more corrupt than the general run of eighteenth-century parliaments. That, at most, was a difference of degree, not of kind. Its tragedy lay in the dilemma of the sectarian situation, a dilemma which Grattan's Parliament inherited and which has yet to be resolved, the dilemma which their opposition to the secret ballot suggests also baffled, if to a lesser extent, the United Irishmen. Protestants formed only about one third of the population. Therefore once people, and not Protestant property and religion, came to constitute the criterion of representation, Protestants would be in the minority. The Catholics demanded equality, but demography dictated that equality meant superiority. There could be no equality between Protestants and Catholics: the only alternative to Protestant superiority was Protestant inferiority. The Catholic reply was that Protestants would have nothing to fear once they gave Catholics their rights, but how could one tell? A glance at Wexford in 1798 and at the feudings in the North hardly proved reassuring. It was only by taking religion out of politics that the dilemma confronting Grattan's Parliament could be resolved. Yet the main step taken by Grattan's Parliament in this direction, the enfranchisement of the forty-shilling freeholders, irrespective of religion, in 1793, which subordinated religious to property criteria, was adopted against its real wishes. This is why Grattan's Parliament, unlike the British parliament, could never be reformed from within. The British parliament was potentially representative of the people as well as the property of Britain, in that its members considered themselves as belonging to the same national community as the non-electors, however intense their contempt for their own lower orders. Most members of Grattan's Parliament did not consider themselves members of the same community as the Catholic Irish. Grattan's

Parliament could have resulted only in a succession of 1798s, not in reconciliation. Grattan's epitaph on the Irish parliament

> With all its imperfections, its temptations and its corruptions, it was potent for good. Because its members sat in Ireland . . . they were influenced by Irish sympathy . . . they did not like to meet every hour faces that looked shame on them

must be considered a masterpiece of wishful thinking. An MP who, like Colonel Robert Ross of Newry, could exclaim in 1798: 'For God's sake, let the innocents be hanged, and when the rebellion is extinguished, a bill of indemnity cures all', reflected much more closely the spirit of an assembly whose members were unlikely to be perturbed by reproachful glances. Lecky's argument that Grattan's Parliament would have passed Catholic Emancipation because 61 of 93 Irish MPs voted for it in 1829 seems to me suspect. Lecky's assumption requires as a first precondition that the Irish parliament would, at some stage, have abolished the rotten boroughs to something like the extent which actually occurred in the Union. By reducing the number of MPs from 300 to 100 and abolishing most of the boroughs, the Act of Union proved to be one of the most sweeping measures of parliamentary reform in Irish history. It may serve as an eloquent epitaph on the reforming zeal of Grattan's Parliament that its greatest reformer should have been William Pitt.

What, then, was the ultimate legacy of Grattan's Parliament? It made no distinctive contribution either to political theory or political practice. The outstanding oratorical ability of a handful of members and the administrative ability of a still smaller number should not be allowed to disguise the mediocrity of the overwhelming majority of Anglo-Ireland's political representatives. In this, at least, they proved as Irish as the Irish themselves. The caste mentality of Grattan's Parliament allowed its members to cooperate cordially with the Scots-Irish, increasingly mobilised in the Orange Order, founded in 1795 and destined long to survive both Grattan's Parliament and Anglo-Irish Ascendancy. Two illusions reinforce each other in the popular historical reconstruction of the last decade of parliamentary 'independence': that Grattan's Parliament was a 'liberal', spontaneously 'progressive' institution, and that the United

Irishmen united Irishmen. However committed to theoretical sympathy for the plight of Catholics some members of the Belfast middle-classes may have been, the Presbyterian farmers, labourers and weavers wanted nothing of such liberal sentimental slush. The Orange Order, not the United Irishmen, represented their gut reaction to Catholic demands.

The mystery of Grattan's Parliament is the mystery of the capacity for self-deception, frequently from the most honourable motives, of later generations of Irishmen, and, not least, of Anglo-Irishmen, who invested it with something of the emotional fervour which the Celts reserved for the Gaelic golden age. Politically, culturally and economically, Ireland became more, not less, integrated with England during the period of 'Grattan's Parliament'. Perhaps the greatest injury inflicted by the Union on the Irish mind was that, by substituting Westminster for College Green, it identified parliament with the struggle for national independence rather than with the struggle for internal reform. It thus allowed nationalists to evade the responsibility of confronting the realities of Irish society by pretending that all internal problems were the product of malevolence at Westminster, and enabled them to idealise, with supreme irony, Grattan's Parliament, the bloodiest repressive institution in modern Irish history.

The Contribution of O'Connell

OLIVER MacDONAGH

'OTHELLO'S occupation's gone.' So a friend told O'Connell on the morrow of the Clare Election, and the eve of his entry into the House of Commons at Westminster in 1830. For thirty years O'Connell had been an agitator outside the walls of the legitimate political system. It was hardly to be expected that at the age of fifty-five a man should take up successfully a new trade, which was the very inversion, so to speak, of his old. He had, moreover, forced himself, by means that were hated in Britain and feared in the House of Commons, into a closed circle. He had, in the eyes of the British political classes, recklessly aroused the passions of the mob, and dangerously weakened the barriers to general dispossession, violence and licence. He would have to make his way against the constant buffets of political, religious and—perhaps most inimical of all—social prejudice.

In many respects Othello did make his way. O'Connell became one of the handful of men who came late to parliament with a large reputation, and retained it undiminished. When one adds to his name those of Cobden, Joseph Chamberlain and Ernest Bevin, one has practically exhausted the category. With his marvellous plasticity, he caught 'the tone of the House' at once. The following passage from his short maiden speech coruscates with the irony, clarity and deceptively simple art which rendered him immediately a parliamentary giant:

What did it [the King's speech] contain? The first point was, that foreign nations continued to speak in terms of peace; but did they ever do otherwise when a war was on the point of breaking out, or even when the war itself had actually commenced? The next information was, that the Russian war was at an end. That was an important discovery indeed; and, of course, none of them knew that before. They were then told that nothing was determined as to Portugal. And why? Ah! they were not told that.

- challenge to power / like boss ? mtn politics vs elite
- extra - constitutional reform?
- involvement of church
- alternative institutions
- assoc. w/ enlightenment + "philosophes"
- liberalism - emphasis on individual liberty in wider sphere - not just Cath find
- "freedoms from" species of liberty
- (Mass) organization - people self disciplined - not "beasts!

Was the character of Don Miguel then doubtful? Did any one doubt that he had usurped the throne of another, and endeavoured to cement his seat by the spilling of innocent blood? If so, why did the government of England shrink from the decision to which it ought to come? They were next told of the partial distress of the country. But was that a fact? He thought that the expressions which had fallen from the three hon. members on the other side who had supported the Address, were—the one, that the distress was general; the second, that the distress was extraordinary; and the third, that the distress was overwhelming. The Chancellor of the Exchequer, however, had made one happy discovery; he had found an 'oasis in the desert'—a country where no distress at all existed: and, who would have thought it?—that country was Ireland.[1]

From this moment until three months before his death in 1847, O'Connell was a major parliamentary figure, one of the significant contributors to the heroic element in the British parliamentary tradition. As telling a tribute to his personal dominance as any of the laughter and huzzas and howls which accompanied his speeches in the 1830s were the silence and murmurs of pretended agreement with which his final broken rambling was heard when he last addressed the House, a trembling, piteous shadow of his former self.[2]

Although O'Connell succeeded as an individual parliamentarian in the great nineteenth-century sequence stretching from Pitt to Gladstone, his position within the parliamentary system was never clear or certain. He was neither wholly within nor wholly without the institutional structure. The political elite would not fully accept and could not fully reject his presence; and he himself was correspondingly ambivalent. He played a major part in the passage of the Reform Act of 1832, in the abolition of slavery and in the whole course of liberal legislation which profoundly modified the social and administrative structure of Great Britain in the 1830s. He kept the Melbourne government in power over several sessions of parliament. Yet Guizot was astonished to discover in 1840 that many of the leading Whigs knew nothing of O'Connell privately. Their relationships with him were a distasteful and jealously limited professional necessity.

Even Le Marchant, an advanced young Liberal and an ex-

f

tremely well-informed political observer, noted in his diary in 1833:

His [O'Connell's] immediate followers are not [a] very creditable looking set. Fergus O'Connor has the appearance of a country attorney. He was involved some time ago in a charge of robbing the mail, and he did not come off with very clean hands . . . Daunt and O'Dwyer have more of a ruffian about them. Lalor shows that he has never been in gentleman's society before. I believe it was only last year that Sir Henry Parnell brought him up to town to give evidence before a Committee of the House, and presented [him] with a coat, being the first he had ever been the owner of, to appear in. Some of the others are not a whit better. They are understood to subsist on O'Connell. His large house in Albemarle Street is their hotel. They live there free of expense, much, as I hear, in the savage style of their own country.[3]

Some of this was simple insolence, vulgar social prejudice of the type more economically displayed by Wellington in his celebrated complaint about the 'shocking bad hats' to be found in the first Reformed Parliament. It also contained an element of the undying resentment of the elite that the closed circle of politics had been broken in 1830. However, the importance of this type of prejudice quite transcends class petulance: it provides us with one of the vital codes for interpreting Anglo-Irish relations in the nineteenth century.

Perhaps the matter may be best explained by an analogy. Irish-Americans in the third quarter of the nineteenth century found themselves, en masse, in a situation of economic, social, and even, in certain senses, civic inferiority. Their collective response was to use their numbers and their local concentration against the established classes. They sought political power, not for particular ends, but for itself. The more they were excluded from society, the more they were driven to assert and advertise themselves in the political arena. But they were caught between two magnets: their solidarity as a distinctive group, and their passion for acceptance as equals, or even as one of the master races, in American society at large. There was also a dichotomy between the idealistic, rebel and working-class strain in the Irish-American struggle, and its opposite, the drive towards achievement, success, conformity and the satisfaction of social aspiration. It is a grave though very common error to regard these antithetical elements as parties within a movement. For the same people were often alternately driven by both these impulses.

Of course one cannot press the analogy closely; there are many glaring dissimilarities between the Irish-Americans in the socio-political structure of the United States and the Catholic Irish within that of the United Kingdom. But it does help to explain the ambivalence and oscillation of O'Connell's parliamentarianism. To gain a footing within the political system, he had had to assault and embarrass it. His leverage—that is to say, his power, to raise agitations—would always draw much of its force from anti-British feeling and a rejection of the established order. Yet one of the great forces which impelled O'Connell forward was resentment of the inferiority which established society had forced on him at various levels in his life. It seems to me significant that O'Connell, in his speech of acceptance in Ennis in 1828, had burst out against the discrimination from which he suffered: as a lawyer, as a gentleman, as a landed proprietor, he was, he said, denied the status which his achievements and inheritance deserved because the religion with which he was identified was stigmatised as 'inferior'.[4] Here we see in miniature the double drive towards defiance and acceptance: antithetical aims perhaps, but also aims powered by a single force, a passion for equality. This helps considerably to explain O'Connell's repeated shifts in objectives and attitudes over the next decade and a half. It certainly illuminates his ambiguous situation within the British parliamentary tradition. He was at once an outsider to, and an enemy of, the system, and yet its upholder and occasional beneficiary.

All this is indirectly connected with O'Connell's second major contribution to the parliamentary tradition: the vast enlargement of its area and modes of operation. In part, this was forced on him by circumstances; in part, it was the fruit of his extraordinary political inventiveness. O'Connell was the pioneer of the modern political party. By present-day standards, the discipline of his party in the House of Commons was loose, constituency organisation weak and the central control over the nomination of candidates inconstant and uncertain. But, by contemporary standards in a situation where MPs, unless they were office-holders or placemen, were independent and un-predictable agents, O'Connell's 'tail' was a phalanx which the leadership could use at will and which, if the support of the clergy were available, possessed an impregnable power-base in at least one third of the Irish constituencies. Although O'Connell's development of constituency and national machin-ery and parliamentary management was necessarily rudimentary, it foreshadowed in almost every single feature the modern political organisation of the party.

A still more important precedent instituted by O'Connell may be seen in his exploration of the whole range of political ex-pedients open to a minority movement in a more or less consti-tutional state. In the strictly parliamentary sphere, his various absolute, contingent and tacit alliances with the Whigs showed how brute votes in the lobbies might be cashed in for specific legislative or administrative advantages. Here the sketch-plans for many of the achievements of the 1880s were prepared. But the most interesting developments of all were extra-parliamen-tary. Even more than in his control of several county and a few borough seats and, in favourable conditions, of up to forty votes in the House of Commons, O'Connell's political strength lay in the threat of mass agitation and, behind it, the threat of mass disorder. Faint harbingers of the Catholic, National and Repeal Associations may be seen in the Wilkes movements and the Methodist church organisation of the late eighteenth cen-tury, but O'Connell's master work, the enrolment and political harnessing of the masses, was essentially new. It was this which gave him his most powerful weapon at Westminster, as of course the equivalent was to aid Parnell when he too—though much more plausibly and effectively—could present himself as holding, single-handed, vast revolutionary forces under leash.

The world's political repertoire was increased still further by O'Connell when he devised or developed—although tenta-tively—the technique of alternative institutions. The Council of Three Hundred (the native representative assembly which he talked of calling) represented at once the ideas of with-drawal in protest from a hostile system, and the inauguration of a rival assembly or anti-parliament. More generally, as the Repeal movement acquired quasi-judicial and quasi-police functions and exercised more and more social controls in towns and countryside, it adumbrated the concept of a second governmental system, growing up beside and gradually superseding the established state. In O'Connell's hands these things were tactical methods of increasing pressure upon the British government and of maintaining discipline at home; but—to look no further afield than Ireland—they also obviously prefigured the essential strategy of Sinn Féin down to 1920. If, therefore, we interpret 'parliamentary tradition' in its widest sense, as dealing with the whole gamut of power-relationships within a parliamentary society and not merely with elected assemblies and their immediate appendages, then O'Connell emerges as a political inventor and enlarger of the first magnitude. In an age of gadgetry and technical innovation of every kind, he was an Edison or a Bessemer in his own field, and his new political technology was broadcast by emigrants throughout the English-speaking world in the succeeding generation.

So far I have considered O'Connell's contribution primarily in Irish terms. But it must not be forgotten that he was also (and also regarded himself as) a major figure in the British radical tradition.

I avowed myself [he wrote to Bentham from Ennis in July 1829] on the hustings today to be a Benthamite, and explained the leading principles of your disciples—the greatest happiness principle —*our* sect will prosper. I begin my parliamentary career by tendering you my constant, zealous and active services in the promotion of that principle. You have now one Member of Parliament of *your own*.[4]

While some of this may be set off as characteristic blarney, the fact remains that O'Connell was the leading utilitarian in the House of Commons during the 1830s. Does this necessarily imply that he was a radical? It may seem strange to stress the radicalism of one who was, by present-day standards, a black conservative on many social, and almost every economic issue. However, all things must be seen in context. O'Connell was one of the great carriers in his own day of the historic liberal tradition of the Enlightenment and the *philosophes;* and much of this tradition lies at the heart of pacific radicalism to this very hour. The centrepiece of early nineteenth-century radicalism was the individual person, his liberty and his equal rights. Its concept of liberty was negative—a series of 'freedoms from'

—freedom from restraints and coercion in almost any form. Its concept of equality was formal—that no man should be penalised in any fashion whatsoever for his colour, his race, his religion or his expression of beliefs. Modern radicals may smile at what seem to them such simplistic interpretations of the *things*, but surely the basic *notions* have only been neatly changed, not taken away. In fact, many of the issues which engaged O'Connell are far from dated. He was a sedulous political egalitarian, an anti-racialist, an anti-imperialist and an unwearying humanitarian reformer. In short, he swam in the mainstream of British parliamentary radicalism, running from Horne Tooke in the 1780s to Michael Foot today. This movement was—and is—an expression of one of the main branches of European radicalism. Setting aside our contemporary forms of social radicalism as anachronistic in O'Connell's day, the great bifurcation then was between the universal, rational and atomistic strain which he represented, and the strain which emphasised the race rather than the person, the group rather than the individual, and instinct and emotion as against reason. It is an oversimplification perhaps, but basically correct, to see the conflict between O'Connell and the more ardent element in Young Ireland as a conflict between these two forms of radicalism—a local engagement, in fact, in the titanic struggle that involved all Europe in the nineteenth century. It is no coincidence that O'Connell (against the inclinations of so-called 'left-wing' Repealers) should have rejected aid from the slave-states of the South as tainted. It is no coincidence that, unlike the *Nation*, he should have placed little or no value upon distinctive cultures. It is no coincidence that he should have greeted the news of Waterloo with: 'The scoundrels of society have now every triumph. The defeats and disasters are reserved for the friends of liberty'; or the news of the Liberal Revolution in Spain in 1820 with: 'I hail it as the first of a series of events useful to human liberty and human happiness.'[6] For to O'Connell and the parliamentary radicals the struggle was universal, and the issues quite transcended race and nation. One of the earliest entries in O'Connell's diary, written when he was twenty-two years old, reads: 'I will endeavour to give liberty to my country and increase the knowledge and virtue of humankind.'[7] It is an arresting and characteristic conjunction. Although he lived for half a century more, he never saw increasing the knowledge and virtue of the human kind as a secondary objective; on the contrary, this was the framework which gave meaning and value to anything which he achieved at home.

If we consider O'Connell in the context of continental Europe rather than of Ireland or Great Britain, we have still not elicited his main significance in the political history of the nineteenth century. He was that rare form of parliamentary radical, a religious believer, and still rarer, a Roman Catholic. In the years 1815–45 the papacy was generally tightening its connections with legitimism and authority. Democracy and representative institutions—the very symbols of contemporary progress—were anathemised, and liberation identified with infidelity. In this situation, O'Connell's long and dramatic political career was of critical importance. It was not merely that he asserted the compatibility, and even the interdependence, of his religion and his radicalism. He also demonstrated that the masses could be led, could be purposively organised, could learn self-discipline; that they were not wild beasts who, uncaged, would harry and destroy the very bases of society. Most important of all, in no less than three great crises, on the Veto issue, support for the Catholic Association and involvement in the Repeal agitation of the early 1840s, he induced the great body of the Irish clergy and episcopate to commit themselves irrevocably to the popular movements. This ensured that in at least one vital region, the 'official Church' had become integrated in the struggle for democratic rights and parliamentary equality. It was also, incidentally, some insurance against those popular movements turning in the direction of plebiscitary dictatorship that one of its major constituents should have an independent base and independent objects. All this was material in holding back any final alliance between the Roman Church and Metternichian reaction. It helped to furnish a shield for the growth of Liberal Catholicism—using the words in their political rather than theological sense—in Western Europe in the 1830s. It rendered O'Connell, in his own lifetime, a master-figure in continental eyes, a pontifex, a bridge-builder. The address of the Catholics of France, delivered by Montalembert to the dying O'Connell, on his way through Paris in March 1847, declared: 'But you are not only a man of one nation, you are a man of all Christendom.'[8] The address was in effect a lapidary inscription, and notoriously the composers of such inscriptions are not on oath. But this particular phrase was no flummery. To Catholic left-wing opinion in France, Belgium, Holland and Germany—indeed to the hopes of Catholic left-wing opinion in almost any continental European country—O'Connell's political exploration was perhaps the crucial experience of the time.

In conventional Irish historiography, the 'parliamentary tradition' is often spoken of in simple antithesis to the 'revolutionary tradition' and physical force. This antithesis has of course some validity. O'Connell's political behaviour was conditioned by his constant rejection of violence or conspiratorial means. His own movements, in turn, were conditioned by his parliamentarianism. What were Conciliation Hall or the reformed Dublin Corporation meant to be if not a variation on Westminster? But, as I have shown, the antithesis, though true, is also shallow. The 'parliamentary method' was not an established form of conduct or code of principles to which O'Connell subscribed. It was, rather, a wide variety of interlocking techniques and concepts which he developed in response to needs. Apart from the clandestine organisation and the gun, there is scarcely any mode of exercising political pressure in a constitutional system which O'Connell did not explore. Moreover, he moved back and forwards across his range of tactics, and employed them in various combinations in a fashion which anticipated, so far as the conditions of his time allowed, the great decade of the 1880s, in which the foundations of the Act of Union were broken. He put together the framework of the modern political party in Great Britain and elaborated its radical tradition. He gave, in his own sphere, the first answers to the question posed by the current cliché, 'the Church in the Modern World', and nurtured, indirectly, the confessional party in Western Europe: in the shape of Christian Democracy, this was to determine, to a significant extent, the character of the parliamentary tradition on the continent. At yet another remove, his work in Ireland influenced the growth of 'boss' politics in the United States, with its deadly challenge to the power and assumptions alike of the Puritan and post-Puritan élite. In all of this we should not expect, and certainly shall not find, finality or neat consistency. O'Connell was a pioneer, the first cartographer of an unknown continent, that of mass constitutional politics and pacific popular democracy.

I am attempting no personal or national evaluation. There were areas of the parliamentary tradition to which O'Connell could never contribute—those of office and government, in particular. There was deep irony in the fact that he, a self-proclaimed political rationalist and individualist, derived the substance of his power from crowds and feelings. On the most critical question perhaps for any democrat, acceptance of opposition as necessary and legitimate, we might well have doubts. Every other manoeuvre in his tortuous career opened debates upon the wisdom or the probity of his conduct—though here, with the entire course of that career long since spread out and a juster appreciation of the mountainous difficulties in his way, history is—or at any rate will be—kinder than those of his contemporaries who wrote the books. He had scarcely an original idea in his mind. Many of his most important innovations represent the reflex actions of a superb political animal; they are not the harvest of thought and planning.

But when all this (and as much more as can be thought of in a depreciatory strain) has been said, O'Connell remains a colossus of the parliamentary tradition. More perhaps than any other man in nineteenth-century Irish life, he belonged, in his own phrase, to the human kind. Even if his work was done upon the ever-melting snow of public passion and excitement, it proved creative. Even if his materials were the miseries and inequities, the insolence and envies, of a petty island, what he made of them had a universal and a lasting meaning.

Famine and the Failure of Parliament

KEVIN B. NOWLAN

IRELAND, throughout the first half of the nineteenth century, remained troubled by political, religious and social tensions. The massive Catholic Emancipation campaign of the 1820s was one expression of the unease in Ireland; the Tithe War, as it was called, of the 1830s was another. Behind the unrest lay deep causes, old memories and grievances as well as the failure of the Act of Union to bring with it clear political or economic advantages. Above all, it was the poverty of so many of the people and the virtually bankrupt condition of so much of Irish agricultural society which constituted the immediate source of instability.

In sharp contrast to Great Britain, Ireland only shared in the great industrial expansion of the nineteenth century in a marginal way. Throughout the first half of the century, and indeed long after, agriculture constituted the basic element in the Irish economy. However, in terms of investment, methods of cultivation and social cooperation between the classes, Irish agriculture remained in a dangerous position in the years after 1815. Subdivision of holdings, high rents, a lack of capital and uncertainty of tenure hampered many small farmers, while, in turn, landlords were often beset by heavy encumbrances and by the difficulty of improving estates which were subdivided into small holdings. It would, of course, be wrong to assume a uniform condition of economic and social distress in Ireland. Some extensive areas, especially in the north and east of the country were considerably more prosperous than those in the west, and there were well-run estates where the relations between landlords and tenants were satisfactory; but the general problem of poverty and insecurity remained a widespread one. This gloomy picture was hardly made any brighter by the shortage of money for land drainage and the tendency for capital to flow out of Ireland for investment elsewhere. Rural unrest, the 'agrarian outrages', were enduring features of Irish society. Another was the frequent recurrence of periods of food shortage, of famine or near-famine, often associated with fever and deficiency diseases.

The Great Famine of the mid-nineteenth century was no isolated occurrence but rather the most disastrous period of shortage and hunger in a half century which had seen a number of periods of distress, frequently associated with failures of the potato crop. The potato had become the principal food of a very large sector of the Irish population. It yielded a large return, was easy to cultivate and, with a population of over eight million in the early 1840s it offered one means of meeting the needs of many in terms of food. The potato was, however, vulnerable to diseases and there were at that time no really effective means of protecting the crop from destruction.

There had been widespread distress in Ireland in 1817 and, on a somewhat more limited scale, in 1822. Again in 1831, 1836–37, there were food shortages, especially in the west, while 1839 and 1842 saw hardship and distress in several areas. To the famines and near-famines must be added the epidemics such as the typhus of 1817–19, and it is well to remember that food shortages and deficiency diseases could also plague the overcrowded cities and towns as well as the countryside. This pattern of recurring periods of shortage presented the authorities in London and Dublin with a problem which could not be ignored even if, at times, efforts were made to minimise its significance. From 1817 onwards legislation had been put through parliament to meet distress, mainly by way of advances or loans to finance public works and to aid local relief committees. Considerable emphasis was placed by successive British governments on local responsibility as the primary responsibility for the relief of distress. This concentration on local self-help rather than on governmental intervention was, of course, characteristic of the social thinking of the time as expressed, for example, in the Irish Poor Law of 1838. It was to prove an important precedent for policies adopted during the Great Famine.

Liberal economic thinking and practice profoundly influenced the failure of parliament to attempt to resolve some of the major ills of Irish society. This ensured that, throughout the 1830s and 1840s, Irish popular politics were coloured by the conviction that Irish interests were being neglected at Westminster. Equally important, it was felt that the Irish Catholic majority was still regarded by the government and the Ascendancy as socially inferior and politically suspect. While the main stress in the O'Connellite Repeal movement of the 1840s was on political issues, especially the restoration of the Irish parliament, the implications of the political agitation were clear : the Union parliament had failed to legislate in a manner which was calculated to do justice to Irish social and economic needs.

It is well known that the great Repeal agitation of 1843 exercised a considerable influence on government policy towards Ireland. The Tory Party, under the able and firm leadership of Sir Robert Peel, had been in office at Westminster since 1841. Peel's response to the unrest in Ireland was to introduce measures such as the Maynooth Bill in 1845 and to establish the Devon Commission to enquire into the Irish land system. Yet another expression of Peel's thinking about Ireland was the abortive land measure of 1845 which would have provided some small compensation to tenant-farmers for improvements to the land; but, as the debates on the reform proposals showed only too well, there were many members in both houses of parliament who continued to view with deep suspicion any proposals to alter the existing order in Ireland. Already, on the eve of the Great Famine, it was evident that, while relatively minor changes could now be expected from both British parties, the Whigs and the Tories, no really radical reforms were likely in Ireland.

With the autumn of 1845 came the first alarming reports of a potato blight. By the end of October it had struck at the crop in at least eleven Irish counties; but the uneven incidence of the new disease made it difficult, in 1845, to determine the true extent of the disaster. Indeed, this lack of precision was to take on a political significance in the parliamentary debates of 1846 on the issue of the repeal of the Corn Laws. Oddly, the first immediate political consequence of the potato failure was to be seen in the context of internal British politics rather than in the context of Irish affairs. By 1845 Sir Robert Peel had moved away from the traditional Tory policy of agricultural protection and, as a result, he had come to question the utility of the Corn Laws which imposed duties on the import of grain from overseas into the United Kingdom. The Irish crisis provided Peel with a strong argument in favour of abolition. He argued that it would be impossible to tax the import of foodstuffs at such a time. The Corn Laws would, therefore, have to be suspended but, once suspended, he went on to contend, they could never really be imposed again, given the strength of the opposition to them in Britain.

We now know that the issue of the repeal of the Corn Laws was to split the Conservative Party into rival factions and to lead to the fall of Peel from office in the summer of 1846. By joining the issue of distress in Ireland with an essentially British question, he made the very extent of the food crisis in Ireland a matter of dispute in the parliamentary debates. In the long-drawn-out struggle in Westminster over the Corn Laws, the Tory friends of agricultural protection questioned the extent of the potato failure in Ireland, saying that Peel had exaggerated its seriousness for party purposes. Peel, the O'Connellite members, the radicals and the Whigs all rejected the ultra-Tory case, but some obscurity attached to the issue because of the contradictory reports from Ireland and the patchwork character of the actual crop failure. The impact of that first partial failure was also probably blunted by the experience of repeated limited failures of crops in Ireland over the previous thirty or forty years. For many members of parliament Ireland, though a part of the United Kingdom, was a remote, somehow alien country and, even when the Famine reached its climax in 1846–47, a sense of urgency about Irish problems was often missing at Westminster. In Ireland, too, the first reports of the potato blight produced few symptoms of serious alarm. It was only slowly that the food question and the full realisation that the country faced a social collapse came to dominate Irish politics. As late as the summer of 1846, the main issue under discussion in the Repeal Association was the dispute on policy matters between the O'Connellites and the Young Irelanders—on the question whether or not the Association should in future co-operate with the British Whigs.

It may be argued that Peel took an unwarranted risk, in parliamentary terms, by confusing Irish distress with the Corn Law question and that such a device might well have impeded the prompt relief of suffering in Ireland. In fact, however, the measures taken by the Peel administration were about adequate to meet the limited problem of 1845–46, though of no value as a contribution towards the basic ills of Irish society and the long-term needs of the poor.

Measures were put through parliament for relief works, which were to be financed in the traditional way, partly from local sources and partly from the imperial exchequer. In apparent defiance of the principle that a government should not interfere with the free operations of trade, Peel authorised the importation of Indian meal on the government's account and the sale of the meal to the needy through local relief committees—a measure, in effect, of price control. Although Irish opinion was somewhat critical of the steps taken, especially the unwillingness of the government to make the Irish crisis a full United Kingdom responsibility, it may fairly be said that the approach of Peel and his ministers to a near-famine situation in Ireland showed a greater flexibility and realism than was displayed by their Whig successors when faced with the major tragedy of 'Black '47'. Peel, as a man of his time, was deeply influenced by current economic teachings on non-intervention in economic affairs by the state, but, as a remarkable administrator, he could escape, if only to a limited degree, from the narrow confines of the accepted doctrines of political economy.

Sir Robert Peel was forced out of office in June 1846 with the Tory Party fatally divided. He was succeeded by Lord John Russell at the head of a Whig minority government which, however, could normally rely on the support of the Peelites and the Irish Repealers. However, the fact that it was a minority government seems to have made the new Prime Minister excessively prudent in his approach to new legislation. His weak initial position helped to strengthen his natural hesitancy. And even when the Whigs emerged somewhat stronger in numbers from the 1847 General Election, his leadership remained unimpressive and we know that he sometimes lost the initiative in the cabinet to stronger forces such as Lords Palmerston and Lansdowne.

Lord John's accession to office was, at first, quite well received in Ireland. O'Connell, though he had some reservations, still hoped to obtain substantial reforms from the Whigs, but events were soon to disappoint his hopes. Russell's early comments on the Irish scene were promising. He told parliament that there was a need for long-term reforms in Ireland, for measures to better regulate the relations between landlords and tenants, to help land reclamation and to put the parliamentary franchise in Ireland on a basis of equality with Great Britain. Apart, however, from some limited aid for land reclamation schemes, his modest programme for long-term improvements never became a reality.

From May 1846 onwards reports had been coming in of the very widespread recurrence of the potato blight. It is now known that throughout the whole country the potato crop of 1846–47 was totally destroyed. With little or no reserves to call upon, a large section of the smallholders, the cottiers and the poor of the towns were defenceless when faced by this second recurrence of the potato blight. At no time was government prepared to close the ports to the export of grain and other foodstuffs, so that food left the country as the potato crop rotted. The closure of the ports would have represented for ministers and parliament an unacceptable measure of state intervention with the free working of economic forces.

The attitude of his government to what was to prove to be a major food crisis in Ireland was defined by Russell in parliament at the beginning of August 1846. I think it is fair to say that no really fundamental criticism of this approach was expressed from the Peelite benches in parliament. Keeping close to classical economic principles, Russell argued that it could never become an established practice for the government to provide food for a whole population at an uneconomic price. It was the task of private enterprise to supply the market needs. The only safe way, therefore, for the state to intervene in a time of emergency was to assist locally organised relief schemes through treasury loans which would have to be reimbursed from a local rate. His orthodox principles clearly defined, Russell made his Poor Employment (Ireland) Act the foundation of his arrangements to meet the total failure of the potato crop. The wages paid to the destitute on the public works would enable them, it was expected, to buy food on the market.

The Poor Employment Bill passed virtually undebated

through parliament and it aroused little comment, to begin with, in Ireland. The rapid deterioration in the food position, the inadequacies of the retail trade, the rising food prices, the poor wages on the public works and the uselessness of these works for the old, the sick and the very young soon revealed the tragic limitations of the government's measures to meet the famine. We know that this policy was not inspired by some sinister and cruel desire to destroy the Catholic Irish. Russell and his supporters in parliament believed in remedial legislation but they were hampered by the economic and social prejudices of the day and by the fact that a disaster in Ireland had not the same immediacy for them and for many of their parliamentary opponents as a disaster in Great Britain. Among some members of both houses might be detected a certain distaste for Irish affairs which could, under pressure, take on a critical or at least an unsympathetic flavour.

In the crisis months of the winter of 1846–47 the British government saw the Irish landlords and, indeed, the Irish as a whole as being primarily responsible for the situation and for resolving it. British legislators found it hard to recognise that Ireland was an integral part of the United Kingdom and to draw the necessary consequences from that recognition. Men such as Russell regarded the British government as a wise humanitarian force in Ireland doing its best to make good the inadequacies of others. That a different view was taking shape in Ireland is hardly surprising. The dissatisfaction with the government's approach also found expression among the officials in Dublin Castle.[1]

Eventually, under pressure from Ireland, some concessions were made to permit advances from the treasury towards the improvement of privately owned agricultural land as well as towards the cost of sometimes rather useless public works. Such concessions, however, did nothing to counter the effects of rapidly rising food prices and the devices of the speculators, and were no help to the hungry poor who could not obtain employment on the relief works. As the Lord Lieutenant, Lord Bessborough, put it to Russell in January 1847, 'I know all the difficulties that arise when you begin to interfere with trade, but it is difficult to persuade a starving population that one class should be permitted to make 50 per cent., by the sale of provisions, while they are dying for want of them.'[2] All through that critical winter the poor were largely dependent on what they could earn on the relief works; as many as 734,792 were so employed in March 1847. For those unable to work, the only places of refuge were the overcrowded work-houses where the weekly death rate in April 1847 had reached twenty-five per thousand. With the death rate frightening and food prices still rising, the Russell administration had, in the end, to admit the inadequacy of the relief schemes and reluctantly to accept the conclusion that free rations of food would have to be distributed to the hungry. As a temporary measure, the Destitute Poor (Ireland) Bill, better known later as the Soup Kitchen Act, was put through parliament. It was a modest measure, but it at least helped to check the worst evils of famine in the spring and summer of 1847. It came, however, too late to save many from a winter of starvation and sickness and, like so much of the legislation of this time, it did nothing to remedy the basic ills of Irish rural society.

In Ireland disappointment with the United Kingdom's parliament to conquer the food crisis in a generous way grew in 1846–47. Criticism of the Whigs became increasingly vocal in both O'Connellite and Young Ireland circles, while among the landlords, too, the complaint was widespread that the emergency legislation was imposing an excessive burden in taxation on the Irish economy. For a short time it seemed as though many landlords might join with the Repealers in a common front. One of the most hopeful signs of such a union was the creation of an 'Irish Parliamentary Party', as it was called, composed of eighty-three Irish peers and MPs and drawn from the ranks of the Repealers, Tories and Whigs alike. On issues of common concern, they undertook to act in concert in parliament. The party could have proved a formidable pressure-group on such issues as imperial aids for the Irish economy, more generous famine relief schemes and some measure of compensation to tenant-farmers for improvements to the land; but the bold project quickly fell to pieces in the face of sectional interests and party manoeuvres in parliament. With the Irish Parliamentary Party died, too, the last hope of establishing a strong Irish parliamentary lobby in the mid-nineteenth century.

Russell had in 1847 promised to introduce legislation not

merely to amend the Irish Poor Law of 1838, but also to bring forward his proposals to encourage land drainage and to make £1 million available to reclaim waste land in Ireland. Compulsory powers—a striking proposal for the time—would be sought to acquire waste land from uncooperative landowners. The reclaimed land would be sold or leased to small farmers. There was a hint, too, that something would be done to aid tenant-farmers who were faced with eviction from their holdings. The contrast between what Russell promised and what was actually achieved was a measure both of his government's failure to meet Irish problems and of the inadequacy of the new Irish Parliamentary Party. The ambitious land reclamation scheme was abandoned on the grounds that the compulsory acquisition clauses would prove unacceptable to a House of Lords dominated by the landed interest and though a rather feeble bill was eventually introduced in February 1848 to give some compensation to evicted tenant-farmers for improvements made by them, it was soon lost in a select committee and never emerged again.

The Irish Parliamentary Party, in fact, broke up on two issues in that disappointing parliamentary session of 1847. The first was Lord George Bentinck's bill proposing that £16 million should be advanced by the treasury on long-term loans to aid Irish railway schemes both as a famine relief project and as a venture which would strengthen the Irish economy generally. Bentinck was the leader in the Commons of the Tory protectionists—the section which had broken away from Peel on the Corn Law repeal issue. And though Bentinck and his colleagues had questioned the extent of the potato failure in 1845–46, they were now apparently willing, as the anti-Free Trade party, to accept state intervention in economic affairs, on a scale which was quite unacceptable to either Russell or Peel. The Tory protectionists saw in the Irish Party not only a symptom of Irish discontent with the Whigs but also possible allies in any new realignment in parliament. Bentinck and his friends sharply criticised the useless public works. Principles which might be justifiable in ordinary circumstances, he argued, were of no weight in times of famine.

Reactions to the £16 million scheme in Irish Party circles were at first very favourable, but faced with the vigorous rejection of the scheme by Russell, the British Whigs and Peel, the fine unity of the Irish Party began to crumble. When the bill was finally defeated in February 1847, only thirty-seven out of the seventy Irish members present supported the measure.

It needed, however, the government's proposals to amend the Irish Poor Law to finally bring down the Irish Parliamentary Party. The amending bill was not of an exciting kind but it did bring with it the prospect of a less harsh administration of poor relief; therefore the Repeal MPs, though without much enthusiasm, felt that they ought to support it. The Irish conservatives saw in the additional burden of rates, which the bill would involve, a dire threat to the very survival of the Irish landlords. On this measure, the Irish Party divided and disappeared from history.

The alliance between Repealers and conservative landlords had been an uneasy one and it was impossible to hide for long the fact that the interests of landlords and tenant-farmers were not the same. Equally clear was the fact that, in political and social terms, any enduring settlement would mean the end or drastic curtailment of the power of the old Ascendancy. The famine crisis of 1847 was not enough to bring together all elements in Ireland in an enduring national alliance.

Though parliament in 1847 and 1848 proved reluctant to adopt a programme which would have met the Irish crisis in a comprehensive and fundamental way, it is well to remember the scope of the emergency relief measures. By the summer of 1847 some three million people were receiving food rations in Ireland under the Soup Kitchen Act and by the end of 1848, it has been estimated, some £9,536,000 had been expended on famine relief and drainage schemes; and ultimately, in 1853, the principle of imperial responsibility for the outstanding balances was accepted. Against all this must be set the grim toll of death. Between half a million and one million people died as a result of the Famine and the diseases that came with it. Some died in Ireland, others when they reached the shores of North America. The first feeble recognition of the state's obligation to meet a major social crisis in a comprehensive way was not sufficient to avert a disaster.

In Ireland, then, the Great Famine, in social terms, heralded in an era of long-sustained emigration overseas. In political terms, it helped to bring to an end the old O'Connellite Repeal movement which had dominated the early 1840s. The failure of government and parliament to escape from the narrow limits of nineteenth-century social and economic teaching also helped to turn a section of the Young Irelanders away from constitutional to revolutionary or near-revolutionary methods. That rejection of constitutionalism and the abandonment by the radicals of any hope of an alliance with the Irish landlords could already be observed before the end of 1847. As John Mitchel put it early in 1848, 'The country is actually in a state of war—a war of property against poverty.'[3] 1848 was to see a new interest in republicanism against a background of the Famine and the French Revolution of February 1848. Though republicanism was to achieve little immediate influence in Ireland in 1848-49, it was from this source that Fenianism was to spring in the 1850s. The second half of the nineteenth century was to be characterised by a certain dualism in Irish politics —Home Rule constitutionalism on the one hand and a separatist, republican tradition on the other. The tragic events in Ireland between 1845 and 1849 and the failure of men in power to rise above the conventions of their day helped foster that enduring dualism in the structure of Irish political life.

Charles Stewart Parnell

F. S. L. LYONS

THERE is a curiously apt symbolism in the fact that, although the name of Parnell is one of the most famous in Irish history, no one seems quite sure how to pronounce it. Most people, I suppose, would prefer Par*nell*, but there is ample evidence that those of his colleagues who were closest to him used the form *Par*nell. But whichever form of his name we choose to adopt and however much we may learn about him, can we lay our hands on our hearts and say that we really know and understand the man? I suspect that for many of us, and not least those who have posthumously invoked his name for political causes that were not his causes, he most resembles some great monument which we may have been obliged to visit in youth, but which thereafter we simply cease to notice, perhaps because it is so familiar.

It is not, however, simply a case of familiarity breeding indifference, Parnell baffles us, not just because we do not look, but because the more intensively we do look, the more difficult it is to identify the inner drives and motivations which propelled him, comet-like, along the track of his brief, brilliant and ultimately disastrous career. This does not mean that we are absolved from trying to penetrate the meaning of that career. On the contrary, what he did and what he stood for may be more relevant today than they have been for a long time past. But it does mean that at the outset we shall have to reconcile ourselves to the paramount fact about Parnell—that nothing is quite what it seems, and that when we seek to enter his world we shall find the keys to it in two words, paradox and ambiguity.

Take first the element of paradox. When you come to think of it, everything about the man was, or seemed, paradoxical. Here was an Anglo-Irish aristocrat leading a mainly middle-class party; a landlord heading a tenants' revolt; a Protestant winning the devotion of a Catholic people; a parliamentarian walking on the verge of revolution; a withdrawn introvert thrown largely among genial extroverts; an intensely private man condemned to live much of his life in public; an inarticulate orator swaying vast audiences by short, clipped speeches which themselves became major public events; finally, a human being so superstitious that far from wrapping the green flag round him, he insisted that his followers should keep that unlucky colour as far as possible out of his sight.

Of course, paradox, even on this epic scale, is capable of rational explanation. Parnell *was* a very strange man, perhaps even touched—as he himself dreaded—by that mental instability which haunted his family. Yet although he would undoubtedly have stood out starkly against any setting, we may be quite sure that the particular setting in which he grew up—I mean his heredity and his environment—did much to shape the person he became.

He was born in 1846 into a family that had owned property in Wicklow for several generations. More to the point, it was a family with a tendency to run counter to the normally conservative politics of the landed gentry. A well-known ancestor had opposed the Act of Union, and Parnell's own mother— the daughter of the American Admiral Charles Stewart, who had fought against Britain in 1812—brought with her a strain of anti-British feeling which communicated itself to her son. True, this did not prevent her from sending him to Cambridge. However, he left the university without a degree after a clash with the authorities which, it has been suggested, may have fostered in him that dislike of England—and of Englishmen— that was to be one of his life-long characteristics.

In reality, this dislike went deeper and Cambridge was a symbol, not a cause. Belonging as he did to the Anglo-Irish Ascendancy, Parnell shared to the full their ambivalence: unable to identify with those whom they regarded as their inferiors in Ireland, they were equally quick to resent the attitude of superiority which the English governing elite adopted towards all Irishmen, regardless of ancestry or class. To this attitude Parnell had his own riposte. 'These Englishmen despise us because we are Irish,' he said once to his brother John, 'but we must stand up to them. That's the only way to treat an

Englishman—stand up to him.' With that single phrase he defined his whole philosophy of politics.

In formulating such a philosophy—if that is not too grand a way of describing the down-to-earth pragmatism of an essentially unintellectual man—Parnell owed probably as much to his environment as to his inheritance. Not only was his Wicklow homeland still resonant with romantic echoes of '98, but the family seem to have been not unsympathetic towards the resurrection of the revolutionary idea embodied in the Fenian movement of the 1860s, and Parnell himself later testified that it was Fenianism which had originally turned his thoughts towards politics. Certainly, the first significant words he spoke in the House of Commons pointed that way. Elected in 1875, mainly because of his name and his willingness to pay his expenses, he startled public opinion, Irish as well as English, when in the following year he blurted out his belief that the Fenians who had killed a policeman in Manchester when attempting the rescue of two of their comrades in 1867 had committed no murder.

This speech, which may have sprung from instinct rather than calculation, did more than anything else to draw Parnell out of the shadows. In 1877, though still a political novice, he was elected President of the Home Rule Confederation of Great Britain in place of the 'father' of Home Rule, the ageing and increasingly ineffective Isaac Butt. The phrase 'Home Rule', though used with irritating vagueness by people with radically different views as to what it really meant, had been common currency since 1870, when Butt first began to gather support for what was then loosely described as 'federalism'. By this was meant little more than that an Irish parliament should be reconstituted to look after purely Irish affairs, while the parliament at Westminster should, as hitherto, continue to be the legislative authority for all large, imperial issues.

This was an idea which could, and did, attract much support from middle-class, conservatively-minded Irish nationalists. What is more surprising is that it also attracted support from some Fenians. The official leadership of the Irish Republican Brotherhood did, it is true, hold aloof from Butt, though they respected him for his devoted and sometimes successful efforts to defend Fenian prisoners in the treason trials of the mid-

1860s, but there were others, frustrated by revolutionary stagnation, who sought to build a bridge between constitutional politics and the physical-force movement by infiltrating the Home Rule organisation and even by joining Butt's parliamentary group. Once there, however, they took a line with which Butt, who had a profound respect for the House of Commons, had no sympathy whatever. Their approach was simple and, within limits, effective. It was to draw attention to Irish grievances by making it impossible for parliament to proceed with English business and by this 'obstructionism' to win from the government a more positive policy of reform for Ireland.

Towards this group Parnell almost instinctively gravitated. Indeed, a speech he made in the summer of 1877 seemed to indicate that he might be prepared to go even further.

I do not believe in a policy of conciliation of English feeling or English prejudices . . . What did we ever get in the past by trying to conciliate them? . . . Why was the English Church of Ireland disestablished and disendowed? Why was some measure of protection given to the Irish tenant? It was because there was an explosion at Clerkenwell and because a lock was shot off a prison-van at Manchester. We will never gain anything from England unless we tread upon her toes; we will never gain a single pennyworth from her by conciliation.

This was the kind of over-simplification Fenians understood. Not surprisingly, they did their best to persuade him to join them, but they did so in vain. True, in 1878–79 complex and secret negotiations (in which Irish-American Fenians took the initiative, but to which the IRB refused to be a party) led to the loose and ambiguous understanding known as the 'New Departure'. The essence of this was that individual Fenians might be free to support a campaign to obtain conditions for the Irish tenant-farmers, or eventually to lend their aid to the winning of other reforms by constitutional action, but that these would be regarded as merely a means to the ultimate goal of independence which, it was assumed, would still have to be won by the threat, or the reality, of physical force.

Parnell himself always denied that he had ever entered into any kind of treaty or formal alliance with the Fenians and, though there is a conflict of evidence, this rings true. At that period the Fenians had little enough to offer him. They were divided and disorganised, and while they did undoubtedly represent a still vital element in Irish nationality, they were in no position to translate their ideas into action, except by infusions of Irish-American money. The money was certainly important, but Parnell, though he listened attentively to the emissaries who sought him out and whom he impressed by his exemplary silence, nevertheless held impassively to his own course. 'We used to say', said one of them ruefully, 'if ever there was a man for a secret society, this is the man—he can hold his tongue . . . But I could never discover that Parnell had the least notion of joining us.' This was, indeed, Parnell's own view, though he put it more brutally. He had no mind to lead a revolution like George Washington, he told a friend, because Ireland was not America—it was too small to run away in.

All the same, a real revolution was developing, towards which, whether he liked it or not, he would have to define his attitude. By 1879 much of the country was in the grip of agricultural depression and the West especially was facing its most severe famine since the 1840s. The vast majority of Irish farmers were tenants, holding their small plots on precarious leases and, despite Gladstone's well-intentioned but ineffective Land Act of 1870, they were still vulnerable to eviction if they could not pay their rents. In the depression years of the late 1870s arrears of rent had become formidable; inevitably, evictions multiplied, and so too did reprisals, taking the form of 'outrages', directed not only against landlords and their agents, but also against 'landgrabbers' who dared to take farms from which their fellow-tenants had been expelled. To organise these angry and desperate men for their own defence, and also to keep their violent impulses within bounds, there emerged during 1879 the Irish National Land League. The driving-force behind it was Michael Davitt. Davitt, who was the same age as Parnell, was himself the son of evicted tenants who had emigrated to England. There, he had been drawn into Fenian activities and had in consequence served a spell of harsh imprisonment at Dartmoor. On his release he had become closely associated with the New Departure, but the plight of his fellow-countrymen, and especially those of his native Mayo, soon transcended all other considerations. For him politics reduced themselves to two basic necessities: firstly, to protect the tenants in their holdings, and secondly, in the long term, to make them the owners of their farms.

Yet, though Davitt's ultimate aim was in the truest sense revolutionary, it was implicit in his conception of the New Departure that this should be carried through so far as possible with the aid of the more advanced parliamentary leaders. Therefore, before 1879 was out, he persuaded Parnell to become President of the League. In so doing he linked the mass movement to the parliamentary agitation, with profound consequences for both of them. That autumn Parnell began to preach his basic doctrine of self-reliance to peasants hungry to absorb it. They must keep a firm grip on their homesteads, he told them. 'You must help yourselves and the public opinion of the world will stand by you.' But it was part of that ambiguity which was central to his whole approach to politics that he allowed his hearers to remain uncertain of how far he thought self-reliance should go. Early in 1880, while raising funds in America, he seemed to be saying that there were virtually no limits. To abolish landlordism, he asserted, would be to undermine English misgovernment, and he is alleged to have added :

When we have undermined English misgovernment we have paved the way for Ireland to take her place among the nations of the earth. And let us not forget that that is the ultimate goal at which all we Irishmen aim. None of us, whether we be in America or in Ireland . . . will be satisfied until we have destroyed the last link which keeps Ireland bound to England.[1]

Ironically enough, Parnell's seemingly militant American tour came only a few weeks before the General Election of 1880 brought him such an accession of strength that, although still only a minority of about twenty-five activists could be counted as his devoted followers, he was elected Chairman of the Irish Parliamentary Party. He was now poised to bring maximum pressure to bear upon the Liberal government which had been returned to power after an electoral campaign in which foreign policy had loomed larger than Ireland. He did so by mobilising the full force of Irish discontent behind the pressure for legislation to redress the balance in the tenants' favour. 'The measure of the Land Bill next session', he said in a famous speech at Ennis in September 1880, 'will be the measure of your activity and energy this winter.' The farmers, he insisted, must refuse to pay unjust rents or to occupy farms from which others had been evicted. Characteristically, he urged action against backsliders which, while being non-violent, was likely to be highly effective in country districts or small towns where everyone knew everyone else. This was, of course, the boycott, the 'moral Coventry', which, he suggested, perhaps ironically, was a more Christian and charitable method of dealing with a defaulter than shooting him.

It was too much to hope that this advice would be universally accepted. As the crisis deepened in the winter of 1880–81, a penumbra of violence gathered round the League and its leaders. For that very reason, Parnell's own insistence on non-violence was of paramount importance, since it enabled him to balance between parliamentarism and extremism, or rather to import into parliament the atmosphere of extremism which in turn had a direct bearing upon government policy. It was not surprising either that his enemies should have labelled him a rampant revolutionary, or that his friends should have been mystified by the ambiguity which was so central to his strategy that it seemed to have become almost second nature.

The crucial phase of this part of his career fell in 1881 and 1882. During that period Gladstone's government strove to put down violence by coercion while at the same time passing a Land Act which in effect made the tenant a co-partner in the soil with his landlords, regulated the rents he might be charged, and went much further than any previous legislation to protect him from eviction. Since the coercive measures came first, the Irish Parliamentary Party resisted them with such furious obstruction that the normal procedure of the House of Commons had to be changed and the closure of debate instituted. Among Parnell's followers there was a militant section which wanted to manipulate this situation by causing the party to withdraw from parliament and either intensify the agitation in Ireland or drum up support for it in America.

If we are to understand Parnell's subsequent actions, it is essential to realise why he resisted this desperate course which in all probability would have provoked a major conflict with the authorities. Basically, it was because he set the positive gains from the Land Act above the dubious gains to be made from a direct confrontation with the government. But, almost certainly, it was also because he sensed that the rewards to be reaped from parliamentary pressure would not stop short at the Land Act. At the same time, it was necessary for him to remain in contact with his left wing, both as a reinsurance in case he had miscalculated the effectiveness of parliamentary pressure, and because, without responsible leadership, there was a real danger that the agitation would slide into anarchy. His plan therefore was to ensure that the Land Act passed through parliament, to persuade the Land League to 'test' the act on certain selected estates, and to continue to attack the government in fiery speeches which were chiefly designed to impress his more extreme followers in Ireland and America.

The difficulty was that the speeches impressed the government at least as much as they did his own followers. Consequently, in October 1881 Parnell was shut up in Kilmainham Prison, along with the other leaders of the Land League. When he was arrested, Parnell is said to have remarked that 'Captain Moonlight' would take his place; and it was true that, with the officers of the League in jail, the 'wild men' had their own way, with the result that the number of murders and other outrages increased sharply. From prison, Parnell authorised the publication of a 'No Rent Manifesto', calling on the tenant-farmers to launch a general strike against rent; this may have been an attempt to reassert the authority of the League over the perpetrators of indiscriminate violence, but the evidence suggests that Parnell himself regarded it as an idle gesture. At any rate, it gave the government the opportunity to suppress the League, and since the tenants were already showing a marked preference for taking advantage of the Land Act, there was no longer much reason for Parnell and his colleagues to remain in prison. In May 1882, therefore, they were released after having agreed to the so-called Kilmainham 'treaty'. The basis of the understanding was that the benefits of the Land Act would be extended to classes of tenants hitherto excluded from it, and that coercion would be dropped; in return, Parnell would use his influence against outrage in Ireland and would cooperate 'in forwarding Liberal principles and measures of general reform'.

Scarcely had Parnell left prison than the new Chief Secretary for Ireland, Lord Frederick Cavendish, and his Under-Secretary, T. H. Burke, were stabbed to death in the Phoenix Park. The assassins were members of a secret society, the 'Invincibles', who had no connection either with Parnell or with the Land League, but inevitably the crime impelled the government towards renewed coercion. Yet, while the Phoenix Park Murders probably intensified anti-Irish feeling in England, they did not break the accord which had been reached between Parnell and the Liberals and they did not deflect him from his parliamentary work—though it seems that at the moment of assassination he was so shaken as to contemplate resigning. In the event, two circumstances soon combined to strengthen his position. The first was the disillusionment of his left wing; the success of the Land Act deprived them of an occupation and increasingly they left the stage to him. The other was the change in the franchise after 1884 which, together with the subsequent redistribution of seats, made it virtually certain that Parnell would lead a united party of more than eighty Irish members after the next election. For the time being, therefore, he needed no mass-movement at his back. The simple fact that he would shortly be the leader of an effective 'third force' in the House of Commons meant that both Conservatives and Liberals had to take account of him; his own bargaining position was correspondingly improved.

It was improved still further by the General Election at the end of 1885, which gave the Liberals a majority of 86 over the Conservatives, but which put Parnell at the head of an Irish party which also numbered 86. This extraordinary coincidence momentarily placed Parnell in control of the balance of power. When, at the end of the election, Gladstone's decision to introduce a Home Rule Bill for Ireland became known, it was natural for contemporaries to assume that his conversion was tactical. In fact, it was due much more to a deep conviction that the Irish question must be taken out of English politics. He would have preferred the Conservatives to have dealt with it, but since they refused to touch it, he had no option but to attempt it himself. In so doing he helped to define and harden English attitudes to Ireland. From an English point of view, the fundamental issue was whether or not Irish Home Rule was a threat to the integrity and security of the Empire. Not only

Conservatives, but important sections of the Liberal Party as well, felt that it was, and when Gladstone introduced his bill in the summer of 1886 its defeat was already inevitable.

In retrospect this may seem strange, especially when we recall that Home Rule involved no more than a modest grant of local self-government to Ireland, with all important matters still reserved to the imperial parliament. Why then was the opposition so intense, why was the danger to the empire felt to be so great? It was partly because many Englishmen quite genuinely regarded the Irish as unfit for self-government and dreaded the impending chaos they were sure would result from Home Rule, but still more because they could not bring themselves to trust Parnell, who, for his part, still preserved his habitual ambiguity. During the debates he accepted Gladstone's bill as 'a final settlement', but in the run-up to the election he had used other language. The sole plank in his party's platform, he had said, was 'national independence'. Did Home Rule fall within that definition or did it not? No one knew for certain, but the famous words he uttered in Dublin, and which are now inscribed on his statue, certainly gave food for thought: 'No man has a right to fix the boundary to the march of a nation.'

But if Parnell's ambiguity thus remained, the crisis of 1885–86 affected him and his party in two quite clear and distinct ways. First of all, the fact that the major English parties had taken up well-defined attitudes meant that not only his own freedom of manoeuvre, but that of the whole generation that came after him, was drastically curtailed. If Home Rule in future could only be had from the Liberals then willy-nilly the Irish would be at the mercy of their allies. But there was a second sense in which the Home Rule crisis left its mark upon the constitutional movement. By apparently accepting the notion that self-government could now best be achieved if the Irish Parliamentary Party behaved as if it were just another British party, Parnell was accentuating that drift away from his own grass-roots which had been begun by the Kilmainham 'treaty'. It is highly significant that when agrarian war flared up again with the launching of the 'Plan of Campaign' in October 1886, Parnell at once dissociated himself from it and continued to hold aloof throughout the four years of its operation. Tactically, this may have been wise. But it is arguable that strategically, and in the long term, it marked the first stage in the debilitation of the Home Rule cause and of the Irish Parliamentary Party.

However, all this was hidden for the time being. It was hidden partly because the measures taken to suppress the Plan of Campaign by the Tory government which had been returned to power in the post-Home Rule Election of 1886, so alienated Liberal opinion that nationalists and Liberals were driven closer together than they had ever been. But it was hidden also because Parnell and his colleagues were subjected to yet another form of pressure. In April 1887 *The Times* published in facsimile a letter purporting to be Parnell's, in which he appeared to have condoned the Phoenix Park Murders. Other similar letters were likewise printed, but when Parnell pressed for a Select Committee to clear his name, he was given instead a judicial commission charged with investigating the whole history of the past ten years, with the implication that its business was to establish whether or not there had been a direct connection between Parnellism and Irish crime. The key lay in the letters alleged to have been written by Parnell, and when the Dublin journalist, Richard Pigott, admitted to having forged them, the case against the Irish leader collapsed. His prestige rose to unprecedented heights. He was feted by the Liberals, he visited Gladstone to discuss the next Home Rule Bill, it seemed only a matter of time before he became head of an Irish government. Yet he himself remained unmoved, sceptical and, as always, ambiguous. At the very pinnacle of his popularity he warned his fellow-countrymen not to expect too much from parliamentary action. 'The most advanced section of Irishmen,' he said in May 1889, 'as well as the least advanced, have always understood that the parliamentary policy was to be a trial and that we did not ourselves believe in the possibility of maintaining for all time an incorruptible and independent Irish representation at Westminster.'

So the ambiguity persisted. But now a different kind of ambiguity was to be revealed—with devastating effect. In December 1889 Captain W. H. O'Shea entered divorce proceedings against his wife, citing Parnell as co-respondent. At first his colleagues believed that this was just another conspiracy which would fail as deservedly as the *Times*-Pigott conspiracy had failed, especially since Parnell allowed it to be known that he would emerge from the affair without stain; but when the case came on in November 1890, what some people had known or suspected for years at once became plain—that Parnell and Katharine O'Shea had been lovers for a decade, that she had born his children, and that from at least 1886 onwards they had lived together continuously. The case was not contested, mainly because Parnell and Katharine wanted above all else to get married; but also, it was disclosed many years later, because they believed that Captain O'Shea could be bought off by a share of the substantial fortune Mrs O'Shea was expecting to inherit from a recently dead aunt. This scheme miscarried, but it helps to explain why Parnell gave the assurances he did.

When the assurances apparently proved false there was an immediate reaction. In England, the Nonconformist conscience was clamant and the Liberal-Nationalist alliance at once came under strain. In Ireland, the Church, though circumspect in its opposition, was bound to throw its weight against a proven adulterer. But what, for most Irishmen and virtually all Liberals, proved decisive was the warning administered by Gladstone to the Irish Parliamentary Party, first privately, then publicly, that they must in effect choose between Parnell and Home Rule. The first instinctive reaction of his most prominent followers was one of loyalty to their chief, and Parnell was re-elected Chairman, though it is fair to add that many members were ignorant of the Liberal pressure when they re-elected him. But gradually the implications sank in and when Parnell showed himself utterly impenitent, a majority of the party braced itself, after a week of tortured debate in Committee Room 15, to place the policy above the man and to repudiate his leadership.

The man, however, refused to surrender and the fight was carried to Ireland where it raged for another eleven months, only temporarily to be stilled by Parnell's death at Brighton in October 1891. During that last disastrous coda to his career, Parnell refused what seemed favourable terms for a temporary retirement: 'If I go, I go for ever,' he said, and he may well have been right. He also appeared to be making a deliberate appeal to 'the hill-side men'—that is, to the Fenians who certainly came out strongly in his support.

I have not misled you [he said in Dublin]. I have never said that this constitutional movement must succeed . . . We stand at the parting of the ways . . . if our constitutional movement of to-day is broken, sundered, separated, discredited and forgotten, England will be face to face with that imperishable force which . . . gives me vitality and power. And if Ireland leaves this path upon which I have led her . . . I will not for my part say that I will not accompany her further.

Yet, even to the very end, the familiar ambiguity remained, for despite three successive by-election defeats he still continued to look to the next general election to restore his fortunes and refused to regard parliamentary pressure as outmoded. Most probably, he was trying to navigate back to that dangerous but exhilarating position he had occupied between 1879 and 1882, when he had a great popular movement at his back and no entangling Liberal alliance to hamper him in the House of Commons. But circumstances, both political and personal, had vastly changed since then, and in a sense the most important thing about his downfall was its negative aspect—that it demonstrated the limitations of independent opposition by an Irish party at Westminster.

On the other side of the balance sheet, there were, of course, positive achievements. To Parnell primarily belongs the credit for the creation of a parliamentary group which, in its prime, became a splendid and dedicated party. To Parnell again was mainly due the transformation of Home Rule from a vague aspiration to a policy endorsed by one of the two great English parties. To Parnell, finally, did his countrymen owe the restoration of their self-respect through their involvement in the normal procedures of modern democratic politics. Since this was to be perhaps his most important legacy, there is a certain irony in the fact that to the generation which came after him he figured mainly as a romantic hero betrayed by his own followers under pressure from the English enemy. Myths, as we have good reason to know, are potent in Irish political culture, but this myth is not only misleading but also unnecessary. The real Parnell was big enough, and hard enough to understand, without the additional confusion of having to see him through rose or red or (what he would himself have shuddered at) green spectacles. He was a complex political animal function-

G

ing in a complex political situation. The best tribute we can pay him is to see him in his own context and judge him on his own terms.

The Irish Parliamentary Party

F. S. L. LYONS

MY task in this essay is to reverse the normal order of celestial events. I have to describe not a death followed by a resurrection, but a resurrection followed by a death—or, more accurately, a seeming death followed by a seeming resurrection and this in turn by a total and final oblivion. The splendid parliamentary instrument fashioned by Parnell was, as we all know, shattered in 1890 by the split in the party which had been precipitated by the O'Shea divorce case and which continued with unabated ferocity not only up to the fallen leader's death the following year, but right through the remainder of that decade. It is the aftermath and the consequences of this split which must be the point of departure for my survey of the fortunes of the Irish parliamentary tradition between the two catastrophes of 1890 and 1918.

It is customary for historians to contrast the bitter, internal feud among the parliamentarians with the exciting new developments which were so radically transforming the country during that same decade of the 1890s. It is certainly true that neither private impulses nor public initiatives owed much to any of the three groups into which the Irish Parliamentary Party had split after 1891. Thus the Conservatives, in power for most of this period, were able to pass an important measure of land purchase, to set up the Congested Districts Board, to establish the Department of Agriculture and Technical Instruction, and to confer upon Ireland a system of local government based on elected county councils—all without really effective intervention by, or pressure from, the Nationalist MPs at Westminster. It was the same at home. These were the years of the foundation of the Gaelic League, of the literary revival and the establishment of the National Theatre, of the first beginnings of Connolly's labour movement, and of Griffith's formulation of the doctrines of Sinn Féin—but to such diverse and ultimately crucial manifestations the Irish party, or parties, were seen to be indifferent, if not actively hostile. It is, I think, beyond question that if we are to seek for the first symptoms of disenchantment with constitutional nationalism we shall find them in these years when the youth and imagination and energy of the nation, repelled by the barren faction fights of the parliamentarians, turned in disgust and with relief towards other forms of self-expression.

It was characteristic of the disarray into which Parnell's heirs had fallen that when in 1900 they did manage to reunite, they did so incompletely (T. M. Healy being excluded from the love-feast), and did so only because they were driven by irresistible external impulses to come together again or vanish for ever. Not even the parliamentarians could celebrate the centenary of '98—with its inevitable emphasis upon *United* Ireland—without embarrassment at their own obvious disunity. Nor could they with conviction champion the Boer cause in the House of Commons or draw stirring morals for Ireland from the war in South Africa without reflecting that what they said or did would gain greatly in dignity and effectiveness if they said or did it as a unified party. But what brought them to their senses most of all was what had made them great in their heyday—a recrudescence of the land agitation. This was mainly the work of William O'Brien who, as one of Parnell's chief lieutenants, had always been closely identified with the fortunes of the Irish tenant-farmers. In the mid-1890s O'Brien had withdrawn from parliament in revulsion from the sordid and incessant feuds of his former colleagues and soon afterwards had launched a new movement in the west of Ireland to protect the small farmers from the encroachments of the large cattle-ranches. His movement spread rapidly and at the turn of the century he found himself at the head of a nation-wide organisation, the United Irish League. This gave him great influence in the country and he used it to maximum effect by exerting pressure upon the parliamentarians to abandon their futile quarrels and seek a real reconciliation.

O'Brien undoubtedly expected that if the party were reunited under the auspices of his League it would remain subordinate to that League. However, like most contemporaries, he had been deceived by the verbal civil war among the parliamentarians into underestimating their toughness and resilience. For the long ordeal of the split, painful and injurious as it had been, had in some ways actually strengthened the claims of constitutional nationalism to speak for and to the Irish people. Most notably, although the deposition of Parnell had, as O'Brien remarked, 'replaced one-man power by eighty-men powerlessness', there was, even in this, an element of positive achievement. For Parnell's one-man power had been the power of a dictator. In deposing him by the eminently parliamentary method of a majority vote taken after a week of agonising but highly responsible debate, the party—at least the anti-Parnellite section of it—had vindicated an essential principle of constitutional government.

Granted that this was so, it might be argued that the fruits of that achievement turned to ashes because of the triple division into which the party floundered before Parnell had been many months in his grave. Obviously, the achievement *was* diminished in the sense that public opinion was alienated by the endless and seemingly petty bickering over control of funds, of constituency organisations, of newspapers, of committees, and all the other paraphernalia of democratic politics. However, this was not the whole story; nor was the bickering so entirely petty as it appeared. The largest of the three sections, the group led first by Justin McCarthy and then by John Dillon, was in fact fighting on two fronts and for two different, but equally important, principles. First, in insisting that there could be no peace with the tiny Parnellite minority except on the basis of reunification, Dillon and his friends were continuing to uphold the concept of majority rule. They never showed themselves so magnanimous or so far-sighted as when they agreed, as part of the process of burying the hatchet, that the Chairman of the reunited party should be Parnell's successor, John Redmond. In this they chose more wisely than they knew. At the time Redmond was widely regarded as somewhat suspect— an impulsive, unreliable weathercock of a politician. It was only gradually that his true quality emerged and that the party came to realise that it had in him a leader who was not only lucid and articulate in debate and in committee, but was also a genuinely reconciling force.

If in fighting Parnell's followers and then agreeing to serve under the Parnellite leader, the majority section displayed a high degree of self-abnegation, in the more squalid and disagreeable conflict with Tim Healy they defended a second principle no less vital to the survival of the parliamentary tradition. This was their resolute refusal to allow the fact that clerical influence had contributed to Parnell's downfall to influence the situation after Parnell had disappeared from the scene. Although Healy and his small group of relations and followers stood for other things besides clericalism (for example, for the freedom of individual constituencies from central control), and although they were not even openly and professedly a clerical party, the evidence suggests most strongly that such support as they gained in the country came largely from the priests who had learned to look upon Healy himself as the champion of Catholic morality outraged by Parnell's liaison with Katharine O'Shea. That this support—never, admittedly, on a massive scale—did not become truly formidable was mainly due to the tenacious resistance of John Dillon.

The party which reunited in 1900 was, therefore, very similar to the one which Parnell had led in his prime. It remained, as before, essentially middle-class and middle of the road, vaguely liberal in its political attitudes, decidedly conservative in its social composition and outlook, and retaining so many senior members who had grown up under the shadow of the 'Chief' that the leadership, not just in 1900 but also when the end came in 1918, still consisted almost entirely of men who had first entered politics in the Parnellite high noon. It was ironical, however, that the one new recruit of front-bench calibre who did join after 1900, the Ulster Catholic, Joe Devlin, probably did more than anyone else to re-establish an element of strident Catholicism in the party's make-up. Devlin, who was an able administrator as well as a fine speaker, owed his powerful influence in Irish politics not merely to the fact that he took over the running of the United Irish League, but also to his prominence in the Ancient Order of Hibernians. That institution was avowedly sectarian, and although Redmond and Dillon may have looked somewhat askance at it, it undeniably played a vital role in organising the Catholic vote, especially in the Northern counties. This is not to say that the party thereby became a clerical party or that there was any serious foundation for the Unionist taunt that Home Rule would mean Rome rule. What Devlin really personified was an enduring characteristic in a country where religion was still a deeply divisive influence. Sectarian organisations were inevitable where sectarian rivalries still abounded. Just as an Ulster Unionist politician could ignore the Orange Order only at his peril, so no nationalist party in a predominantly Catholic society could pretend that the Hibernians did not exist; if they had not existed, it would probably have been necessary to invent them.

It remains true that an undercurrent of uneasiness about the Hibernian connection continued to eddy through the party, especially among its highly critical supporters in the Young Ireland branch of the United Irish League, right up to 1914, but this was less significant than it might have been in quieter times, because the situation which the party confronted between reunion and the onset of the Home Rule crisis in 1912 was one of such extraordinary difficulty that sectarian frictions were among the least of its worries. It faced, in fact, three different but related problems. The first of these, paradoxically, sprang from what seemed to be one of its most glittering achievements. This was the virtual, though not quite final, settlement of the land question by the Wyndham Act of 1903, which, by facilitating the sale of whole estates on terms relatively favourable to the landlords and with state-aided loans for the purchasers, did more than any previous legislation to convert the small farmer from tenant into owner. True, the act's financial clauses were so unsound that they had to be revised in 1909, and true also that the completion of the purchase operation, North and South, had to wait until after 1922; nevertheless, the Wyndham Act was a turning-point and was seen to be such even at the time. The way towards this reform had been prepared by the famous Land Conference of 1902, at which representatives of the landlords and of the tenants (the chief of the latter being William O'Brien and John Redmond) agreed upon the main terms on which land legislation should be based. The Wyndham Act owed much to the Land Conference and while the act was passing through parliament its author, the Chief Secretary, George Wyndham, was in frequent, if unobtrusive, contact with Redmond.

But no sooner was the act passed than criticism of it began

to spread—formidable criticism, voiced by such heroes of the Land War as Dillon and Davitt, and by the Irish Parliamentary Party's newspaper, the *Freeman's Journal*. Part of the complaint was a technical argument that the landlords were receiving too good a price, but behind this lay a much more fundamental point. The critics of the act, especially Dillon, felt profoundly that to settle such an age-long battle on the basis of agreement with the landlords was a most dangerous precedent which, if carried to its logical conclusion, would deprive the nationalist movement of its cutting-edge. Too much preoccupation with short-term material benefits, thought Dillon, would dull men's appetite for Home Rule, while Tories bringing gifts could accomplish in a few years what Tories bringing coercion had never been able to do. For William O'Brien, on the other hand, the new policy, which he labelled 'conference plus business', was capable of almost indefinite expansion and, in fact, in the years following the Wyndham Act, efforts were made to reach further agreed solutions in such matters as university education and the devolution of a measure of local self-government to an elected Irish council. These failed to materialise, but the dangers seemingly inherent in any attempt to harmonise the interests of the declining Protestant Ascendancy and those of the rising nationalist majority so impressed the party leaders that they took a stern and uncompromising line with O'Brien, who, after several years of quarrelling with his former colleagues, finally left the party for ever in 1909. His bitterness was almost pathological, and so intense as to make him lose most of what political judgement he still possessed, but the fact that he had great influence in Co. Cork, and was soon joined by that other political nonconformist, Tim Healy, allowed him, from 1910 onwards, to lead an independent parliamentary group of about ten members which continued thereafter to be an unrelenting thorn in the flesh of the official Irish Parliamentary Party.

These internal divisions have to be seen against a rapidly changing background which itself provided the party with the second of its problems. If one turns aside from the *Freeman's Journal* and some of the more solid provincial newspapers of these years, and reads instead the *Irish Independent*, or D. P. Moran's *Leader*, or Griffith's *United Irishman* and (later) *Sinn Féin*, or the various productions of the Gaelic League, one cannot but be struck by the volume and unanimity of the attacks upon the party, even though the individuals and papers that joined in this free-for-all had generally little in common except a shared hostility towards, and contempt for, the parliamentarians. Their diverse motives included the simple jealousy of the *Irish Independent* (which was Healyite in its politics), the self-conscious cultural nationalism of the Gaelic League, the withering contempt of Moran for what he regarded as the excessive anglicisation of MPs who lived too much in London, and Griffith's perpetual insistence that self-reliance and abstention from the imperial parliament should be the key ideas of the future. When we add to all this that these were also the years of the rise of a much more vocal and aggressive labour movement, and of the reorganisation of the IRB into a conspiratorial machine for which the Irish Parliamentary Party was simply irrelevant, it is easy to see that despite the party's firm hold on the constituencies (in 1908 it beat off a Sinn Féin challenge at a by-election without too much difficulty), its appeal to the energy and imagination of youth was steadily draining away.

To restore its prestige the party badly needed to be able to play once more the old parliamentary game Parnell had played in 1885–86, when he held the balance of power between the two great English parties. However—and here the party faced its third problem—between 1900 and 1910 Redmond and his cohorts were hopelessly outnumbered by the large majorities enjoyed by the governments then in power. The fact that in 1906 the long Conservative domination was swept away by a Liberal electoral landslide was only superficially a comfort. A shadowy Liberal alliance had survived from the 1890s, but the Liberals were no longer prepared as a party to commit themselves wholeheartedly to Home Rule. On the contrary, they had many others needs and interests to consider and were in any event soon preoccupied by the threat to their programme posed by the wrecking tactics of the House of Lords. Their one concession to their supposed allies—the Irish Council Bill of 1907 —fell so ludicrously short of Home Rule as to provoke a howl of rage even among Redmond's most loyal supporters. Social legislation, admittedly, was relatively easy to come by—for example, the Irish Universities Act of 1908 and the 1909 Land Act—but, as the years rolled on, it became dismally clear that only some drastic, almost magical, reduction in the size of the Liberal Party would enable the Nationalists to resume their traditional role and press their traditional demand.

The breakthrough came in 1909 when the situation was transformed by the decision of the House of Lords to reject Lloyd George's radical budget of that year. In the ensuing crisis the two General Elections of 1910 shattered the Liberal supremacy in the House of Commons and left the two main parties so evenly matched that Redmond was able to achieve what seemed an ideal position of balance. Yet it was also a position of great peril. The budget itself, which contained liquor taxes and licence duties adversely affecting the makers, the sellers and the consumers of drink, was extremely unpopular in Ireland, and Redmond would only be able to justify his refusal to oppose it root and branch if he could demonstrate that he had used his electoral power to compel the Liberals so to deal with the House of Lords as to clear the way for the introduction of a Home Rule Bill.

The sequel showed that he could do this, but only at a price. The Liberals, driven by the budget crisis towards that confrontation with the Lords which had been threatening since 1906, did succeed in limiting the veto power of the Upper House, in that the Parliament Act of 1911 ensured that any legislation passing through the House of Commons in three successive sessions of the same parliament would automatically become law. When, therefore, the government introduced a Home Rule Bill in 1912, it was, theoretically, at least, certain of reaching the statute-book by 1914. But it was precisely at this point that certainty dissolved into doubt and frustration. The bill may seem to us in retrospect to have been a modest enough affair, scarcely calculated to bring not merely Ireland, but Britain also to the verge of civil war. It offered Ireland a local parliament, indeed, with control over strictly Irish business, but in such large imperial matters as peace and war and the Crown, and in the vital fields of taxation and tariffs, it reserved the major decisions of policy to the imperial parliament at Westminster, where Ireland would continue to be represented, though in reduced numbers.

It is probably true to say that to most Irishmen this programme seemed reasonably adequate from its first unveiling at least up to the time of the Easter Rising. But it never really stood a chance of being considered on its merits. In north-east Ulster, and among Unionists elsewhere in Ireland, it was enough that Home Rule threatened the British connection for it to be resisted tooth and nail. There immediately began again, but this time much more intensively, the preparations to resist Home Rule which had first appeared in 1886—the solemn affirmations, the drilling (and later, the arming), even the preliminary steps towards forming a separate government should the hated legislation actually pass into law.

These preparations were deadly serious and it is a major criticism of the Nationalist leaders that they were never able to rid themselves of the notion that the Ulster Unionists were bluffing and that their resistance would crumble if put to the test. That would still have been a gross miscalculation if Irish, or even Ulster, Unionists had stood on their own. However, from 1912 onwards they received the most public and explicit assurances from the leaders of the Conservative Party that there was no limit to the support which Irish Unionism could look to receive from British Conservatism. The motives for such support were of course by no means exclusively altruistic. Bonar Law, who in 1911 had succeeded Arthur Balfour as the Conservative leader, was doubtless influenced to some extent by his family connection with Ulster, but he and his colleagues were guided by calculation as much as by emotion. On the one hand, and at the level of principle, they seem to have been genuinely alarmed by Home Rule as a threat both to the safety and to the integrity of the Empire. On the other hand, however, as politicians excluded from office since 1906, and baulked of defeating Liberal legislation by the restriction of the veto power of the House of Lords, it was an obvious, if hazardous, tactic for them to use the Ulster issue as a means of forcing the government towards an early general election, from which they expected, not without reason, to win the majority that would bring them back to power. However, in their obsessive hatred of the Liberals, the Conservatives went too far. Although some of their leaders, including, eventually, Bonar Law himself, seem to have thought that the Liberal government would crack under pressure which stopped just short of violence, others saw no cause to be so lily-livered and did not shrink from conspiratorial devices—the most dangerous being the partially successful attempt to tamper with the loyalty of the army—which, if world war had not intervened, might well have brought civil strife to Britain as well as to Ireland.

The Liberals did not quite crack under this formidable pressure, but they went near enough to doing so to make it perfectly clear that for most of them, including the Prime Minister, Asquith, and also, probably, Lloyd George, the cause of Ireland was no longer a crusade, but a nagging nuisance to be got rid of with the minimum of fuss. Thus, although they did not abandon the Home Rule Bill, they began to consider modifying it almost from the moment of its introduction with the object of enabling a variable number of north-eastern counties to opt out of the jurisdiction of a Dublin-based parliament. This manoeuvre, though originally intended by the Unionists as a means of making Home Rule for any part of Ireland impossible, soon achieved an independent life of its own and Redmond was driven, step by step, to concede the possibility of what he regarded as a temporary partition of the country, but which others would certainly wish to make permanent. In going so far as even to contemplate partition, he was taking a grave risk not only of alienating his own supporters, but of losing credibility among the Englishmen with whom he had to deal. It is impossible to study the history of these crowded and dramatic years without feeling that the rigid and passionate Carson imposed himself far more effectively upon British politics than the courteous but ultimately flexible Redmond. The upshot was that, although Home Rule did struggle onto the statute-book in September 1914, it was with two serious qualifications. One was that the act itself was suspended for the duration of the war, and the other was that it was made clear that when the time came for putting it into operation special provision would have to be made for north-east Ulster.

The consequences of this failure had already begun to make themselves felt before the last act of the parliamentary drama (or farce) had been played. If Redmond had been able to carry Home Rule for the whole of Ireland he would have ridden high indeed and most criticism would have been silenced. Even Pearse, it is well to recall, had spoken on a Home Rule platform in 1912. But when Redmond began to compromise, and when the Ulstermen formed their volunteer force to fight for the Union, the position of the Irish Parliamentary Party was greatly weakened. Conversely, that of the more militant nationalists was correspondingly strengthened. True, when an Irish Volunteer movement sprang to life in the South in imitation of—and, of course, potentially in opposition to—the Ulster Volunteers, it was initially intended to be purely defensive. Before long, however, it was penetrated by the IRB, and although Redmond moved belatedly to bring it under his own control, he was unable to prevent a significant minority from breaking away from the main body and taking with them their share of the weapons previously landed at Howth and Kilcoole.

The outbreak of the war, though superficially it put the Irish question into cold storage, in fact operated still further to the disadvantage of the Irish Parliamentary Party. This was partly Redmond's own doing. Identifying himself with the Allied cause, he sought similarly to identify with it a resentful and reluctant country. With recruiting mishandled, casualties mounting and conscription looming on the horizon, dislike of the war turned very easily into detestation. Redmond and Dillon might go through the motions of discussing with the British government the transfer of power when Home Rule should eventually be put in operation, but the men who were at that moment plotting the Easter Rising had a very different end in view. Even though, as we know, Irish opinion was at first hostile to the Rising and only became sympathetic when the executions and the deportations made their full impact, it is certainly no exaggeration to say that the Irish Parliamentary Party had begun to lose ground in the country long before the ghost of Roger Casement came beating on the door.

After the Rising, and in the two and a half years between then and the General Election at the end of 1918, what had been a gradual decline in the party's fortunes turned into a catastrophic rout. Historians have found many reasons for this collapse. Among the most important are : the failure to achieve an agreed constitutional settlement immediately after the Rising, even though Redmond had further compromised his position by conceding the right of six counties to opt out of Home Rule, as he wrongly thought, temporarily; the fact that the existence of a war-time coalition government in Britain (in

which, for a time, both Carson and Bonar Law were included)
deprived Redmond of his position of balance; the growing war-
weariness in Ireland and the almost universal dread of conscription, exploited by Sinn Féin with conspicuous ability in the
spring of 1918; the remarkable efficiency, both of Sinn Féin
propaganda and of Sinn Féin organisation; above all, perhaps,
the crucial decision at the Sinn Féin Convention of 1917 to
merge the very diverse movements led by Griffith and de Valera
and to combine them in the demand for an independent republic
in the election campaign of the following year, which resulted
in a crushing triumph for Sinn Féin and the virtual obliteration
of the Irish Parliamentary Party.

Behind these specific and perfectly valid explanations lie
others, more intangible but no less important. We may best
sum them up by saying that the Irish Parliamentary Party continued to be dogged by its past, while itself unable to adjust to
the demands of a rapidly changing present. The Parnell split
had inflicted upon it a wound from which it never fully recovered. This was so, not just because it drastically shook the
confidence of the people in their parliamentary representatives,
but also because the fatal habit of internal dissension continued
right up to 1914 and deflected the party's attention from significant changes in the climate of opinion in Ireland. The two most
momentous of these were the cult of Gaelic nationalism and the
cult of violence. Each was, in certain important ways, diametrically opposed to the reconciling, one might almost say the
ecumenical, function which the party at its best was admirably
fitted to perform. With the coming of the war and the acting
out in 1916 of Pearse's vision of the blood-sacrifice, the combination of Gaelicism and of violence became powerfully attractive, and when over this floated the flag of the Republic, it is
easy to see how the party, confused and battered as it had been
for so long, should have drifted in the revolutionary gale onto
the reef on which in 1918 it eventually broke up.

Yet to end the story by simply recording the death of the
party at the hands of violent men would be to simplify, and so
to falsify, history. For when the dust of battle cleared away
four years later no independent all-Ireland Republic was any-
where in sight. And bitter as this and the partition of the island
both were to those who had fought for such an ideal, perhaps

we can see more clearly now what was hidden from them. This is that the parliamentary tradition and those other things which went with it—an independent judiciary, the rule of law, an incorruptible civil service—so far from having been snuffed out, had rooted themselves more deeply in the life of the country than anyone could have imagined. Indeed, we may go further. We may say that the party, which in its prime had contributed so mightily to the solution of the land question and thus to the transformation of Irish society in the two or three generations before 1914, contributed no less to the growing political maturity of the nation. It did this most obviously by its conduct and practice during some forty years of hard and exacting parliamentary labour; it worked in the same direction by establishing and fostering other representative institutions (notably the successive national organisations) and by the stimulus it gave—especially in local and parliamentary elections —to democratic action and discussion at every level of political involvement. Transcending even these achievements was the fact that when it went, it went not as the victim of a military *coup d'état,* but after straightforward defeat at a general election. This in turn paved the way for the creation of Dáil Éireann, but Dáil Éireann had scarcely started to function before, almost unconsciously, it began to utilise and to build upon the constitutional tradition it inherited. If to the survivors of the old Irish Parliamentary Party this seemed the last and most intolerable irony, to us, looking back, it may rather stand as the last and perhaps the highest tribute.

The First Dáil and After

BRIAN FARRELL

THE First Dáil was delivered out of a British general election. Its birth would have been impossible without a British act of parliament. The Representation of the People Act of 1918 created an entirely new electorate within the United Kingdom. In Ireland the voting register jumped from 701,475 to 1,936,673; allowing for all those men who had been killed in the war or had died since the previous general election in 1912, this electoral reform meant that something like two out of every three of those on the register were due to vote for the first time. It was this great body of new voters—younger men and women, in the main—who swamped the traditional support of the old Irish Parliamentary Party and swept Sinn Féin to victory. Sinn Féin gave birth to the Dáil.

Sinn Féin was a new party. The name belonged to a small political ginger-group established by Arthur Griffith in 1905. This original Sinn Féin was as much a cultural as a political force. Its political programme was based on the re-creation of the 1782 constitution. It represented an ingenious attempt to marry the old Irish parliamentary ambition for legislative independence with the contemporary Austro-Hungarian experience of dual monarchy. Griffith thought that an independent and united Ireland might be achieved by creating a distinct King, Lords and Commons of Ireland—but that the sovereign would also happen to be King of England. It was a slightly more elaborate version of the Home Rule proposals being canvassed in the years before the First World War. Arthur Griffith's Sinn Féin was a powerful propaganda vehicle; it had a formative influence on a whole generation of Irish men and women. As an organisation, it was a political failure. By early 1916 it had only half a dozen branches outside Dublin. It had no institutional responsibility for the military development of the Volunteers. And it was only by accident that the name was tagged on to the Easter Rising—in an effort to associate two discredited enterprises.

But in the aftermath of the Rising, Sinn Féin became a portmanteau title for a wide popular movement that could embrace all shades of advanced nationalist opinion in Ireland. That, of course, included the physical-force men; it would be a mistake to think that they were the only, or even the decisive, element in this new Sinn Féin. It was a broadly based grouping that managed to bring together dissident parliamentarians, incipient anti-partitionists and Sinn Féin monarchists on its constitutional wing with ex-prisoners and 1916 veterans on the militant wing (although not all of these latter were uncritical advocates of any early recourse to arms again). Essentially, then, Sinn Féin was, and remained, a political rather than a military movement.

The Volunteers were its military arm; their role was supportive rather than dominant. Indeed, between Easter 1916 and the 21 January 1919 when the First Dáil was inaugurated in the Dublin Mansion House there was little overt militancy on the Irish side. No British soldier and only one policeman was killed in the whole period, although the very day that the Dáil first met also saw Dan Breen's Soloheadbeg incident usher in a more violent phase in the struggle. But immediately after the failure of the Rising—and it *was* a failure—the main effort was political. Sinn Féin in 1917 and 1918 devoted its energies to organisation, to propaganda, and to the task of converting Irish opinion to demand a carefully undefined political independence at the war's end. This was not just an aim in itself but the fertile field in which the seed of a vigorous economic and cultural programme of self-development could be planted.

In the light of subsequent events, in the romantic glow of 'four glorious years' of freedom-fighting, it takes an imaginative effort to understand and recreate what was happening in Ireland in these years. We have tended to concertina the events of those crowded years into a single, clear-cut, military campaign—stretching uninterruptedly from 1916 to limited political independence in 1922. The ensuing disaster of the Civil War has cast a cloud of confusion and a blanket of bitterness over this seminal period in Irish political development. We have misunderstood both the aims and achievements of Irish leaders in the period.

Despite the rhetoric of the 1916 Proclamation and the ideological vigour of the 'Democratic Programme' of the First Dáil, the Irish leaders were not revolutionaries—certainly not in a political sense. It might well be argued that their most revolutionary commitments were in the cultural sphere: in their vision of a new, integrated, Gaelic Ireland. And it was precisely here that they were least effective. Although there are fine phrases about the need to change social and economic structures in the manifestos, the mainline tradition of Sinn Féin continued to be cautious and conservative. The 'Democratic Programme' did not represent the social and economic ideals of the First Dáil. Most of its members had not read the document in advance; the few who had seen it in draft were reluctant enough to subscribe to it, and there was a last-minute redrafting of the document only hours before the Dáil met. The 'Democratic Programme' was in fact a tactical device designed to secure political support for the new Irish legislative body within the international socialist movement and to enhance Irish Labour's standing abroad. Economically, the new Sinn Féin remained firmly wedded to the reformist parliamentary tradition which had created its opportunity; typically it used the Volunteers to suppress local efforts to attempt an immediate sharing out of land in the West. Politically, Sinn Féin attempted to duplicate the institutional framework it was dedicated to destroy. Even more than Stormont, the Dáil was from the outset a Westminster import.

The fact is evident from even a cursory examination of the constitution, standing orders, and proceedings of Dáil Éireann in its formative years. The documents sketch an outline of the British system of cabinet government and, despite all the difficulties of these years, a consistent effort was made to maintain 'Westminster standards'. This was not just a matter of respecting such traditional conventions as the priority given to parliamentary questions, the acceptance of rulings by the Ceann Comhairle, or even the attempt to depersonalise proceedings by using constituency titles rather than deputies' names. All of these were important indications of the normalcy of British procedures for the young Irish political leaders. They were not the only evidence. There was also, from the beginning, a determined effort to establish and emphasise that the Dáil, with its firm electoral mandate, was the only legitimate source of authority and to place that civil authority clearly above the actual force wielded by IRA Volunteers in the field. The Dáil and its leaders, it might be said, did not seek to destroy the institutional status quo in Ireland; they sought to take it over. The creation and functioning of the Dáil courts provides an interesting and successful case study of how the policy operated with a careful concern to preserve as far as possible the existing and accepted system. Sinn Féin was working to create a polity within a polity —making the Dáil rather than the House of Commons the main arena for Irish political communication, control and competition.

Of course, the old ambiguity about the role of force in the Irish representative tradition—a theme so often mentioned in this series of essays—was a dominant concern. In theory the Volunteers became the armed force of the Dáil; in practice, through Collins and Mulcahy, a system of staff control was established within the Volunteers which blurred the issue of civil political control. There is some evidence that the command structure operated without much reference to the nominal Minister for National Defence, Cathal Brugha, and this may well have been a considerable contributory factor in the subsequent Civil War division.[1] In the period after the Treaty debate Collins deliberately evaded and confused the theoretical issue by combining both military and civil command in his own person. But throughout the life of the First and Second Dála, while it was the men in the field who made the essential tactical decisions of a guerrilla war, the general principle of civil control and the authority of the elected representative government were upheld. It was the politicians who negotiated the Treaty; it was the failure of the politicians to resolve and reconcile their deep disagreements on the Treaty in the Dáil that provoked the Civil War.

The story of that agonising cleavage on the Treaty debate is investigated in detail by Professor Lyons in the final essays in this volume. It is enough here to make three points: (1) that the original impulse was to attempt to contain the dispute within the limits of a parliamentary debate; (2) that in the main the military commanders awaited the outcome of that debate before initiating any action in the field; (3) that despite the disaster of the Civil War, the Irish parliamentary tradition was resilient enough eventually to encompass, neutralise and institutionalise the dispute within the structures of a competitive political party system.

It is this final development which makes the Irish experience unique among the new nation-states of the twentieth-century world. The earlier stages of the liberation struggle followed a pattern familiar enough : the attempted coup or bloody protest in arms, the creation of a national-front organisation from the disparate elements of resistance to an imperial occupying power, the fragmentation of these elements in a civil war at the moment of independence. All of this can be paralleled in the post-colonial and post-occupation period of a wide variety of states. Typically, the next phase has been either the imposition of military rule by the young reforming commanders of the liberation army or the assumption of governmental power by a single authoritarian party. Both developments are the reflections of the fragility of constitutional conventions in periods of intense political activity. The existing system has neither the resources nor the support to carry the load of decisions and choices imposed by the transition to political independence : it first bends then breaks under the burden. In Ireland, by contrast, a sturdy, stable and developed political culture sustained the infant state through its traumatic early years.

I have already suggested that this early success in achieving stability was primarily part of Ireland's British inheritance from the nineteenth century—a parliamentary inheritance which Irish leaders and parties in Westminster had done much to shape. It might be asked why the same parliamentary inheritance has failed to contain the chronic community suspicions and prevent political instability in the North. The answer, in part, is that the political divergence in the political development of the two parts of the island since 1921 owes something to the fact that the two new Irish parliaments—in Dublin and in Belfast—sprang from different branches of that Westminster tradition.

Repeatedly through the nineteenth century, as earlier essays in this book have documented in some detail, Irish nationalist

MPs found allies on the Liberal side of the House of Commons; in the same way the Unionists gravitated towards the Conservatives. This was partly a matter of interest—the original basic cousinship of the landed gentry shading into a shared involvement in financial and commercial development. It can also be partly explained as an instinctive, although calculable, attraction of nationalists towards a critical and reforming party and of the Unionists towards those who shared with them an innate belief in their natural right to rule. Stated in such broad and simple terms, the analogy may seem crude. But it does provide a useful point of departure for a brief concluding survey of the pattern of the Irish parliamentary development after the creation of the original Dáil Éireann.

The Government of Ireland Act of 1920 provided the Northern Unionists with a basic constitutional document. It enshrined all the structures of the Westminster model. There was a Governor to represent the Crown whose main duties were liturgical—to summon, prorogue and dissolve parliament and to give the formal royal assent to bills. There was a Senate whose pace and functions reflected the sedate and sleepy ceremonial of the House of Lords. And, finally, the fifty-two members of the Northern House of Commons ranged in clear-cut party blocs. The only considerable technical innovation marking a deviation from the British model—the proportional representation system of voting—was eradicated as soon as legally possible. The resultant single-party regime thus established has often been both attacked and defended in terms of the British model from which it was derived. It might be more useful to distinguish the liberal and conservative versions of that model.[2] The liberal version of the British constitution lays stress on representation, on consent, on answerability, on control of government; its political values reflect the experience of men who have spent more time in opposition than in government. The conservative version is closer to what is sometimes called the Whitehall model of the British constitution; it emphasises the right of the executive to make decisions, the binding force of law, the need to preserve an established order which is presumed to be just and legitimate. The Unionist Party's bland assurance that its 'natural' majority gave it a right to rule in perpetuity; its aggressive attachment to jingoistic symbols, songs and speeches; its entrenched resistance to any attempt to attenuate the powers of its own executive—all of this, including its enthusiastic if ambiguous loyalty to the Crown, is intelligible within the conservative version of the British parliamentary model.

In the South there was no such clearly acceptable and 'natural' constitutional model. One of the first actions of the new provisional government in 1922 was to establish a committee to draft a written constitution. This very decision represented a substantial departure from the main British tradition, and the nine men initially entrusted with the task of framing a suitable basic law for the Irish state were consciously critical of many aspects of British political usage. In particular, they (and their political masters in the early Irish cabinets) deplored the artificial character of parliamentary party conflicts, sought to create a more direct and active role for the people in public affairs and tried to erect some safeguards against executive dominance. Moreover, they were committed in a formal way to secure the rights of the political (and, largely, religious) minority in the South by promises given by Arthur Griffith to a group of representative Southern Unionists at the time the Treaty was signed. As a result, the Free State constitution had a modern and even a continental cast. There were some innovations in the draft : the provision for proportional representation, for the legislative referendum and initiative, and for expert 'extern' ministers in government who would be freed from the constraints and uncertainties of the usual partisan parliamentary support. None of these strayed far from British liberal ideals; nor could they disguise the fact that the constitutional language cloaked the basic framework of British cabinet government. Political events soon showed that the Irish system would operate along the same lines as its Westminster counterpart.

For what differentiated the development of the Irish parliamentary tradition on the two sides of the Border was not merely constitutional theories and provisions but political realities and the values underlying them. In the North the same entrenched party remained in power. The preservation of its governmental monopoly depended largely on its capacity to retain an existing majority support. In effect, the Northern

Unionists—like, for instance, the Democrats in the Southern United States—were always more conscious of the need to please and appease extreme activists within their own ranks than to lean across a sectarian—or racial—divide in order to secure new sources of support within the minority.[3] In the North the political divide coincided with a deep cultural and religious cleavage in society; for majority political leaders wall-building was a more rewarding activity than bridge-building.

In the South a new political elite emerged into a fluid political situation.[4] There was no fixed and certain majority to hand. It had to be created. The first part of the Civil War campaign was not military but electoral. The outcome of that 1922 'Pact' Election was a decisive victory in terms of votes and seats for the pro-Treaty wing of Sinn Féin. But the result also established the existence of a large body of citizens unwilling to accept that settlement. The stage was set for the fixing of an irreconcilable gulf. But though the Civil War scarred the political development of the new Irish state, it did not destroy the established political and civic culture. Yet civil wars are notoriously destructive of that civil trust which is the bedrock of stable, legitimate political systems. They encourage those who possess power to adopt strategies of permanent repression; they tempt military leaders to claim an active and dominant part in politics; they entice opponents of the regime into a posture of extreme intransigence. How and why was Ireland so soon spared such results?

Fundamentally, the split on the Treaty was tactical, personal, emotional. The shorthand term 'pro-Treaty' obscures the fact that no one defended the settlement as an absolute ideal.

In the Treaty debate Griffith could say, 'We have done the best we could for Ireland'; Collins could call it 'not the ultimate freedom that all nations aspire and develop to, but the freedom to achieve it'; Kevin O'Higgins could argue, 'I hardly hope that within the terms of this Treaty there lies the fulfilment of Ireland's destiny, but I do hope and believe that with the disappearance of old passions and distrusts, fostered by centuries of persecution and desperate resistance, what remains may be won by agreement and by peaceful political evolution.' On the other side, while the Treaty was rejected, the main speakers did not rule out the idea of some negotiated settlement with Britain; de Valera offered Document No. 2 as an alternative device; Erskine Childers put his finger on the fact that 'The sole question before the nation, Dáil Éireann, and the delegation was how is it possible to effect an association with the British Commonwealth which would be honourable to the Irish nation.'

Clearly, though the split was deep and bitter, it was not ideological, in the long term not unbridgeable. The polarisation was well-nigh complete; it did not have to remain fixed. It cut across other cleavages in Irish society. Other ties and other identifications—of class, of region, of social and economic interest, of religion—remained from which different political and personal loyalties and alliances could be created.

Thus, although the Treaty issue provided two poles around which most political opinion quickly clustered, these poles were not impossibly far apart. It was not only possible but necessary to secure the middle ground, where the two positions shaded into each other, in order to gain and retain governmental power. Over time, in that process of competition for support the two poles moved closer together. The ground was set for a bi-polar political party system. For ideological reasons associated with Labour's refusal to become identified with the new Sinn Féin, as well as for technical electoral reasons associated with the proportional representation method of voting, Labour established a special place in the Irish scheme of things and prevented it developing as a purely two-party system.[5] Nevertheless, Ireland has remained attached to the most marked characteristic of the British two-party system—single-party government. But this development of competitive political parties from a civil war situation depended on the way in which that crisis was handled.

Although the new government of the Irish Free State did adopt repressive measures towards anti-Treaty activists (and, indeed, the internments and executions have become part of Irish political folklore and reference), there was no enthusiasm to adopt such policies permanently. Even their most violent opponents recognised that neither cabinet nor army had much joy in the work. It was commonly suggested on the Republican side that the Free State was implementing a coercive policy dictated by the British government. This was one undoubted source of pressure. The activities of the Irregulars were another.

But there was also an Irish community demand for a restoration of order. There was no majority in the new Ireland for any revolutionary settlement. Nor was there a fertile field in which any ideological group could sow the seeds of major socio-economic change. On the contrary, largely as a result of the Land Acts, a substantial and influential section of the rural community—and Ireland was still overwhelmingly an agricultural country—as well as the urban middle-class, had a vested interest in preserving the existing social order. They had no intention of seeing their own, relatively new, possessions destroyed in pursuit of some theoretical formula. When that order and those possessions were threatened by a group lacking the legitimacy of an electoral mandate, there was ample support for a short-term policy of governmental repression.

Part of the price paid was an extension in the numbers and influence of the military. The large standing army, forged out of a guerrilla force of freedom-fighters on the urgent anvil of internal disorder has often been a potent threat to the political stability of new states. In Ireland that threat never got beyond the limits of the army crisis of 1924—an attempted political initiative, a declaration of intent, far short of any determined effort at mutiny by senior army officers. Certainly the episode was serious. It involved the resignation of two cabinet ministers, the removal of three of the most senior officers in the army, the appointment of a new head of the armed forces and the resignation of nine deputies from the Dáil. Yet, far from shaking the stability of the young Irish government, this army crisis served to confirm the established acceptance of the idea of legitimate civil control.

There were two remaining threats to the creation of an open competitive party system in the South. One was posed by the still unresolved issue of national boundaries. The final report of the three-man Boundary Commission was leaked to the press in 1925. It proposed a border that fell far short of the repeated claims put forward by Dublin; it was made to appear that the Free State's government's representative, Eóin Mac Néill had subscribed to the settlement. With little room to manouevre, Dublin was forced to accept a line that virtually secured the existing boundary. It was an unpopular and unpalatable decision. The Cosgrave administration lost further support in the Dáil and in the country. Yet the fact that any government, so soon after independence, could survive acceptance of such terms is indicative of the undemanding character —evidence of the non-ideological context—of Irish politics. Politics is perceived as a series of contests and compromises, not as a moral battle-royal of absolute demands and immutable principles. The dominance of gradualism, the willingness to accept what cannot be changed, the commitment to empirical solutions, is paramount. On the Border issue, as on the army issue, it was enough that a ministerial head should roll. The government itself did not fall; the regime remained intact.

There was still one more obstacle to the recreation of political normalcy. An influential group of leaders and a large body of their followers continued to deny that the regime itself was truly legitimate. The main opposition was not only outside the Dáil; it rejected the right of the Dáil to speak for the people.

Within the Dáil, the small Labour Party played out a conventional role as the major parliamentary opposition with force and vigour. In the Senate, too, there was a healthy, experienced and well-informed body of criticism for governmental measures from an organised group mainly associated with the old Southern Unionist interest. Together these two sets of representatives helped to establish and maintain an institutional parliamentary opposition. But the real centre of opposition to the government—the anti-Treaty Republicans—remained outside the Oireachtas.

While that situation persisted there was an air of unreality and an undercurrent of instability about parliamentary affairs in Ireland. It threatened to weaken government; it offered no possibility of growth to the extra-parliamentary opposition.

The abstentionist group, still called Sinn Féin, became progressively weaker through the early 1920s. The record of the party's decline has been documented :

Its membership was dwindling, its financial position grew steadily worse and its performance at the polls showed little likelihood of it receiving an over-all majority from the electorate. On the other hand the Free State was functioning, it was internationally recognised and it retained the support of a majority of the people. It was not surprising then that various elements within the Republican movement began to question the Party's performance and the efficacy of its policies.[6]

First the military wing broke away. Then disagreement on the political side over the Border issue led to a split. There was a certain inevitability about the way in which the issue of the Oath was moved into the centre of the debate and then the Oath itself downgraded to an empty formula. It enabled de Valera to break with Sinn Féin and found his own Fianna Fáil party and then to lead that party into the Dáil. Such a bald summary scarcely does justice to a more complex process of reappraisal, fragmentation and regrouping; it does serve to underline the point that a large body of voters understood, accepted and supported the view that, whatever the cost, a political party could only hope to be effective within a parliamentary context.

By now, with two large parties competing for majority support, that parliament had moved even closer to its Westminster origins. Many of the experimental and continental features of the Irish Free State constitution were abandoned virtually without trial. Few of the 'extern' ministers were ever appointed; all were staunch party men. Neither the referendum nor the initiative were ever used to ascertain the people's opinion; both were abolished when de Valera tried to invoke these constitutional provisions to jettison the Oath. The elaborate schemes to give the Senate some power and purpose were gradually modified. The constitution itself, although it was the fundamental law for fifteen years, remained throughout its life, like the British constitution, wholly flexible and subject to amendment simply by act of parliament. Alone among the innovations, proportional representation was preserved.

So, by the later twenties, the main outline of the new Irish political system was established. It needed only one more event to prove conclusively that the surface attachment to the British liberal parliamentary model was securely rooted in political realities: there had to be an alternation of parties in government, a peaceful transfer of power. This was achieved with a minimum of strain and tension after a bitter election campaign in 1932. Just ten years after the new state was established, within a decade of the Civil War, the reins of government changed hands and all the institutions of the state—army, police, bureaucracy—accepted the transfer as normal. In a sense the transition was already implicit in 1927 when Fianna Fáil agreed to accept the rules of the parliamentary game.[7] There could be no greater tribute to the strength of the Irish parliamentary tradition than that it could advance in independence so smoothly.

FROM WAR TO CIVIL WAR
IN IRELAND

Three essays on the Treaty debate

F. S. L. LYONS

17

The Meaning of Independence

SINCE these three essays are written to commemorate the signing of the Anglo-Irish Treaty in December 1921, I must begin by making clear what I understand by the word 'commemorate'. When we commemorate events of the past and the men who took part in them, it seems to me that we are simply recognising that those events and those men were of exceptional significance in history and deserve, therefore, to be remembered. In this present instance, indeed, I would go further. I would say that because the lives of everyone now living in Ireland have been, and are still being, directly affected by what happened in the early 1920s, then commemoration becomes something more than just a pious gesture to ancestral shades.

But if so, it has to be a particular kind of commemoration. When we reflect upon those bygone events—upon how the foundation of the state and the division of the country had their origins, upon the suffering, the destruction and the enduring bitterness—then, however tempting it may be to take sides, surely we cannot look back either in anger or in satisfaction, but only in compassion. Our business is not to praise or to blame, but to understand—always, and above everything, to understand.

Even if Irish history had proceeded along very different lines since 1921, if we could have contemplated recent developments with unmixed pride and joy, it would still be necessary to use any moment of commemoration as an occasion for solemn reflection. But in the present situation, with the dire past still overhanging the dire present, the need to go back to fundamentals and consider once more the meaning of independence, asserts itself with almost intolerable urgency. The theories of revolution, the theories of nationality, the theories of history, which have brought Ireland to its present pass, cry out for reexamination and the time is ripe to try to break the great enchantment which for too long has made myth so much more congenial than reality.

If I begin by suggesting that part of Ireland's predicament stems from a wrong reading of history, this is not to say that I think historians themselves are primarily to blame, or that they need parody Yeats's famous question :

> Did that play [or book] of mine send out
> Certain men the English shot?

On the contrary, historians have never aspired either to such influence or to such arrogance. Their whole endeavour for many years has been to withdraw passion from history and to turn the light of reason upon even the most recent and turbulent past. Nevertheless, as a patriot such as Thomas Davis well knew, history can be made an essential ingredient of nationalism, and to this day the cool rationality of the professionals is still apt to be brushed aside by those who want only to rifle the archives for purposes of propaganda.

We can see this most clearly if we dwell for a moment upon one of our most cherished generalisations. I am referring to the truism that if you look at Irish history from, say, the late eighteenth to the early twentieth centuries, you will observe a steady oscillation between peaceful methods of agitation and methods of physical violence. Superficially, this is true enough—constitutionalism punctuated by insurrection appears to have been a regularly recurring pattern. Unfortunately, it is also too simple a pattern, and dangerous in its simplicity. It is dangerously simple because it assumes that peaceful agitation and violent agitation are two opposing poles with no resting-place in between. Obviously, if you believe this, and if you think you can demonstrate at any particular point in time the failure of one of these two modes of action, then a seemingly inexorable logic compels you to adopt the other. Perhaps the most lethal over-simplification of this kind to have occurred in our own day has been the tendency to assert that constitutional agitation 'failed' and then to build upon that glib assertion the even more disastrous proposition that violence will therefore always hold the key to success.

Is it not high time we began to query the inevitability, not to say the crudeness of such logic? A theory of society which depends upon the members of that society recognising no middle ground between extremes seems to me excessively naïve.

Most people, I suspect, do not live by the hard, clear light of abstract dogmas explicitly stated. Instead, they willingly inhabit a murky, grey world where the only fixed points are a wife, a family, a farm or a job, and the only ambition is to get through life with the minimum of unpleasantness. But, you may say, whoever claimed that revolutions are made by the dull, grey masses? Is it not perfectly obvious that revolutions are made by minorities whose superior insight allows them to see to the heart of things and open the eyes of everyman to injustices he had been too blind, too stupid, too downtrodden, to see for himself? And revolutions, some will add, spring not only from minorities, but from the ideas formulated within those minorities by the intellectuals. On this view, the cataclysmic moment comes when some man of genius translates esoteric doctrines into immediately comprehensible slogans—'land' or 'bread', for example—to which the people will joyfully rally, so that what began as a conspiracy will end as a mass movement. It is essential, of course, that the transition from conspiracy to mass movement should somehow be made if the revolution is ever to be successful. That the thing can be done history has demonstrated repeatedly. It can be done because, although, as I have suggested, most people wish only to be left in peace, there is a limit to the exploitation of their passivity. 'Man', as La Fontaine's wolf long ago found out, 'is a wicked animal. When you attack him, he defends himself.' In short, violence is inherent in each of us. For some—the minority, especially its ardent youth—that violence can be activated by idealism. For the majority it needs to be related to realisable needs and desires. When the abstract idealism of the minority and the material interests of the majority are in unison, then you have a truly revolutionary situation.

If we apply these general remarks to the Irish experience, we shall see that they make nonsense of the traditional, rigid distinctions between constitutional and violent action. If we ask, for instance, what was the one real revolution carried out in Ireland during the nineteenth century, the answer is obvious. Certainly, it was not Robert Emmet's promenade in 1803, nor the abortive risings of '48 and '67. It was the land agitation which did more than anything else to transform Irish society. But if we ask further whether that was a peaceful or a violent

H

agitation, the reply must be that it was both. The parliamentary drive for the amendment of the land laws would not have succeeded had it not been for the mass movement in the countryside, and the mass movement in the countryside would have foundered in indiscriminate outrage had it not been shaped and controlled by the parliamentarians.

The plain truth is that we have to reckon with violence as one of the weapons (by no means the only one) of insurgent nationalism. The great debate among nationalists, at least from Young Ireland onwards, was less about the morality of the use of force than about its practicality—and by this I mean not only whether it would lead to a massacre of ill-armed Irishmen by British troops, but whether it would result in such a dramatic transformation of the situation as to justify the bloodshed and suffering it would undoubtedly cause. This great question faced every kind of nationalist at every stage in the nineteenth century. It was still an open question when the parliamentary pressure for Home Rule entered its critical phase between 1912 and 1914, and the question grew steadily more insistent as it became clear that Ulster Unionists and British Conservatives were themselves prepared to use force to defeat the ordinary processes of government. As well as being an urgent question it was also a complex one, and no analysis of the situation in Ireland on the eve of the First World War will carry the least conviction if it is stated simply in terms of violence versus non-violence, or, for that matter, of absolute versus partial independence. Not merely were there many different, conflicting, shades of opinion, but the situation itself was so fluid that the views of individuals frequently changed under the impact of events. When later we have to deal with the agonising debate on the Treaty and with the bitter decision which then confronted Irishmen—whether it was or was not permissible to set bounds to the march of a nation—we shall only understand the cruelty of the dilemma if we first realise the profound confusion out of which that dilemma arose.

Broadly speaking—and even this may be an over-simplification—four fairly well-defined attitudes had emerged by 1914, and the history of the subsequent years is largely composed of the action and reaction of those attitudes upon each other. The dominant strain in nationalist thinking was undoubtedly still that embodied by the Irish Parliamentary Party, whose leader, John Redmond, seemed to have crossed the frontier of the promised land when Home Rule finally reached the statute-book in September 1914. True, the self-government Redmond had achieved was decidedly modest—little more, indeed, than glorified local government—and even the gilt of this concession was somewhat tarnished by its suspension until after the war and by the fact that amending legislation to provide separately for Ulster still hovered in the wings. Nevertheless, the restoration of an Irish parliament did seem imminent (few then envisaged a long war) and the Irish Parliamentary Party was widely acclaimed for having triumphantly crowned its long career of constructive work for Ireland.

We know now that these high hopes were illusory. Even before 1914 the party had been assailed by critics from within and without. These were only temporarily silenced and were soon to acquire fresh ammunition. Redmond and his colleagues, in spite of—or rather, because of—the fact that they had grown grey in the service of their country, had been curiously insensitive to the currents of change that had been eddying through Ireland since the turn of the century. They had virtually ignored the Gaelic revival; they had neglected the claims of labour, and in the great Dublin dispute of 1913 their dislike of the employers had been exceeded only by their hatred of Larkin; they had been quick to resent the appearance of new political rivals but strangely inept in disposing of them. Part of this rigidity was the natural conservatism of old age and middle class, but part sprang from an attachment to the parliamentary game as played by British rules which was presently to render them dangerously vulnerable. Indeed, their vulnerability had already been revealed before the war, when they had shown themselves unable to maintain the unity of Ireland in face of resistance from the Ulster Volunteers and when they had failed to grasp the significance of the counter-movement of the Irish Volunteers in the South until it was too late. Once the war had started they were still more fatally exposed. Committed by Redmond at the outset to support of the Allies, their credibility waned fast as recruiting was mishandled, casualties mounted, and the menace of conscription grew nearer.

Yet, despite all this, it is probably true that up to 1916, and

possibly even later, Redmond's conception of Home Rule—
limited self-government by an Irish parliament within the
Empire—represented for most Irishmen not just an attainable
but also a desirable ideal. There were, however, other conceptions. The one which, until then, had been most persistently
and articulately advanced was the curious amalgam of fantasy
and commonsense called Sinn Féin. When Arthur Griffith began
attacking the Irish Parliamentary Party at the turn of the century he did so primarily on the ground that so long as Irishmen
continued to go cap in hand to London for every improvement
in their lot they would never develop that self-reliance which
he saw as the only foundation for national independence. But
his actual definition of independence was clouded by ambiguities which would haunt him to his dying day. Stripped of his
cherished but obscure allusions to the 'constitution of 1782'
and to the Austro-Hungarian 'Ausgleich', what he seemed to
be saying was that the crucial revolutionary act would occur
when the elected Irish representatives withdrew from Westminster, and, having formed their own parliament in Ireland,
proceeded to enact all those social and economic reforms with
which the Sinn Féin programme was so liberally endowed. But
it was far from clear how this secession should be carried out,
what place physical force might have in achieving it, or even,
supposing it to have been achieved, what kind of independent
Ireland would emerge. Doubtless there were good tactical
reasons for such vagueness. Griffith clearly felt it to be salutary,
for, though he called himself a separatist and had for a time
belonged to the IRB, his policy was aimed at those who were
about equally dissatisfied with the posturing of the Parliamentarians and the rhetoric of the Republicans. However, given the
prominence of the 'constitution of 1782' in his thinking, it is
reasonable to assume that he accepted a continued connection
with the Crown as politically inevitable, even if personally distasteful.

To more extreme men Sinn Féin, thus loosely defined, may
have marked an improvement an old-style Home Rule, but it
was a far cry from absolute independence. Absolute independence still meant, in theory at least, what it had meant to Wolfe
Tone, to the more radical of the Young Irelanders, and to the
Fenians—an all-Ireland Republic. This was the aspiration to

which the IRB was oath-bound and towards which it began to shape its course within weeks of the outbreak of war. Yet even this clear-cut aim dissolves into uncertainty on closer inspection, for the Republic meant different things to different people. To Pádraig Pearse, and to the many who had come to revolutionary politics through the Gaelic League, it meant, in Pearse's own formula, that Ireland free was Ireland Gaelic and Ireland Gaelic was Ireland free. But how this was to be reconciled with the creation of an all-Ireland Republic which must necessarily embrace large numbers of people indifferent, or actively hostile, towards the Irish language was not, and never has been, satisfactorily answered.

For that matter, not all Republicans believed that Gaelicisation, however desirable, was automatically the highest priority. For James Connolly and those who thought like him, an Irish Republic meant essentially a workers' Republic. From a socialist viewpoint, an Irish insurrection would be but a local incident in the international class war, and for organised labour to participate in it was justifiable only if the destruction of English rule was the prelude to the destruction of capitalist power. But Connolly, although enormously significant as a forerunner, and imposing himself on his contemporaries by sheer force of personality, was more vulnerable than the cult now surrounding his name would lead one to suppose. Intellectually almost too sophisticated for the simple men he led, his trade union support weakened by the debacle of 1913, deprived of the vital Belfast base by long-standing sectarian rivalries among the workers, preaching urban socialism in a predominantly Catholic and rural country, and controlling a Citizen Army barely two hundred strong, he brought to the revolutionary cause almost as many liabilities as he conferred benefits. His intelligence, his energy, the fanatical devotion he inspired among his followers—these certainly represented an accretion of strength. But the social and economic upheaval which he saw as the ultimate outcome of the struggle was equally far removed from the essentially political vision which inspired most of his fellow-Republicans (though Pearse was probably nearer to him than the others) and from the bourgeois industrial state which loomed so large on Griffith's horizon.

We shall never know if these major differences of opinion would have been resolved by the men of 1916, since the firing-squads silenced the argument almost before it had begun. We can say, though, that the strange alliance between the Gaelic romantic, Pearse, the politically-orientated zealots of the IRB and the Marxist Connolly did produce in the Proclamation of Independence a conflation of most of the 'advanced' ideas then circulating among the most extreme nationalists. But they appear in a rather crude and undigested form. Thus, while there are certainly overtones of Connolly's socialism in that document, they are vaguely expressed and the central place is reserved for the declaration of the sovereign independent Republic. Yet even this was less categorical than it seemed, for we now know that even at the height of the Rising Pearse and others contemplated the possibility that the price of German aid might be a German princeling on an Irish throne, in which event the Republic would presumably have reverted from established fact to its familiar status of pious aspiration.

Perhaps it is unfair to seek precision in a document which was primarily rhetorical. That the men of 1916 should have produced a rallying-cry rather than a programme was not surprising, since, of course, the chief of them believed that their contribution to the cause would be a political martyrdom not a military victory. The aftermath of the Rising certainly simplified the situation in several ways. Most obviously, the executions and internments that followed the collapse of the rebellion began to swing Irish feeling about the insurgents from initial hostility towards passionate sympathy. But two other consequences of 1916 were no less important. One was that the failure of the British government to achieve a Home Rule settlement after the Rising was crushed dealt a well-nigh fatal blow to constitutional nationalism. The Irish Parliamentary Party would struggle on desperately for another two years, but it would thenceforward be increasingly on the defensive. The other consequence of 1916 was perhaps less immediately obvious, but was nevertheless profoundly significant. It was that the shooting of Connolly, combined with Larkin's absence in America, meant not only that labour was deprived of its most outstanding leaders, but that the social democratic strain in the movement was thereafter muted. The Republic indeed remained at the centre of revolutionary thinking, but less was heard of the *workers'* Republic.

In the period between the executions and the Sinn Féin triumph at the General Election of 1918, the tendency to concentrate upon the single political objective of the Republic (for which, at least up to 1919, it was hoped to obtain international recognition at the Peace Conference) was intensified. There remained, however, one difficult and damaging ambiguity. Although the Rising was in fact the work of a small group inside the IRB, the contemporary impulse, both official and popular, was to call it the Sinn Féin rebellion. In the sense that Sinn Féiners had no doubt participated in the Rising and that Griffith himself, though not taking part, had been swept into the internment net, the misnomer was not altogether unjustified. Nevertheless, it remained true that Sinn Féin and the IRB stood for different things and were led by different people.[1] If they were to be fused into a single revolutionary force it was urgent that they should be brought together very quickly. The great significance of the Sinn Féin Convention of 1917 was that it did precisely this, though not without private discussions which were arduous, sharp, and ominous for the future. Briefly, that Convention did two things. Firstly, it enabled de Valera, the embodiment of 1916, to replace Griffith as head of the organisation and thus to bring the Sinn Féin and Republican wings of the movement closer together; since de Valera soon afterwards became President of the Irish Volunteers, it was obvious that consolidation and centralisation were already taking shape. Secondly, the Convention ratified the formula which opened the way to the spectacular electoral victory of Sinn Féin a year later. Devised by de Valera, that formula read as follows:

Sinn Féin aims at securing the international recognition of Ireland as an independent Irish republic.

Having achieved that status the Irish people may by referendum freely choose their own form of government.

This was admittedly a compromise. And like most compromises it achieved a short-term success while leaving a fundamental problem unresolved. By 1917 the cult of the Easter Rising was already well-established. Men had died for the

Republic. Therefore the Republic was a sacred cause. But suppose circumstances demanded that more men should die for the Republic—would not the cause become still more sacred and its defenders still more fanatical? If so, what chance would there then be for alternative forms of government to be discussed and freely chosen on their merits?

No doubt in 1917 such questions seemed academic. Yet, if the zealots meant what they said and actually succeeded in establishing their Republic, was it not morally certain that this would encounter the armed resistance of Britain and that 1916 would be re-enacted on a larger, bloodier scale? Between 1917 and 1919 events, aided by the frailties and foolishness of British policy, brought such a confrontation steadily nearer. Intermittent coercion, the failure to achieve an agreed settlement, the menace of conscription, all combined so to augment support for Sinn Féin that at the General Election of 1918 they captured 73 out of the 105 Irish seats. This gave them the basis for putting into operation the quintessential Sinn Féin policy—to abstain from Westminster and to set up their own assembly in Ireland.

With the opening of the First Dáil on 21 January 1919 a recognisably new phase in Anglo-Irish relations had begun. The Republic had ceased to be an aspiration and had apparently become, or was in process of becoming, a fact. How the British government reacted to this development and how an initially confused situation became a situation of deadly warfare between the two countries will be dealt with in my next essay.

I shall conclude this essay by drawing attention to the way in which what I have already described as the simplification of a complex problem was carried much further by the work of the First Dáil. This happened in both a negative and a positive sense. Negatively, it is now known that although the Dáil seemed to be following in the footsteps of the men of 1916 by promulgating a Democratic Programme, the Programme itself, as presented to the Dáil, was markedly less radical than in its original form. The watered-down version was, it seems, substituted at the behest of Michael Collins, among others, on the significant ground that potentially controversial domestic issues should be postponed until full independence had been achieved.

On the positive side, the Dáil not only approved a Declaration of Independence ratifying the Republic proclaimed in 1916, it also did two other things. First, it set on foot its own ministries and law-courts which, fugitive and harassed by the British authorities as they soon were, nevertheless did mark the beginning of actual government of Irishmen by Irishmen—an initiative which perhaps did more than anything else to root the revolution firmly in the lives of the people. Secondly, in August 1919 the Dáil decided to re-emphasise its republicanism by requiring all its own members and the Volunteers to take a solemn oath of allegiance to the Republic. At the time this was rightly seen as a means of bringing the Volunteers more firmly under the Dáil's control, thereby preventing them from being dominated by the IRB, which, by its constitution, was bound to regard its own Supreme Council as the government of Ireland 'until Ireland secures national independence and a permanent republican government is established'. Whether the oath would succeed in achieving that particular object time alone would tell. Its bearing upon the concept of independence is what immediately concerns us, and this was very direct and important. By as it were institutionalising the loyalty of Irishmen to the Republic, the oath helped to make more rigid an already hardening situation. Everything in the future would turn upon whether the country would accept the sacrifices that such rigidity was sure to exact, or whether in the end ordinary and unheroic men and women would exert an irresistible, contrary pressure towards being allowed to live an ordinary and unheroic existence.

18

Days of Decision

I have already indicated in my previous essay that what had really occurred in Ireland between 1916 and 1919 was a drastic simplification of an extremely complex problem: the pressure of events had driven Sinn Féin and the Republicans together, had eliminated the Irish Parliamentary Party, and narrowed the Irish question down to the simple assertion of the Republic to which Dáil Éireann, its members and its soldiers stood pledged. But at the beginning of 1919 the Republic, despite the election campaign and despite the Dáil's solemn affirmations, still represented a romantic ideal which had yet to be realised in fact. The establishment of the Dáil ministries and of the Sinn Féin courts went some way towards that realisation, but they led a precarious, often subterranean, existence, and, while they were no doubt essential to the emergence of an independent state, their existence could logically have been compatible with other than republican forms of government. What we have to do now, therefore, is to examine how this ideal concept of a sovereign independent Republic fared in the harsh light of everyday reality. In particular, we have to consider the forces, inside as well as outside Ireland, which worked powerfully against it.

To all appearances the verdict of the General Election of 1918 was, as we have seen, an overwhelming vote in favour of the Sinn Féin programme everywhere except in the north-east corner of the island. But here precisely lay the rub. The Republic envisaged by the men of 1916 and ratified by the Dáil in 1919, was an all-Ireland Republic. Yet the north-eastern counties, which on every previous occasion had been stirred into a frenzy by the mere mention of minimal Home Rule, were certain to resist a Republic to the last gasp.

Lloyd George was perfectly well aware of this. Whenever, between 1916 and 1920, he turned towards the Irish problem, some form of partition invariably suggested itself to him. However, the General Election of 1918, which had so transformed the situation in Ireland, had directly affected his position also. True, he swept back to office at the head of a renewed coalition ministry, but the great bulk of those who supported that ministry were Conservatives, and within the ministry itself the weight of experience and authority was decidedly on the Conservative side. Exactly how this change in the balance of political power would work upon British attitudes to Ireland only time would tell, but two points may be made here at the outset —one fairly obvious, the other strangely neglected, even by historians. The less obvious, but still crucial, point is that the very size of the Conservative Party in the House of Commons meant that a wholly Conservative government was once more a real possibility and that Lloyd George, although a powerful asset as 'the man who won the war', could conceivably be a wasting asset if his Irish policies ran too far ahead of what Conservatives regarded as feasible. This did not necessarily mean that the Conservative view of Ireland would be so strongly coloured by Ulster Unionism as it had been before the war. The great political strength of Ulster Unionism in the crisis of 1912–14 had been that its ally, the British Conservative Party, was so frustrated and maddened by six years' exclusion from office and by the loss of the veto power of the House of Lords, that it was prepared to utilise Ulster resistance to Home Rule in Ireland as a means of overthrowing the Liberal government in Britain itself. By 1919, however, with the Liberals hopelessly split between Asquithians and followers of Lloyd George, the Conservatives no longer needed to play the Orange card, at least not with the reckless abandon with which they had been prepared to play it in 1914.

We need not, of course, deduce from this that British Conservatism had suddenly become a model of sweet reasonableness where Ireland was concerned. On the contrary—and this is the second way in which their electoral revival of 1918 affected the situation—Conservatives still clung to two fixed positions, of both of which Lloyd George had to take careful account if he wanted to remain at the head of his coalition. One was that although they may no longer have wished to use Ulster for their own political purposes, they were not prepared to see Ulster compelled into union with the South; if the Ulstermen were prepared to accept a form of Home Rule for themselves, that might be another matter, but they must not be coerced. Their second fixed position was that they were still—indeed, as a result of the war, perhaps even more so—the party of Empire. What this meant in plain terms was that although they might and did recognise that a continually festering Irish sore involved weakness and danger for Britain, they would in no circumstances whatever accept an Irish settlement on republican lines which, in their view, would be ruinous to the integrity of the Empire.

Thus, although actual battle was only very gradually joined during 1919, we can see that from the outset of the struggle two fundamentally different concepts opposed each other. On the Irish side a belief that only through the establishment of the Republic could absolute dependence and separation from Britain be achieved. On the British side an equal belief that an Irish Republic would involve a double threat: strategically, in that an independent country so near to England would constitute a hazard to defence; and, in the broader sense, that where Ireland was allowed to lead, others—notably India—might be tempted to follow. With the armed conflict that resulted from the clash of these diametrically opposed viewpoints we are not here directly concerned, though we have always to bear in mind that as the conflict reached its crescendo of horror and violence in the latter part of 1920, what was happening in the streets and in the countryside made the ultimate task of reconciliation far, far harder. It did so in several ways. First, the guerrilla character of the war itself and the methods used by both sides in fighting it, meant that bitterness between the two countries was greatly intensified. In Ireland resentment at the activities of the Black and Tans and the Auxiliaries undoubtedly had the effect of rallying support for the Sinn Féin forces; and when these forces were actually able to control parts of the country and to set the machinery of the Dáil administration in motion, it was natural enough that ordinary men and women, anxious only for a quiet life, should turn towards those who seemed best able to provide it. If that involved supporting the Republic—then up the Republic!

The British attitude was necessarily less straightforward. On the one hand, there was deep anger at the tactics of the IRA, and particularly at the frequent assassinations carried out by

Collins's 'squad'. On the other hand, there was an enormous weariness with a sordid struggle from which no honour could possibly be gained, and a growing sensitiveness on the part of the public, especially among influential sections of the press, towards the brutalities of which the forces of the Crown were undeniably guilty.

It would, however, be a mistake to equate this revulsion with weakness. On the contrary, there is evidence in the cabinet discussions in the latter part of 1920 of a genuine hesitation between the horns of an all too familiar dilemma—whether to intensify coercion or to elaborate reform. In the classical tradition, both policies were in the end applied simultaneously. Hence, while the Black and Tans and the Auxiliaries went about their work in their usual way, the Government of Ireland Bill laboured through parliament, finally becoming law just before Christmas. This provided for the establishment of two parliaments in Ireland—one for the six north-eastern counties and one for the rest of the country. The powers to be granted to these local bodies were not very impressive, while important subjects, including ultimate financial responsibility, were to be reserved to the imperial parliament at Westminster, where the two parts of Ireland would have a reduced representation. The act also envisaged the creation of a Council of Ireland, representative of the two regional parliaments, in the naïve hope that cooperation at this level might lead to unification. The act, once passed, met a predictable fate. It was accepted grudgingly by the six north-eastern counties as the best guarantee they could get of their continuing attachment to the United Kingdom, but in the South it was contemptuously ignored, except that the machinery it provided for a general election in May 1921 was utilised to return the Second Dáil, which was overwhelmingly and intransigently Sinn Féin in its composition.

Yet the Government of Ireland Act did have an indirect effect upon the relations between the British government and the insurgents in the South, for it was known that if the act were not put into effect by the appointed date in mid-1921, the penalty would be the imposition of Crown colony government upon the twenty-six southern counties. This could of course only have been done by redoubling the military effort then in progress, and some ministers would probably have welcomed such an all-out campaign. Others, sickened by the continuing tale of horror, cast round anxiously for a truce, and Lloyd George himself, by the close of 1920, was on the look-out for such a possibility. A major difficulty was to find someone with authority to speak for Sinn Féin who was not either a wanted man or actually in prison. A way out was opened by the return of de Valera from his American mission at the end of the year. Almost at once he began to receive indirect overtures for a truce. The approach to the cease-fire, which did not come until 11 July, was tortuous and protracted in the extreme, reflecting the difficulties in which both men were entangled.

De Valera himself was anxious to ease the burden of the struggle upon the people, and there seems little doubt that the truce did not come a moment too soon for the IRA, which was overstrained and particularly short of arms and ammunition.[2] On the other hand, he could not approach the bargaining-table having agreed in advance to conditions which would not only disarm his forces, but surrender the objective—the absolute independence—for which those forces were fighting. Lloyd George equally was in a dilemma. Although an intensification of the war was militarily possible, it might be politically disastrous, not only in alienating still further an already distressed public opinion, but in weakening the coalition government which was deeply confused about Ireland and wanted desperately to achieve some sort of settlement. But—and this was where Lloyd George was as trammelled as was de Valera on the other side—it could not be a settlement which struck at the security or the integrity of the Empire.

It is not surprising, therefore, that the preliminaries were difficult or that a great variety of helpers, ranging from George V to General Smuts, was pressed into service. And even when a truce was arranged and de Valera finally met Lloyd George face to face, the obstacles to a settlement seemed insurmountable. Yet the necessities of the situation were so urgent that, despite all setbacks, a formula was eventually hammered out which at least enabled an Irish delegation to go to London. It was a formula which left a great deal hanging in the balance. The delegates, it was finally agreed, were to meet their British counterparts, 'with a view to ascertaining how the association of Ireland with the community of nations known as the British

Empire may best be reconciled with Irish national aspirations', but this offered no light or leading as to just how this eminently desirable objective might be achieved.

There had, however, been signs in the Irish camp that extreme rigidity of doctrine might not be indefinitely maintained. De Valera himself, while not abandoning the concept of absolute independence, had made little reference to the Republic in his correspondence with Lloyd George and had already begun to formulate his thesis of 'external association', suggesting that an independent Ireland might accept 'a certain treaty of free association with the British Commonwealth group', as with a partial League of Nations, though even this, he was careful to add, would depend upon such an arrangement securing for the nation 'the allegiance of the present dissenting minority', by which, of course, was meant the Ulster Unionists. A little later in parliament he reminded deputies that the creation of the First Dáil had been a vote for freedom and independence rather than for a particular form of government 'because we are not republican doctrinaires'.[3]

Nevertheless, he did not have to look outside his own cabinet to find potential, or even actual doctrinaires, for two of the ministers, Austin Stack and Cathal Brugha, were among the most unyielding exponents of the national demand in its most extreme form and it was ominous for the future that neither of them was willing to serve on the delegation that was about to open negotiations for a settlement. At the time, undoubtedly, much more significance was attached to the fact that de Valera himself decided not to go to London. Of the various explanations advanced for this crucial decision, those which carry most conviction are that by staying at home he could best ensure that the final vote for peace or war would be taken in Dublin, well away from the mesmeric influence of Lloyd George, and also that he would be better able to continue to preach the gospel of external association to his still only half-converted Republican colleagues.[4] If the main intention was to reserve to the cabinet in Dublin the ultimate responsibility of choice, there was a fatal ambiguity about the instructions issued to the delegates. Their credentials, approved by the Dáil and the cabinet but for obvious reasons not formally accepted by the British government, described them as 'envoys plenipotentiary' from the elected government of the Republic of Ireland 'to negotiate and conclude with the representatives of His Britannic Majesty George V a Treaty or Treaties of association and accommodation between Ireland and the Community of Nations known as the British Commonwealth'. Yet, though these seemed as full powers as could be imagined, the delegates also received explicit orders to submit to Dublin the complete text of any draft treaty about to be signed and to await a reply.

We shall see presently what fearful consequences flowed from this seeming contradiction in the instructions. Although it was reasonable to suppose that the delegation *would* refer back to Dublin when the critical moment arrived, it was a very strong delegation and its leading members, Griffith and Collins, had both become accustomed to the exercise of authority in the recent struggle. They could, therefore, be expected to show a good deal of initiative and independence in the negotiations. Of the other three delegates, Gavan Duffy and Eamon Duggan were lawyers (Gavan Duffy had drafted the Declaration of Independence of 1919 and had also been a Dáil envoy to the Paris Peace Conference), whereas Robert Barton's principal function was to safeguard Irish economic interests. The delegation was accompanied by a team of secretaries, and not the least significant feature of the developing situation was that the chief of these was Erskine Childers, an able man but by then an implacable Republican and, unfortunately, one between whom and Griffith little love was lost.

The British team confronting this group was formidable indeed. Besides Lloyd George himself it contained, among others, Winston Churchill, Austen Chamberlain and Lord Birkenhead. Although the main burden of presenting the British case naturally fell upon Lloyd George, it is important to note that the Conservatives were very strongly represented. The Prime Minister's deliberate intention was to involve his Conservative partners in whatever decisions might be taken. There was a risk that this might increase the difficulty of reaching any decisions at all, but it did help Lloyd George to withstand anti-Irish pressures from the Tory back-benches, though, even so, he was to have his awkward moments.

Broadly speaking, the negotiations which began on 11 October and continued until early December, revolved round three issues : the British demand for naval and related facilities; the constitutional position of the new Irish state; and the question of the 'essential unity' of Ireland. Curiously enough, the first of these, which involved no less than the retention by Britain of certain naval stations on the south and west coasts and which could in time of war have made nonsense of Ireland's claim either to neutrality or to independence, was dealt with quite promptly, mainly because the Irish delegates took the view that British concern for defence was a legitimate anxiety, at least in the early stages of Irish independence.

It was far otherwise with those two inextricably tangled questions of what was to be the constitutional standing of the Irish state and whether that state was ultimately to consist of thirty-two or twenty-six counties. The Irish intention was to make Ulster the pivot of their strategy. Rather than repeat the mistake of Redmond in accepting partition, they would break off the negotiations on this vital question of maintaining the unity of their country. But from the British viewpoint the broad constitutional issue was at least as important. They must be clear that the new Ireland remained within the Empire, and for them the crux of the matter was whether the Irish accepted or did not accept the obligation of allegiance to the Crown. Griffith, following the line agreed in Dublin, advanced de Valera's alternative of 'external association', arguing that Ireland could not accept the Crown for internal purposes, but that she might recognise the king as head of the association of Commonwealth states. This, which was to form the essence of the Statute of Westminster ten years later, was much too novel and obscure to impress, let alone convince, Lloyd George and his colleagues and they continued to insist upon allegiance to the Crown.

What could the British offer in return? Lloyd George went to work on a familiar tack. If, he suggested to Griffith, the Irish could meet him satisfactorily on the constitutional question and thus enable him to bring his own diehards to heel, he would pledge himself to fight those same diehards in order to secure essential unity on Ulster. To achieve this fundamental aim, Griffith, after a private interview with Lloyd George, drafted a letter explaining how far he would be prepared to go if assured of Lloyd George's support on Ulster. As amended by his anxious colleagues it was, on the face of it, cautious enough. In it Griffith agreed, provided he was satisfied on other points, to recommend that Ireland should consent to a recognition of the Crown as head of the association of free states of the Commonwealth and that she should join in 'free partnership' (the terms of which would be defined later) with the Commonwealth. Subsequently he, and the rest of the delegation, were persuaded to change this to 'free partnership with the other states within the British Commonwealth', which meant something seriously different.

What is baffling about this exchange is how the Irish delegates, and Griffith especially, can really have believed that Lloyd George could make any significant impact on the Ulster position. Nothing in remote or recent history suggested that he could. De Valera had made no headway when he had met the Ulster premier, Sir James Craig, earlier in the year. Lloyd George, when he met him now in November, made no headway either. Apart altogether from the traditional resistance of Ulster Unionists to any connection with the South—which went far deeper than any nationalist seemed able to grasp—the six north-eastern counties had been in a state of turmoil for months past. Their long, and as yet ill-defined, border was easily penetrated by the IRA, which then, as later, regarded itself as having a special duty to defend the Catholic, nationalist minority, while the Unionists, anxious to maintain their little state intact at all costs, engaged in pogroms against the Catholics which caused large loss of life and considerable displacement of population. How Lloyd George hoped to conjure the 'essential unity' of Ireland out of this situation passes all understanding.

Perhaps, after all, he never really expected to do so. What he did conjure out of Ulster was the means of outflanking the Irish delegation. He did this by suggesting that perhaps the intractable question of how to deal with Ulster might best be solved if the frontiers between the two parts of Ireland were to be fixed by a Boundary Commission which, it was implied, might well transfer such substantial areas of the six counties to the South as to make a separate 'Northern Ireland' non-viable. The launching of such a proposal at this precise moment was, as we now know, Lloyd George's own initiative, though he himself alleged at different times either that the original suggestion was Carson's or that he, Lloyd George, had been convinced that it had Carson's support.[5] The Irish delegation's response to this offer was that it was Lloyd George's affair and in no way bound them, but that if he found it necessary to use it for tactical purposes they would not queer his pitch. They appear not to have realised that in giving him even this much encouragement they were allowing him to take a long pace back from the brink of the resignation on which he had seemingly been tottering. However, even if they had known, it could scarcely have made much difference. Whatever they might or might not expect to get from Lloyd George, the probable alternative to him was Bonar Law, and from him they would certainly get far less.

What did change the situation more markedly to the Irish disadvantage was that on 12–13 November Lloyd George's compatriot Thomas Jones, a member of the cabinet secretariat, extracted from Griffith an agreement that while Lloyd George was fighting to persuade the Conservative Party Conference, due to meet four days later, to back his policy, Griffith would not let the Prime Minister down by repudiating him. Though this was in no sense a pledge binding on the delegation as a whole, Griffith obviously regarded it as binding on him and it was soon to be used against him at the most critical moment in the whole negotiations. Meanwhile, it began to seem as if the break might not come on Ulster after all, for while Lloyd George was persuading his Conservative friends and critics that Ulster's frontier must be fixed by a Boundary Commission if she opted out of an all-Ireland parliament, the entire future of that parliament was thrown in such doubt by the Irish reluctance to come any closer to the Empire than external association that on 22–23 November Lloyd George came very close to breaking off the negotiations. That he did not do so seems largely due to Jones's strenuous exertions to attract the Irish once more to the conference table, rather than chase them away as Lloyd George, in his then excitable mood, might well have done.

Both sides therefore braced themselves for the herculean effort which eventually carried them over their difficulties and on to the point where the 'articles of agreement for a Treaty' could be signed in the small hours of 6 December. I shall deal with some of the more controversial points arising from that

Treaty in my final essay, but a few general comments need to be made here in conclusion. Perhaps the most important is that when the settlement was still in the balance and the delegates had returned to Dublin for a crucial meeting of the Irish cabinet on 3 December, the discussion was long and bitter, foreshadowing the split that was to divide the country in the months ahead. With the specific details we are not here concerned, but it is plain from the surviving accounts of that meeting that the essential disagreement was between those who saw the Republic —even the 'associated' Republic—in danger of slipping from their grasp and those who argued that they were now in sight of the best terms that could be got and who stressed especially that, if the Crown could not be swallowed in some form, then the foothold in Ulster afforded by the Boundary Commission would be lost. Eventually, after they had received somewhat hasty but unmistakably intransigent instructions, directed especially against the Oath of Allegiance, they returned to London. There, they were confronted by Lloyd George at his most dazzling and his most forbidding. On the one hand, he ruthlessly exploited an already well-tried technique by dealing with individuals or groups rather than with the delegation as a whole, thus intensifying their incoherence. On the other hand, while going some way towards meeting Irish objections to the Oath, and producing also the important concession of tariff autonomy, he then delivered his ultimatum. He had promised, he said, to inform Sir James Craig of the final outcome on 6 December and the date was almost upon them. Two letters to Craig had been drafted. Which should he send—the one announcing peace or the one announcing failure? If he had to send the latter, 'It is war, and war within three days.'

After hours of agonised debate the delegates, despite their instructions to refer back to Dublin, made the grave decision to sign the Treaty. They were, of course, cruelly isolated. To telephone de Valera would have seemed the obvious thing, but de Valera was in Limerick and not readily accessible. To have insisted on returning to Dublin would doubtless have led to yet another round of bitter, and probably barren, dispute. This might still have been justified—and at this distance it is easy to claim it ought to have been done—but in their minds and before their eyes was the vision of Lloyd George with his threat of imminent war. When the terms were as good as those which these exhausted men had won, then, it could equally well be argued, they had a moral duty to sign. And so they took up their heavy burden and came home to angry colleagues, to a situation of dire confusion, and to a new turn of fortune's wheel.

19

The Great Debate

I think it essential now, as we approach the Treaty debates themselves, to bear constantly in mind that the bitter confusion which followed the return home of the delegates is the key to a great deal of what happened in those dark days of December 1921. Outwardly, indeed, and so far as the uninformed public was concerned, the signing of the Treaty seemed to mean the end of a long nightmare. The political prisoners would be released, the British would march away for the last time, and Irishmen would finally be free to follow their destiny in their own way.

However, the rejoicing which welled up in the newspapers as soon as the negotiations were known to have been concluded masked every kind of uncertainty. How the country would go, how the Dáil would go, how even the cabinet would go, remained utterly in doubt until the delegates began to arrive back in Dublin, a process which was not completed until the morning of 8 December, the very day on which ministers were to hold their first full meeting since the Treaty had been signed. Yet already there were ominous signs of coming division. On the evening of 6 December de Valera received the news as he was about to take the chair at a Dante symposium at the Mansion House and he spent the evening in a private inferno of his own, concealing his dismay while he pondered the possible consequences of the delegates' fateful decision to sign without further reference to Dublin. Others were tempted to react more violently and there are indications that a move to arrest the returning delegates for treason had to be quashed by the Minister of Defence, Cathal Brugha. This, if true, was in itself ironic in view of the difficulty with which de Valera had brought him and Austin Stack to accept external association. For if de Valera had been appalled by the news of the Treaty, it needed little imagination to guess what the feelings of these two men might be. Behind them lay the promise of still greater peril, since if they, in their disenchantment, swung back towards the 'isolated' Republic, it was fairly certain that part of the army would go with them. Yet here again difficulties multiplied, for it was equally clear that another part—probably the larger part —of the army would take its cue from Collins, so that it was very possible that one of the first consequences of the Treaty would be the shattering of the force which had fought the War of Independence. An additional complication was that Collins's role derived its special significance from his dominant position in the IRB, for although IRB members of the Dáil might be left free to vote as they thought fit, IRB members of the army would be likely to follow their chief.

All this moved for the time being in the recesses of men's minds. It was only after the long discordant meeting of the cabinet on 8 December that the cracks began to show openly, though the immediate emergence of an open split was prevented, partly by the natural tendency of responsible men to recoil from the abyss, and partly by the persistence, even at this highest level, of the all-pervading confusion to which we must constantly return. Only one thing was clear at the end of that acrimonious discussion : there would be no unanimous recommendation from the cabinet to the Dáil. Four of the ministers— Griffith, Collins, Barton and Cosgrave—were for acceptance of the Treaty; three—de Valera, Brugha and Stack—were for rejection. The situation was, however, far more complex than this simple counting of heads would seem to imply. For among these seven—indeed, among those who found themselves on the side—motives and aims varied. Since broadly the same spectrum was to be exhibited when the Dáil came to debate the Treaty, it may be well to try to distinguish its colours at the outset.

The pro-Treaty and the anti-Treaty arguments each divided into two main branches. The most extreme pro-Treaty position was probably that of Arthur Griffith who, both in the cabinet and in the Dáil, insisted that, apart altogether from his own obligation of honour to stand by what he had signed, the Treaty was in itself a good settlement and gave Ireland full self-government. In this Griffith was quite consistent with his original Sinn Féin doctrine, but it is probably true to say that the majority of those who ultimately came down on the Treaty side did so on less idealistic grounds. To them the Treaty was the best that could be got at that moment and its chief virtue was that it offered the means of further growth. Michael Collins expressed this view in a famous phrase when, during the Dáil debates, he observed that the Treaty gave 'not the ultimate freedom that all nations aspire and develop to, but the freedom to achieve it'. Essential to this notion of further growth was the tariff autonomy which Lloyd George had conceded at the last moment and which both Cosgrave and Barton regarded as a major aspect of the settlement, though it is fair to add that Barton, in a most moving speech, emphasised that he signed the Treaty under the absolute conviction that the alternative to not signing would be an immediate resumption of the war.

On the anti-Treaty side the complexities were, if anything, more intricate. The simplest and most ruthless logic was to reject the agreement because it did not concede the fully independent and 'isolated' Republic. This was a view that was bound to be popular in the Dáil because that very young and inexperienced body had been elected in May 1921 primarily to conduct the war against Britain. However, the truce had come in July and hot-blooded Republicans had been condemned to live in a fog of incomprehension and negotiation ever since. To such people rejection of the Treaty and resumption of the war would come almost as a relief. But it would come also as a solemn vindication of principle. The oath to the Republic was regarded by the dedicated Republicans as absolutely binding and as inhibiting them completely from considering any alternative suggestions. The minister who put this most forcibly in the Dáil was Austin Stack, but it was reiterated over and over again by other speakers, and by none more categorically than the women whose husbands, sons or brothers had perished between 1916 and 1921.

Yet this same simple view of the Republic had already been outpaced by events. We saw earlier that in the long fencing-match between de Valera and Lloyd George which had preceded the despatch of the delegation to London, the 'isolated' Republic had been conspicuous by its absence. Had it been otherwise there would have been no delegation and the truce must surely have broken down. If in December the Dáil was debating a compromise peace, then, as Collins truly remarked, it was because 'it was the acceptance of the invitation that formed the compromise'. Moreover, throughout the actual negotiations themselves the hinge upon which everything turned at the most crucial moments had not been whether the delegates would carry off the 'isolated' Republic in the teeth of Lloyd George and his colleagues, but whether they could convince the British team that external association would be an acceptable alternative to dominion status.

That they tried to do this up to the very last hour no one has seriously disputed, though the Treaty itself was eloquent of their defeat. It was, however, a defeat which cut much more sharply at the roots of de Valera's position than of Griffith's. Had the gamble on external association succeeded in London, there might indeed still have been diehard Republican opposition in the Dáil, but a policy put forward by a united cabinet in full control of a united army would in the end have been an irresistible policy. The gamble having failed in London, de Valera was left with two bleak alternatives. Either he would have to side with the extreme Republicans and face a situation where diplomacy must once more yield to war, or else he would have to make a last desperate bid, but in vastly more unpromising circumstances, to rally support behind the still mysterious concept of external association.

It speaks volumes for his courage and tenacity that he did make the effort to rally such support, but it is not surprising that he failed. It had been hard enough to convince the diehard Republicans in the cabinet that external association, by relegating the Crown to purely outside functions, really did mean that, internally, Ireland's status as a Republic would be unimpaired. It was immeasurably harder to convey the same sophisticated point to a large, passionate and deeply disturbed assembly. De Valera's initial attempt to do so was by circulating to the private session which followed the public session of 14 December the hurriedly drafted outline of his alternative to the Treaty. This, immediately christened 'Document No. 2', was discussed in detail the following day (still in private session) and it continued to crop up in the public debates thereafter. De Valera's proposal was not helped by the fact that, in an honest attempt to facilitate comparison, he had composed it in a form resembling the Treaty, nor by his decision to amend it subsequently, so that when Griffith caused both versions to be released to the press early in January, the impression was conveyed to the public that their demented representatives were trying to choose between no less than three variations upon what still seemed to the man in the street to be remarkably similar proposals.

This was in fact a wrong impression, and those who attacked Document No. 2 as merely 'a quibble of words' were not quite fair to the author or to his document, nor did they take sufficient account of the circumstances in which it was framed. If, indeed, Document No. 2 is laid alongside the Treaty the differences are more marked than the resemblances. For while it was true that de Valera's proposals did not diverge essentially from those of the Treaty on the important questions of north-east Ulster and defence (though as regards the latter he wanted the situation reviewed after five years), it was abundantly clear from the opening clauses of his draft that dominion status, as defined by the Treaty, was to be jettisoned together with the Oath, and that, as Document No. 2 stated, 'The legislative, executive and judicial authority of Ireland shall be derived solely from the people of Ireland.'[6] It was no less clear that Ireland's association with the Commonwealth would be strictly limited to Defence, Peace and War, Political Treaties 'and all matters now treated as of common concern amongst the states of the British Commonwealth'.

The fundamental purpose of Document No. 2 was to exclude Britain from interfering in the internal affairs of the new Irish state. In the light of what actually happened when the new state began to function, the fear of a continued British presence which breathes through these proposals may seem now to have been exaggerated. However, we must not be wise after the event. When Document No. 2 was written the British were ensconced in the country and even if they went from the South they would still remain in the six north-eastern counties. Moreover, they had had many centuries in which to sink their governmental roots deep into Irish society. Could one be sure that these roots really would be pulled up overnight? Was dominion status truly a sufficient protection against the insistent pressures of law and custom and geography? For that matter, what sort of freedom did dominion status actually confer when it involved not only the Oath of Allegiance, but also the right of the Crown to appoint the Governor-General and the obligation upon the new state to allow its citizens right of appeal in legal matters to the Judicial Committee of the Privy Council?

The fact that within the Commonwealth the tide towards greater freedom had begun to flow strongly, and was to flow yet more strongly in the years ahead, is in a sense irrelevant to the argument; or rather, it obliges us to define it differently. We may fairly say that, at bottom, the argument concerning the Treaty was an argument about mutual trust. What Griffith, Collins, O'Higgins and the rest were really saying was that the Treaty was a genuine act of reconciliation and that in accepting it Ireland would be asked also to accept the assumption (it could not, at that time, be more than an assumption) that the British would loyally observe their side of the bargain. What de Valera was in effect replying was that, given the long history of broken promises which lay between the two countries, the only way of doing business with perfidious Albion was to embody in a written instrument the safeguards necessary to ensure that the Irish Free State would function as a *de facto* Republic.

The trouble with Document No. 2 was that it fell between two stools. Because it was not explicitly republican no 'extreme' nationalist could really feel affection for it. But because it did break so radically with the Treaty it opened up the bleak prospect of renewed war with Britain. It was much debated at the time, and has been ever since, whether or not rejection of the Treaty—either simple rejection or the substitution for it of Document No. 2—would in fact have led to a reopening of hostilities. This nightmare brooded over the deliberations of the Dáil and it was beyond question a main cause of the deep anxiety with which the country awaited the outcome of the seemingly endless argument. Since events turned out as they did turn out, any answer one may make to this question can only be hypothetical and subjective, but an answer must, nevertheless, be attempted.

I believe that the balance of the evidence tilts towards the view that if the Treaty had been rejected or if external association had yet again been proffered as an alternative, the British response would have been violent. Against this it may be argued that British public opinion was eager for peace at any price, and that no British government was likely to resume a struggle which offered so little chance of decisive victory and which could easily prove an international embarrassment. This seductive reasoning is, however, vulnerable on several grounds. That British public opinion should have been revolted by a war fought—as the war had been fought in 1920–21—with brutality but without a credible political solution being offered simultaneously was natural enough; but that British public opinion should still be revolted by a brutal war after a credible political solution had been offered *and rejected* was a much more dubious proposition. Nor was it any more certain that international disapproval would be a deterrent, for Britain's statesmen would be guided by considerations of a different kind. All the British negotiators had emphasised that imperial unity was for them the rock upon which they must at all costs stand. Although, if a break came, Lloyd George himself might no longer be in a position to carry out his threat of immediate and terrible war, there were others who would not flinch at the prospect, especially those Conservative leaders who had taken their political lives in their hands in forcing their party to swallow the Treaty and who would have neither the ability (nor, probably, the will) to restrain the backlash that would develop if the Treaty were to be rejected.

As for the argument that a resumption of the war would be pointless since it would lead to the same sort of squalid stalemate as before, even that cannot be accepted without question. No doubt morale in the IRA was good and perhaps also—though against this there remains a question-mark—the country would have faced the prolongation of its ordeal with stoic heroism. On the other hand, the truce, though a welcome breathing-space, had had to be paid for. Some of the war-time losses were replaced by new recruits, but not all veterans looked with an approving eye on the so-called 'Truceoliers' whose discipline and effectiveness under fire had yet to be tested. Arms and ammunition were, as always, a problem, and fresh injections of American money would be needed if they were to be bought in sufficient quantities; but, as Collins learned while the negotiations were actually in progress, this could not be counted upon with certainty. Worse still, perhaps, was the difficulty of reconstituting a guerrilla force after its members had, like Collins himself, come out into the open after the cease-fire. Moreover, it has to be remembered that the British military effort had probably not reached its full capacity when the truce came. We now know, from cabinet records and other sources, that during the truce plans were being laid for a far more massive blow than any that had yet been struck. We also know that in 1922, while Griffith and Collins were trying to stretch the Treaty to the uttermost in framing the new constitution, and while the country was drifting towards civil war, not only did they meet the most rigid resistance from the British cabinet in their attempts to 'bend' the Treaty, but some members of that cabinet (notably Churchill) were quite ready to contemplate a new military intervention if the Irish provisional government showed itself in fact unable to govern.

It seems then that the hazards of rejection were real enough; the existence of these hazards, and the fact that they overshadowed the Dáil debates, may in part explain what must seem to us in retrospect a remarkable feature of those debates. This was the failure to discuss adequately two fundamental matters: the question of the British bases and the problem of Northern Ireland. Of what may be called the front-line speakers on either side, the one who grasped most fully the implications of granting naval facilities on Irish soil to the British forces was Erskine Childers. This concession, he pointed out, would make nonsense of Ireland's claim to independence. 'What is the use', he asked, 'of talking of equality, what is the use of talking of a share in foreign policy, what is the use of talking of responsibility for making treaties and alliances with foreign nations which may involve the country in war?' In short, neutrality would be impossible while Ireland remained thus implicated in British quarrels elsewhere. More, much more, was to be heard of this argument seventeen years later when de Valera's government, by negotiating the British evacuation of the ports in 1938, prepared the way for a declaration of Irish neutrality in 1939 which might otherwise have been impossible. At the time, however, most deputies seem to have accepted the argument that defence was a vital British interest and therefore one which it was not unreasonable to concede even if—which is, of course, doubtful—it had been possible to withhold.

The strange silence on Northern Ireland is harder to account for. Dr Maureen Wall has calculated that of 338 pages of debate on the Treaty printed in the Dáil report, only nine are devoted to the issue of partition and that, of these nine, two-thirds were contributed by three deputies from Co. Monaghan.[7] The explanation of this strange lapse seems to be twofold. On the one hand, there was a general disposition, even among those who favoured Document No. 2 as against the Treaty, to assume that the Boundary Commission would take care of the problem in due course and that the six north-eastern counties would eventually drop like a ripe plum into the lap of the Free State. On the other hand, it is necessary to insist, anti-partionist propaganda notwithstanding, that in 1921, as for many years thereafter, the problem of the Border was a secondary problem because the nature of the new state which was to emerge in the South was itself in question. So long as the very issue of independence remained in doubt, unity was bound to be regarded as a peripheral matter.

Day after day, therefore, the debate revolved around the Treaty—how it came to be accepted, how far it could be bettered, what could be substituted for it, whether its rejection would be followed by war. Endlessly, cyclically, with increasing bitterness and frustration, the discussions continued. As they did so, there was a marked, perhaps inevitable, decline from the undeniably high level of the opening exchanges to the wounding cut-and-thrust which followed. Up to the moment when the debate was adjourned for Christmas it was conceivable that, had a vote been taken, it might have been narrowly in favour of rejection. During the recess, however, the pressures in the country for acceptance were greatly intensified. So also were the bad feeling and the misery with which men watched the approach of an apparently inevitable collision. Here, for example, is a passage, typical of many, from an eyewitness account appearing in the Sinn Féin weekly paper, *Young Ireland*, written at the very end of 1921, when the split in the Dáil had become painfully obvious :

Feelings of despair were uppermost in my mind as I walked home. Here were the elected representatives of the people of Ireland with daggers drawn against one another—for try as I could to get rid of the impression, it made itself felt in my mind : a tragic gulf had been dug that day in the parliament of the nation, and the nation would suffer . . . Deep sorrow filled me. I prayed that before it was too late the great tragedy which I saw hovering over our beloved country would be averted. That unity of purpose and unity of action might return. To secure unity I would welcome war back again—to secure unity I would take a thousand oaths of allegiance.[8]

Republican apologists who complain that opinion was 'manufactured' at this crucial point have an uphill task to prove their case. Some pressure, some influence, there undeniably was, but no official leverage could possibly have produced the breadth and depth of feeling that now emerged in support of the Treaty. It was to be found in the business community, among the farmers, at the county councils and other elective bodies, in the Church, even in a number of Sinn Féin clubs and executive bodies. At bottom this massive upsurge of opinion was the expression at once of an enormous weariness with war conditions and of an overpowering anxiety that the country should draw back from the verge of anarchy and that law and order should once again prevail. As *Young Ireland* put it at the time:

The will of the majority should be the governing factor throughout the whole scheme of government. There is at present, as far as we can see, no government operating in our country . . . We are not influenced in this matter by the Treaty. Whether the Treaty is rejected or not, it is evident that we must have some form of government in the country. It is no longer a question of freedom, so much as of government.[9]

In the same vein spoke the main national newspapers. Even the *Irish Times*, which might have been expected to voice the apprehensions of Southern Unionists, in fact pledged their support for the Treaty in the belief that they would receive fair treatment under the new regime—a belief, incidentally, that was to be fully justified in the event. The country was calling, said the *Irish Times*, 'for an end of *de*struction and a beginning of *con*struction. . . The Irish people are knocking impatiently on the door of freedom. Will their own janitor refuse to open it?'[10]

It cannot be said, however, that the Dáil showed itself unduly responsive to this groundswell of opinion. The numbers ranged on opposite sides remained so close that Collins and others resorted to various kinds of semi-secret negotiation to produce an agreed settlement. It was all in vain. The gulf remained un-bridgeable and the decision had to be faced. When it finally was faced on 7 January the majority for the Treaty was no more than seven—64 votes in favour, 57 against.

It is hard now, in the light of what was so soon to follow, to describe that decision as a 'victory'. It marked a fundamental division in the national movement and all those present were aware both of the fact and of its terrible implications. And as the drama moved towards its conclusion, with Griffith replacing de Valera as President and the lines of imminent conflict being etched more deeply by the hour, men looked across the widening chasm with no sort of rejoicing but rather, in some cases, with actual tears.

At that point, where dignity and restraint had not yet dissolved under the stress of civil war, we shall take our leave of them. We may do so, at this remove of time, with an enhanced respect for the honesty of purpose and devotion to country of those who participated in the great debate, irrespective of the banner under which they ultimately served. We may perhaps feel also that this crucial episode in Irish history illustrates as no other can the perils that lie in wait when men fall under the sway of ideology. The urge to define, to be precise, to reduce the manifold complexity of life to the compass of a written instrument, is in politics more often than not an urge towards self-destruction. We, who look back over the barren generation which followed the Civil War, and who contrast the high hopes of 1916, or even of 1919, with the realities of poverty, ill-health and bad housing which dogged the new state almost to our own day, may be especially drawn towards the plea with which Kevin O'Higgins ended his speech to the Dáil: 'The welfare and happiness of the men and women and the little children of this nation must, after all, take precedence of political creeds and theories.'

Notes and Bibliographies

Chapter 1

Notes

1. The claim is made in S. E. Finer, *Comparative Government*, London 1970, 62.
2. P. H. Pearse, *Political Writings and Speeches*, Dublin 1924, 323–4.
3. This and following quotations from *Thomas Davis: Selections from his Prose and Poetry*, ed. T. W. Rolleston, Dublin n.d., 280, 281, 271.
4. Thomas Davis, 'Ballad Poetry of Ireland' in *Essays Literary and Historical by Thomas Davis*, ed. D. J. O'Donoghue, Dundalk 1914, 366–7.
5. Basil Chubb, *The Government and Politics of Ireland*, Oxford, 1970, 44.

Bibliography

In general
G. A. Almond and J. S. Coleman, ed., *The Politics of Developing Areas*, Princetown 1960
Lucian W. Pye and S. Verba, ed., *Political Culture and Political Development*, Princetown 1965
Harry Eckstein, ed., *Internal War*, New York 1964

For Ireland
Basil Chubb, *The Government and Politics of Ireland*, Oxford 1970
Brian Farrell, *The Founding of Dáil Éireann: Parliament and Nation-Building*, Dublin 1971
David E. Schmitt, 'Aspects of Irish Social Organisation and Administrative Development', *Administration* XVIII, 4 (Winter 1970)

Chapter 2

Notes

1. For details of the changes compare Gearóid Mac Niocaill, *Ireland before the Vikings* and Donncha Ó Corráin, *Ireland before the*

I

Normans with Kenneth Nicholls, *Gaelic and Gaelicised Ireland in the Middle Ages* (all Dublin 1972).

2. See D. A. Binchy, *Críth Gablach,* Dublin 1941, 79–80, 102, 104–5.

3. *Audacht Moraind,* edited with German translation by Thurneysen, *Zeitschrift für celtische Philologie* XI (1917). Mr Fergus Kelly is preparing a new edition. I owe the observation on the king's function in this tract to Mr Terence P. Walsh. For the 'Prince's Truth' see Myles Dillon, 'The Archaism of Irish Tradition', *Proc. Brit. Acad.* XXXIII (1947).

4. See the *Annals of Ulster* I, ed. W. M. Hennessy, Dublin 1887, *s.aa.* 779, 803, 850 (the chronology for this period is a year behind); see also F. J. Byrne, *The Rise of the Uí Néill and the High-Kingship of Ireland* (O'Donnell Lecture, N.U.I., 1969), Dublin 1970.

5. For the connection of the *óenach* with the old Irish harvest festival see Máire Mac Néill, *The Festival of Lughnasa,* London 1962.

6. Binchy, *Críth Gablach,* 19–20 (para. 35, 38); see also Eóin Mac Néill, 'The Law of Status or Franchise', *Proc. RIA* XXXVI (1923), 302.

7. *The Metrical Dindshenchas* IV, ed. Edward Gwynn, Dublin 1924, 160–63.

8. Binchy has stripped the historical óenach Tailten of its legendary accretions in his article 'The Fair of Tailtiu and the Feast of Tara', *Ériu* XVIII (1958).

9. See *RIA Contributions to a Dictionary of the Irish Language, A,* fasc. I, s.v. *airecht;* Binchy, *Críth Gablach,* 69, 73, 77; Myles Dillon and Nora K. Chadwick, *The Celtic Realms,* London 1967, 98; *'Cenéla airechta',* ed. Kuno Meyer, *Zeitschrift für celtische Philologie* XII (1918).

10. Quoted by Mac Néill, *Early Irish Laws and Institutions,* Dublin [1935], 152.

11. See Nicholls, *Gaelic and Gaelicised Ireland,* 21–31, 187.

12. Gearóid Mac Niocaill 'The Heir Designate in Early Medieval Ireland', *Irish Jurist* 3 (1968); Donncha Ó Corráin, 'Irish Regnal Succession : a Reappraisal', *Studia Hibernica* XI (1972).

13. *Beatha Aodha Ruaidh Uí Dhomhnaill,* ed. Paul Walsh, I (1948), 112–9, 242–7; II (1957), 224.

14. Cited in *The Bardic Poems of Tadhg Dall Ó hUiginn II,* ed. Eleanor Knott, London 1926, 187.

Bibliography

D. A. Binchy, *Críth Gablach* (Dublin 1941; revised repr., 1970)
D. A. Binchy, 'The Fair of Tailtiu and the Feast of Tara', *Ériu* XVIII (1958)

F. J. Byrne, *The Rise of the Uí Néill and the High-Kingship of Ireland* (O'Donnell Lecture, N.U.I., 1969), Dublin 1970

F. J. Byrne, *Early Irish Kings and High-Kings*, London 1973

Myles Dillon and Nora K. Chadwick, *The Celtic Realms*, London 1967

Eóin Mac Néill, *Early Irish Laws and Institutions*, Dublin [1935]

Máire Mac Néill, *The Festival of Lughnasa*, London 1962

Gearóid Mac Niocaill, *Ireland before the Vikings*, Dublin 1972

Kenneth Nicholls, *Gaelic and Gaelicised Ireland in the Middle Ages*, Dublin 1972

Donncha Ó Corráin, *Ireland before the Normans*, Dublin 1972

Chapter 3

Notes

1. A. J. Otway-Ruthven, *A History of Medieval Ireland*, London 1968, 174.

2. A 'liberty' was an area in which a subject of the King of England was given full control, by the King, of all administration and all jurisdiction, to the exclusion of royal officials. It lay outside the shire system but, like the shire, sent two representatives to parliament.

3. H. G. Richardson and G. O. Sayles, *The Irish Parliament in the Middle Ages*, Philadelphia 1952, 7.

4. For this incident, see *A Contemporary Narrative of the Proceedings against Dame Alice Kyteler prosecuted for Sorcery in 1324 by Richard de Ledrede, Bishop of Ossory*, ed. Thomas Wright, London 1843, 17.

5. For the text of the Remonstrance in translation, see E. Curtis and R. B. McDowell, *Irish Historical Documents, 1172–1922*, London 1943, 34–6.

6. Text in *Statutes and Ordinances and Acts of the Parliament of Ireland* I, ed. H. F. Berry, Dublin 1907, 333–63; see Curtis, *Hist. Med. Ireland*, 2nd ed., London 1938, 215–17.

7. *Ibid.*, 216.

8. For these corrections to Curtis, see G. O. Sayles, 'The Rebellious Earl of Desmond', in *Medieval Studies presented to Aubrey Gwynn, SJ*, ed. J. A. Watt, J. B. Morrall and F. X. Martin, Dublin 1961, 203–29 and 216, n.88, though Sayles misquotes Curtis on the dating.

9. *Annals of Grace*, ed. R. Butler, Dublin 1842.

10. Curtis, *Hist. Med. Ireland*, 216.

11. M. Hayden and G. A. Moonan, *A Short History of the Irish People*, Dublin n.d., 165–6.

12. In *Irish Jurist* 1, 2 (1966).
13. M. V. Clarke, *Medieval Representation and Consent: A Study of Early Parliaments in England and Ireland*, London 1936, chap. 4.
14. J. F. Lydon, 'William of Windsor and the Irish Parliaments', *English Historical Review* 80 (1965).
15. For the proctors, see H. G. Richardson and G. O. Sayles, *The Irish Parliament in the Middle Ages*, 183–6.

Bibliography

General

Antonio Marongiú, *Medieval Parliaments: A Comparative Study*, trans. S. J. Woolf, London 1968. An excellent European survey, with special references to Italy

The 'Stubbs tradition':
William Stubbs, *The Constitutional History of England,,* Oxford 1873–78. Later editions and reprints
R. F. Treharne, 'The Nature of Parliament in the Reign of Henry III', *English Historical Review* 74 (1959)

The 'Maitland tradition':
F. W. Maitland, The 'Introduction' to his *Memoranda de Parliamento, 1305*, London 1893. Reprinted in *Historical Essays of F. W. Maitland*, ed. H. M. Cam, Cambridge 1957
H. G. Richardson and G. O. Sayles. See their many publications on English and Irish parliamentary history, in particular *Parliaments and Great Councils of Medieval England*, first published in *Law Quarterly Review* 77 (1961); separately, London 1961

Surveys and general commentaries:
Peter Spufford, *Origins of the English Parliament*, London 1967. Selected documents with commentaries. Useful
E. B. Fryde and Edward Miller, ed., *Historical Studies of the English Parliament* I (origins to 1399), Cambridge 1970. A collection of valuable papers by authorities with differing viewpoints
Radcliffe and Cross, *The English Legal System*, 5th ed. by Lord Cross and G. J. Hand, London 1971, chapters I–IV. A concise account of the development of parliament in its legal context.
J. G. Edwards, *Historians and the Medieval English Parliament* (David Murray Foundation Lecture, 1955), Glasgow 1960

J. G. Edwards, *The Commons in Medieval English Parliaments*
(Creighton Lecture in History, 1957), London 1958

Ireland

Sources :

*Statutes and Ordinances and Acts of the Parliament of Ireland, King
John to Henry V* (half-title : *Early Statutes of Ireland*) and its con-
tinuations (4 vols), ed. H. F. Berry and J. F. Morrissey, Dublin 1907–
1939
Parliaments and Councils of Medieval Ireland I : *1312–1388*, ed. H. G.
Richardson and G. O. Sayles, Dublin 1947

Commentaries :

Maude V. Clarke, 'Irish Parliaments in the Reign of Edward II', *Royal
Historical Society Transactions*, 4th ser., 9 (1926); repr. in her *Four-
teenth-Century Studies*, Oxford 1937, repr. 1969
Maude V. Clarke, *Medieval Representation and Consent: A Study of
Early Parliaments in England and Ireland, with Special Reference to the
Modus tenendi parliamentum*, London 1936
G. J. Hand, 'The Forgotten Statutes of Kilkenny: A Brief Survey',
Irish Jurist 1, 2 (1966)
J. F. Lydon, 'The Irish Church and Taxation in the Fourteenth Century',
Irish Ecclesiastical Record 103 (1965). Valuable for light on clerical
proctors
J. F. Lydon, 'William of Windsor and the Irish Parliament', *English
Historical Review* 80 (1965). Enlightening
Edmund Curtis, *Richard II in Ireland*, Oxford 1927. Discusses the sub-
missions of the Gaelic chiefs and their attendance at parliament. Im-
portant, and cites the relevant documents
J. F. Lydon, 'Richard II's Expeditions to Ireland', *Royal Society of
Antiquaries of Ireland Journal* 93 (1963). This concentrates on the
military aspect and is a necessary complement to Curtis's account above.
H. G. Richardson and G. O. Sayles, *The Irish Parliament in the Middle
Ages*, 2nd ed., Philadelphia 1964. Authoritative
H. G. Richardson and G. O. Sayles, *Parliament in Medieval Ireland*
(Dublin Historical Association), Dundalk 1964. Admirable summary
of their work published at Philadelphia
John A. Watt, 'The First Recorded Use of the Word "Parliament" in
Ireland?', *Irish Jurist* 4, 1 (1969)
   I am indebted to Dr Art Cosgrove, Dr Seymour Phillips and, in a
very special way, to Professor G. J. Hand, all of University College,
Dublin, for reading the script and suggesting changes and emendations

Chapter 4

Bibliography

The principal sources for the fifteenth century are: *Statutes and Ordinances and Acts of the Parliament of Ireland: King John to Henry V*, ed. H. F. Berry, Dublin 1907

Statute Rolls of the Parliament of Ireland: Henry VI, ed. H. F. Berry, Dublin 1910

Statute Rolls of the Parliament of Ireland: 1–12 Edward IV, ed. H. F. Berry, Dublin 1914; *12–22 Edward IV*, ed. J. F. Morrissey, Dublin 1939

Supplementary material can be found in:

Parliaments and Councils of Medieval Ireland, ed. H. G. Richardson and G. O. Sayles, Dublin 1947

For the submissions to Richard II see E. Curtis, *Richard II in Ireland 1394–5*, Oxford 1927

The standard work on the medieval Irish parliament is H. G. Richardson and G. O. Sayles, *The Irish Parliament in the Middle Ages*, Philadelphia 1952; 2nd ed. 1964

Their conclusions are summarised in the pamphlet *Parliament in Medieval Ireland* (Dublin Historical Association), 1964

M. C. Griffith, 'The Talbot-Ormond Struggle for Control of the Anglo-Irish Government 1414–47', *Irish Historical Studies* II (1941) deals with the quarrels inside the administration in the early fifteenth century

The declaration of 1460 can be conveniently consulted in E. Curtis and R. B. McDowell, *Irish Historical Documents 1172–1922*, London 1943

A. Conway, *Henry VII's Relations with Scotland and Ireland*, Cambridge 1932, includes a chapter on Poynings' Parliament. Poynings' Law is dealt with by D. B. Quinn, 'The Early Interpretation of Poynings' Law', *Irish Historical Studies* II (1941), and R. D. Edwards and T. W. Moody, 'The History of Poynings' Law', *Irish Historical Studies* II (1941)

Chapter 5

Notes

1. Later historians of the Irish Tudor parliaments owe an incalculable debt to Professors D. B. Quinn of Liverpool, R. D. Edwards of UCD and T. W. Moody of TCD who in the late 1930s set about the task of assembling the available material and undertook the

Notes and Bibliographies 263

pioneering studies. The fruits of their labours can be seen in the bibliography. One incidental consequence was to draw attention to the considerable lacunae in the material that has survived. From the twenty-one Parliaments we know to have been convened in that period only one of the original statute rolls survives. We have records of the daily proceedings of parliaments only in two cases, and even these are fragmented and terse. Lists of members of parliament do not exist before 1560 and then they are usually lists of those summoned or elected rather than of those who actually attended.

2. The case against which I am arguing here has been put most forthrightly by H. G. Richardson and G. O. Sayles in *The Irish Parliament in the Middle Ages*, 269–81, and in their pamphlet *Parliament in Medieval Ireland*, 23–4. For an ingenuous defence of Poynings' Law as evidence of an incipient popular unionist tradition in Ireland see C. Litton Falkiner, 'Irish Parliamentary Antiquities' in *Essays relating to Ireland*.

3. On the development of the judicial function of parliaments in the fifteenth century see Richardson and Sayles, *The Irish Parliament in the Middle Ages*, 174–6, 214–220.

4. Richardson and Sayles, *Parliament in Medieval Ireland*, 23; cf. A. J. Otway-Ruthven, *A History of Medieval Ireland*, 171–2.

5. That the Reformation legislation as such was not opposed in parliament is a matter of historical fact. The question of interpretation remains. It remains possible to argue that the parliament did not oppose the legislation because it was under constraints of one kind or another. In my view the weight of evidence is against such an interpretation; see my 'Opposition to the Reformation Legislation', *Irish Historical Studies* XVI (Mar. 1969). The anti-papal act of Poynings' Parliament is the 'Act against Provisors to Rome', *Stat. at Large, Ire.* I, 45, (10 Henry VII c.5).

6. Although the elimination of the proctors was effected in a most cavalier fashion, it was probably inevitable given the trend of parliamentary development. They may be offered the posthumous consolation that their exclusion at that stage deprived Protestant clergy, who were soon to replace them in their churches and cathedrals, of the opportunity of replacing them in parliament also. In the long run this particular updating of parliament weakened rather than strengthened the influence of the New English. On the amendment of the faculties and appeals bills see *Letters and Papers of Henry VIII*, IX, no. 43, *SP Henry VIII*, I, 438. The two acts are in *Stat. at Large, Ire.* I, 91–3, 142–57. Though the bills in the form they were transmitted from England have been lost they can

be reconstructed from W. Shaw Mason, ed., 'Collation of the Irish Statutes', TCD MS V 2.7. R. D. Edwards, 'The Irish Reformation Parliament of Henry VIII, 1536–7', *Historical Studies* VI, ed. T. W. Moody, London 1968, is a meticulous and scholarly narrative of this parliament and its immediate historical context. The best succinct analyses of parliamentary opposition in the English Tudor parliaments are in G. R. Elton, *The Tudor Constitution*, 300–1, *The Body of the Whole Realm*, 16–22, and *England under the Tudors*, 170; see also Conrad Russel, *The Crisis of Parliaments*, 38–40.

7. It is clear from the way St Leger and Cusack subsequently interpreted the act that in reviving the idea of declaring Henry VIII King of Ireland they were motivated by deeper purposes than the refutation of the theoretical claim of the Pope to temporal jurisdiction in Ireland. Unfortunately I cannot here undertake the comprehensive treatment the episode requires, or even an analysis of the discussions between Henry VIII, his council in England and the Irish council, which resulted from Cusack's mission in 1541 and which are central to all I have to say here. There is a tendency nowadays to apply the term apartheid to the situation created by Statutes of Kilkenny. Apartheid was the situation created by the penal religious laws after the sixteenth century when Crown jurisdiction extended throughout the whole island. However, to apply the term to the late medieval period is to misunderstand the actual political situation. As distinct from theoretical claims, the Crown neither enjoyed nor attempted to exercise unilateral jurisdiction in Ireland at that stage. Its position was rather like that of the Irish Republic at the present time, which theoretically rejects but, for the purposes of actual jurisdiction, accepts a partition of jurisdiction in Ireland, thus recognising more than one autonomous political unit in the island. Apartheid regulates the relationship between two communities who come *within* the scope of the same constitution and are bound by the same jurisdictional system. The Statutes of Kilkenny, on the other hand, regulated the relationship of one autonomous political community 'the English in the land of peace' with those *outside* the pale of its laws and jurisdiction. (Otway-Ruthven, *Medieval Ireland*, 139, 290–4.)

8. In order to facilitate the attendance of Irish chiefs who were unwilling to risk long absences from their areas St Leger took parliament on circuit. He held a session of over three weeks at Limerick and over a week at Trim in 1542. The O'Briens of Thomond and the MacWilliam Burkes of Connacht came to Limerick. The O'Neills and O'Donnells came to Trim as well as most of the Leinster Irish. The Earl of Desmond also waived his

privilege of absenting himself secured eighty years earlier after the judicial murder of the Earl of the time while attending parliament. (*SP Henry VIII*, III, 292, 306, 362, 371; *Letters and Papers Henry VIII*, XVI, nos 656, 955; XVII, nos 215, 262, 491; XVIII (I), nos 336, 411; *Cal. Carew MSS* I, nos 129, 155, 169.) The inspiration of the legal minds behind the policy for assimilating the Irish to the English legal system is indicated in the Statutes for Munster, a working compromise between the two systems, and in the proposal for the revision of the statute law 'for the Irishry who submit and are in doubt of such uncertain laws'. (*Letters and Papers Henry VIII*, XVII, no. 491; *SP Henry VIII*, III, 398.)

9. Professor Quinn provides an illuminating study of Crown policy in Ireland in relation to the emergence of sixteenth-century European colonialism in *Historical Studies* I, ed. T. D. Williams, London 1958. However, a detailed analysis of Mary's reign would show that his tentative conclusions about the initial stages of the colonial policy in Ireland need modification in two respects: the allegedly favourable attitude of the loyal Anglo-Irish community to conquest and plantation, and the alleged reluctance of Sussex to embark on such a policy. In fact, the attitude in each case was the reverse. In addition the categories he employs to discuss Irish policy proposals need to be modified. He speaks of a category of 'soft' policies which tended to favour conciliation and gradual reformation in Ireland against which were placed the 'tough' policies which tended to favour conquest and plantation. It would be more accurate to invert these categories and to speak of a policy of reformation which tended to favour soft methods and a policy of conquest which tended to be tough. This is an important modification. While official government policy from the reign of Mary onwards might have been relatively tougher and softer in its implementation depending on political exigencies, it was always from that time a policy of conquest and colonisation. On the other hand the alternative policy of constitutional reformation came quickly to be identified with the Anglo-Irish community. This formed the basis for the confrontation between the Crown colonial policy and the national constitutional policy evident from Sidney's period onwards. On all of this and the circumstances in which St Leger and Cusack were ousted see BM Cotton MSS, Titus B XI, f.407 (413), f.415 (466), f.437; PRO Eng, SP 62/1, no. 31.

10. The Anglo-Irish proposals for a parliament are in PRO Eng, SP 62/1, no. 13. For the resentment provoked by the English troops see SP 62/1, no. 61; 62/2, no. 32.

11. The parliamentary copies of the two crucial acts, one for 'ecclesiastical jurisdiction' the other for 'uniformity' are now lost. However, they were available to W. Shaw Mason when he collated them with the printed statutes in the last century. They bore the royal assent given by the Lord Deputy and were endorsed by the Commons 'les cōens assentuz', implying that they had assented after the acts had been sent down to them by the Upper House. But they bore no endorsement to indicate that they had been presented to the Upper House. (W. Shaw Mason, ed., 'Collation of the Irish Statutes', TCD MS, V 2.7.) Instances of the exercise of Crown patronage in the distribution of seats in the Commons are the return of Sir John Alen, former Lord Chancellor, and Sir Francis Agarde, a New English official, for the two borough seats in Kinsale. Sir Henry Radcliff, the Lord Deputy's brother, was returned for Carlingford. (*Tracts relating to Ireland* (Ire. Arch. Soc.) II, app. II.) No returns are shown for nine newly created shire seats. If the government was able to control the majority of these it would probably have had a majority in the Commons. It seems quite probable also that the same measures were used to intimidate members as were apparently resorted to in 1613 when the parliament building bristled with armed government troops. (David Roth, *Analecta*, 78.) I must thank Fr Joseph Jennings, SM, for giving me the benefit of his expertise in ecclesiastical Latin in the translation of Roth.

12. V. Treadwell, 'The Irish Parliament of 1569–71', Proc. RIA, 65 C (1966–67) is an excellent analysis of Sidney's Parliament. However it does not advert to the political tension between the colonial and the constitutional policies as reflected in parliament. Space precludes analysing the act for the attainder of Shane O'Neill, which gives a very good insight into the attitude of the loyal Anglo-Irish, to Gaelic rebellion on the one hand, and to colonial conquest on the other. I should point out, however, that the traditional assumption that this act demonstrates the hostility of the Anglo-Irish to the Gaelic is a complete non-sequitur. On the same basis it could be argued that the attainders of Kildare, Desmond, and Baltinglas demonstrate Anglo-Irish hostility to the Anglo-Irish.

13. The speeches of Stanyhurst and Sidney are in E. Campion, *History of Ireland* in *Irish Histories* I, 194 ff. Richard Stanyhurst's *Description of Ireland* is published in Holinshed's *Chronicles* vi. Stanyhurst's attitude and purpose have been misunderstood by a succession of critics from Geoffrey Keating in the seventeenth century to our own day.

14. A contemporary copy of Walsh's speech is in PRO Eng, SP 63/124, no. 24. It is inadequately summarised in *Cal. SP Ire.* III, 55–8. The logical sequel to Walsh's speech is the 'Discourse on Ireland' presented to James I by Richard Hadsor, the solicitor for Irish causes, in 1603. Hadsor's brief, argued comprehensively though with obvious anomalies, was that constitutionally, juridically, and historically the kingdom of Ireland constituted an autonomous political entity, quite distinct from the kingdom of England. On this basis he suggested a personal union of the three kingdoms 'to unite in your union of England and Scotland, your realm of Ireland unto you in happy amity'. (BM Cotton MS, Titus B X, 179 (174). It is misascribed in the *Cal. SP Ire.*)

Bibliography
Sources

Chronologies:

D. B. Quinn, 'Parliaments and Great Councils in Ireland, 1461–1586', *Irish Historical Studies* III (1942–3)

H. G. Richardson and G. O. Sayles, *The Irish Parliament in the Middle Ages,* Philadelphia 1952

List of members:

J. Hardiman, 'The Statutes of Kilkenny' in *Tracts relating to Ireland*

C. Litton Falkiner, 'The Parliament of Ireland under the Tudors', *Proc. RIA* 25 C(1904–05), 508–41, 553–66

C. Litton Falkiner, *Essays relating to Ireland,* London 1909, appendix

Records:

C. Litton Falkiner, ed., 'The Diary of John Hooker at Sidney's Parliament', *Proc. RIA,* 25 C (1904–05)

F. J. Routledge, ed., 'The Lord's Journal in Perrot's Parliament', *English Historical Review* XXIX (1914)

Legislation:

Statutes at Large, Ireland I, Dublin 1786

D. B. Quinn, ed., 'Bills and Statutes of Henry VII and Henry VIII', *Analecta Hibernica* 10 (1941)

D. B. Quinn, ed., 'The Printed Irish Statutes of 1586', *Proc. RIA* 49C (1943–44)

W. Shaw Mason, ed., 'Collation of the Printed Statutes with the Rolls', TCD MS V 2.7

Agnes Conway, ed., 'Some Acts of Poyning's Parliament' in *Henry VII, Scotland and Ireland,* Cambridge 1932

Miscellaneous:

Edmund Campion, *A History of Ireland* (c. 1571) in *Ancient Irish Histories,* ed. Sir James Ware, Dublin 1809

Sir John Davies, *A Discoverie of the True Causes why Ireland was never entirely subdued . . .* (1612) in *Ireland under Elizabeth and James I*, ed. H. Morley, London 1890

Richard Stanyhurst, *Description of Ireland* (c. 1575) in R. Holinshed, ed., *Chronicles* vi (1587)

Further Reading
Poynings' Law:
E. Curtis, 'Poynings' Laws' in *Henry VII, Scotland and Ireland,* ed. Agnes Conway, Cambridge 1932

R. D. Edwards and T. W. Moody, 'Early History of Poynings' Law', *Irish Historical Studies* II (1941)

D. B. Quinn, 'Early Interpretation of Poynings' Law', *Irish Historical Studies* II (1941)

D. B. Quinn, Introduction to 'Bills and Statutes', *Analecta Hibernica* 10 (1940–41)

H. G. Richardson and G. O. Sayles, *The Irish Parliament in the Middle Ages,* Philadelphia 1952, 269–81

Reformation Parliament, 1536–7:
B. Bradshaw, 'Opposition at the Irish Reformation Parliament', *Irish Historical Studies* XVI (Mar. 1969)

R. D. Edwards, 'The Irish Reform Parliament', *Historical Studies* VI, ed. T. W. Moody, London 1968

Sidney's Parliament:
V. Treadwell, 'The Irish Parliament of 1569–71', *Proc. RIA,* 65C (1966–67)

Economic:
D. B. Quinn, 'The Irish Parliamentary Subsidy', *Proc. RIA,* 42C (1934–35)

Surveys:
C. Litton Falkiner, 'Irish Parliamentary Antiquities' in *Essays relating to Ireland,* London 1909

T. W. Moody, 'The Irish Parliament under Elizabeth and James I', *Proc. RIA,* 45C (1939–40)

Political background, sixteenth century:
R. D. Edwards, 'Ireland, Elizabeth, and the Counterreformation' in *Elizabethan Government and Society,* ed. S. T. Bindoff, etc., London 1961

Margaret MacCurtain, *Tudor and Stuart Ireland,* Dublin 1972

Grenfell Morton, *Elizabethan Ireland,* London 1971

D. B. Quinn, 'Henry VIII and Ireland, 1509–34', *Irish Historical Studies* XII (1961)

D. B. Quinn, 'Ireland and Sixteenth Century European Expansion', *Historical Studies* I, ed. T. D. Williams, London 1958

D. G. White, 'The Reign of Edward VI in Ireland', *Irish Historical Studies* XIV (1965)

English Tudor parliament:
G. R. Elton, *England under the Tudors,* London 1955
G. R. Elton, *The Tudor Constitution,* Cambridge 1960
G. R. Elton, *The Body of the Whole Realm,* Virginia UP, 1969
C. Morris, *Political Thought from Tyndale to Hooker,* Oxford 1953
Conrad Russel, *The Crisis of Parliaments,* London 1971

Medieval Background:
Kenneth Nicholls, *Gaelic and Gaelicised Ireland,* Dublin 1972
A. J. Otway-Ruthven, *A History of Medieval Ireland,* London 1968
H. G. Richardson and G. O. Sayles, *The Irish Parliament in the Middle Ages,* Philadelphia 1952
H. G. Richardson and G. O. Sayles, *Parliament in Medieval Ireland* (Dublin Historical Society), Dundalk 1964

Chapter 6

Notes

1. See for example, F. L. Carsten, *Princes and Parliaments in Germany,* Oxford 1959; J. H. Elliott, *Revolt of the Catalans,* Cambridge 1963; J. P. Major, *Representative Institutions in Renaissance France,* Madison 1960.
2. For a detailed study see T. W. Moody, 'The Irish Parliament under Elizabeth and James I', *Proc. RIA* 45C (1939–40).
3. On the Ulster Plantation, see G. Hill, *The Plantation in Ulster,* Belfast 1877, and T. W. Moody, *The Londonderry Plantation,* Belfast 1939.
4. On Sir John Davies see J. G. A. Pocock, *The Ancient and The Feudal Law,* Cambridge 1957 and Sir John Davies, *A Discoverie of the True Causes why Ireland was never entirely subdued . . .,* London 1612, reprinted in *Ireland under Elizabeth and James I,* ed. H. Morley, London 1890.
5. See H. F. Kearney, *Strafford in Ireland,* Manchester 1959, 74–81.
6. H. R. Trevor-Roper 'The Gentry', *Econ. Hist. Rev. Supplement,* 1953 (also available in abbreviated form in L. Stone, ed., *Social Change and Revolution in England 1540–1640,* London 1965).
7. See H. F. Kearney, *op. cit.*; A. Clarke, *The Old English in Ireland,* London 1966; A. Clarke, 'Ireland and the General Crisis', *Past and Present* 48 (Aug. 1970); T. Ranger, 'Strafford in Ireland: A Revaluation', *Past and Present* 19 (Apr. 1961), repr. in T. Aston, ed., *Crisis in Europe,* London 1965.
8. On the Graces, P. Wilson 'Strafford' in R. Barry O'Brien, ed.,

Studies in Irish History 1603–49 (London, 1906) is still interesting. See also A. Clarke, *'The Graces 1625–41'* (Dublin Historical Association), Dundalk 1968.

9. See A. Clarke, 'The Policies of the "Old English" in Parliament 1640–41', *Historical Studies* V, ed. J. L. McCracken, London 1965.

10. See J. C. Beckett, 'The Confederation of Kilkenny Reviewed' *Historical Studies* II, ed. M. Roberts, London 1959.

For an excellent general survey of the period, Margaret Mac-Curtain, *Tudor and Stuart Ireland*, Dublin 1972, is invaluable.

Chapter 7

Notes

1. Examination of Edward Dowdall, 13 March 1642, in Gilbert, *History of the Confederation* I, 275.

2. 'The Humble Petition of the Catholics of Ireland to the King's Most Excellent Majesty' in Gilbert, *History of the Confederation* II, 131.

3. Richard Martin to Ulick, Earl of Clanricarde, 2 December 1642, in *Memoirs and Letters of Ulick, Marquis of Clanricarde*, London 1757, 296.

4. A. Clarke, 'The Policies of the "Old English" in Parliament, 1640–41', *Historical Studies* V, ed. J. L. McCracken, London 1965.

Bibliography

There are three main collections of contemporary or near contemporary documents illustrating the history of the Confederation of Kilkenny :

J. T. Gilbert, ed., *A Contemporary History of Affairs in Ireland, from A.D. 1641 to 1652*, 3 vols in 6 parts, Dublin 1879

J. T. Gilbert, ed., *History of the Confederation and the War in Ireland, 1641–1653*, 7 vols, Dublin 1882–91

R. O'Ferrall and R. O'Connell, *Commentarius Rinuccinianus*, ed. Rev. Stanislaus Kavanagh, 6 vols, Dublin 1932–49. (M. J. Hynes, *The Mission of Rinuccini*, Dublin 1932, is mainly a summary of this set of Latin documents.)

The general background of the Confederate period may be filled in from three further works :

R. Bagwell, *Ireland under the Stuarts, 1642–60* II, London 1909

J. C. Beckett, *The Making of Modern Ireland 1603–1923*, London 1966

T. Carte, *The Life of James, Duke of Ormond*, 6 vols, Oxford, ed. of 1851. Bagwell and Carte write from the royalist viewpoint. There is no full-scale history of the Confederation of Kilkenny which can be recommended.

A number of recent specialist studies will be found useful for a fuller understanding of Confederate history:

J. C. Beckett, 'The Confederation of Kilkenny Reviewed', repr. in his *Confrontations: Studies in Irish History*, London 1972

A. Clarke, *The Old English in Ireland 1625–42*, London 1966

P. J. Corish, 'Bishop Nicholas French and the Second Ormond Peace 1648–9', *Irish Historical Studies* VI (1948)

P. J. Corish, 'Rinuccini's Censure of 27 May 1648', *Irish Theological Quarterly* XVIII (1951)

P. J. Corish, 'Two Contemporary Historians of the Confederation of Kilkenny', *Irish Historical Studies* VIII (1953)

P. J. Corish, 'The Crisis in Ireland in 1648: The Nuncio and the Supreme Council', *Irish Theological Quarterly* XXII (1955)

P. J. Corish, 'The Origins of Catholic Nationalism', in Corish, ed., *A History of Irish Catholicism* III, 8, Dublin 1968

D. F. Cregan, 'Daniel O'Neill, a Royalist Agent in Ireland, 1644–50', *Irish Historical Studies* II (1941)

D. F. Cregan, 'Some Members of the Confederation of Kilkenny' in *Measgra i gCuimhne Mhichil Uí Chléirigh*, ed. S. O'Brien, Dublin 1944

D. F. Cregan, 'The Confederate Catholics of Ireland 1642–49', *Irish Historical Studies* XVIII (1972–73)

J. Lowe, 'The Glamorgan Mission to Ireland 1645–6', *Studia Hibernica* IV (1964)

J. Lowe, 'Charles I and the Confederation of Kilkenny 1643–9', *Irish Historical Studies* XIV (1965)

Chapter 8

Notes

1. Thomas Davis, *The Patriot Parliament of 1689*, ed. C. G. Duffy.

2. Henry Jones, *A Sermon preach't at Christ Church Dublin Before the Generall Convention of Ireland May 24 1660*, London 1660. Also *A Continuation of the Brief Narrative and of the Sufferings of the Irish under Cromwell*, London 1660.

3. John Bramhall, *A Sermon Preached at Dublin upon the 23 of Aprill 1661 being the day appointed for his Majesties Coronation*, Dublin 1661.

4. Jeremy Taylor, *A Sermon Preached at the opening of the Parliament of Ireland May 8 1661*, London 1661.

5. Jeremy Taylor, *Rules and Advices to the Clergy of the Dioceses Down and Connor*, Dublin 1661.

6. *A True Account of the Whole Proceedings of the Parliament in Ireland*, London 1689, 6–7.

7. J. Hogan, ed., *Negociations de M. le Comte d'Avaux en Irlande, 1689–90* (Irish MSS Comm.), Dublin 1934, 226, 255.
8. Dopping's speech is given in full in an appendix to William King, *The State of the Protestants of Ireland,* London 1691.
9. *Ormonde MSS* II (Historical MSS Comm.), London 1899, 407.

Bibliography

The most thorough treatment and most ample documentation is still Thomas Davis, *The Patriot Parliament of 1689,* ed. C. Gavan Duffy, London 1893. Duffy's edition was based on a series of articles by Davis under the heading 'Irish State Papers No. 1, Statutes of 1689' in *The Dublin Magazine and Citizen* (Jan.–Apr. 1843). These are normally cited as at pp. 25–42, 75–90, 105–34, 182–201. (They are given thus, for example, in the appendix of T. W. Moody, *Thomas Davis: A Centenary Address,* Dublin 1943, 62.) The Duffy edition, however, substantially abbreviates the original articles, omitting among other things, many references to and critical remarks on sources. In particular, it ignores the first section of an important article by Davis, 'Proceedings of the Parliament in Ireland in 1689' in *The Dublin Magazine* (Apr. 1843), 170–82, which contains new material and some correction of his own work on the composition of the parliament and which should therefore be added to the list of references given above. Duffy claimed in 1880 that Davis had left a revised plan for republication but there is little evidence for this (see correspondence of Duffy and Lecky in the Duffy Letters in the National Library of Ireland, and the Duffy Papers in the Royal Irish Academy).

It should be borne in mind that Davis's assessment of the Patriot Parliament was a distortion of historical reality. Even so, his interpretation is of considerable historiographical interest for the important contribution which it made towards rescuing the Irish parliament from the oppressive, reactionary and subservient image it had created for itself during the greater part of the eighteenth century. In choosing to devote so much time to the rediscovery of the Patriot Parliament, Davis did more than reconstruct an historical episode. He helped to rehabilitate and reinforce the Irish parliamentary tradition as the central core of Irish political development.

The best contemporary sources are: William King, *The State of the Protestants of Ireland,* London 1691 and many later editions; J. Hogan, ed., *Negociations de M. le Comte d'Avaux en Irlande 1689–90* (Irish MSS Comm.), Dublin 1934; supplementary volume, Dublin 1958.

The most convenient and thorough modern treatment is J. G. Simms, *The Jacobite Parliament of 1689* (Dublin Historical Association), Dundalk 1966. This is substantially reproduced with detailed references as Chapter 5 of J. G. Simms, *Jacobite Ireland 1685–91,* London 1969, which is the authoritative monograph on the period and which gives a comprehensive bibliography. Two additions to the sources for texts of the 1689 legislation might be noted : a holograph copy of several acts in Marsh's Library, Dublin, and *An Appendix to the Late King James's Acts* . . . Printed and sold by Ebenezer Rider, Dublin 1740

Chapter 9

Notes

1. 3 William and Mary, c. 2 (Eng.).
2. *Cal. SP Dom., 1695: Addenda*, 213.
3. H. F. Kearney, 'The Political Background to English Mercantilism, 1695–1700', *Econ. Hist. Rev.*, 2nd ser. XI (1959).
4. Molyneux, *Case*, Dublin 1698, 105.
5. *Ibid.*, 97–8.
6. *Commons' Jn. (Eng.)*, XII, 331.
7. E. R. McC. Dix, 'List of Editions of Molyneux's *Case*', *Irish Book-lover* V (1914), 116–18.
8. C. Robbins, *The Eighteenth-Century Commonwealthman*, Cambridge, Mass. 1959, 137–43.
9. *Ibid.*, 88–102; B. Bailyn, *The Ideological Origins of the American Revolution*, 1967 Cambridge, Mass., 71–3.
10. *Commons' Jn. (Ire.)* (1798), II, 342.
11. *Ibid.*, 494.
12. *Lords' Jn. (Ire.)*, II, 247–8.
13. Swift, *Works*, ed. H. Davis, IX, 1–12.
14. J. G. Simms, 'Irish Catholics and the Parliamentary Franchise, 1692–1728', *Irish Historical Studies* XII (1960); W. Graham, ed., *Letters of Joseph Addison*, Oxford 1941, 151.

Bibliography

W. Molyneux, *The Case of Ireland's being bound by Acts of Parliament in England, Stated*, Dublin 1698
J. Cary, *A Vindication of the Parliament of England in Answer to a Book Written by William Molyneux of Dublin, Esquire*, London 1698
W. Atwood, *The History and Reasons of the Dependency of Ireland upon the Imperial Crown of the Kingdom of England: rectifying Mr Molineux's 'State of the Case'*, London 1698
J. Locke, *Two Treatises of Government*, ed. P. Laslett, London 1960
J. Swift, 'The Story of the Injured Lady', *Works*, ed. H. Davis, IX, Oxford 1948, 1–12
J. L. McCracken, *The Irish Parliament in the Eighteenth Century*, Dundalk (Dublin Historical Association), Dundalk 1971

C. Robbins, *The Eighteenth-Century Commonwealthman*, Cambridge, Mass. 1959
O. W. Ferguson, *Jonathan Swift and Ireland*, Urbana, Illinois 1962

Chapter 10

Bibliography

J. T. Ball, *Legislative Systems Operative in Ireland*, London 1889
W. H. Crawford and B. Trainor, ed., *Aspects of Irish Social History, 1750–1800*, Belfast 1969
E. M. Johnston, *Great Britain and Ireland, 1760–1800*, Edinburgh and London 1963
J. L. McCracken, *The Irish Parliament in the Eighteenth Century*, Dundalk 1971
R. B. McDowell, *Irish Public Opinion, 1750–1800*, London 1944
E. Porritt and A. G. Porritt, *The Unreformed House of Commons*, New York 1963
PRONI, *Irish Elections, 1750–1832*, n.d.

Chapter 11

Bibliography

The basic work still remains W. E. H. Lecky, *The History of Ireland in the Eighteenth Century* (Vols 2–4), London 1892.
R. B. MacDowell, *Irish Public Opinion, 1750–1800* (London 1944) provides a most useful summary of the political thought of the late eighteenth century.
E. M. Johnston's densely packed *Great Britain and Ireland, 1760–1800* (Edinburgh 1963) pioneers the application of Namierite techniques to Ireland to construct the standard account of the structure of Irish politics at this period.
J. C. Beckett clarifies the ambiguities in the constitutional relationship between Grattan's Parliament and English political institutions in his probing article 'Anglo-Irish Constitutional Relations in the Late Eighteenth Century', *Irish Historical Studies* XIV (1964–65).
G. C. Bolton's admirable study in depth of the *fin de siècle* political scene in *The Passing of the Irish Act of Union*, Oxford 1966, explodes many nationalist myths about the role of bribery in the passing of the Union, while Maureen Wall exposes other myths in her penetrating appraisal, 'The United Irish Movement', *Historical Studies* V, ed. J. L. McCracken, London 1965.
R. R. Palmer, *The Age of the Democratic Revolution*, 2 vols, Princeton

1959–64, contains interesting reflections on Ireland. Suggestions for
further reading:
M. R. O'Connell, *Irish Politics and Social Conflict in the Age of the
American Revolution*, Philadelphia 1965
P. J. O'Farrell, *Ireland's English Question*, London 1971
L. M. Cullen, *An Economic History of Ireland since 1660*, London
1972
M. A. G. Ó Tuathaigh, *Ireland before the Famine, 1798–1848*, Dublin
1972
P. J. Jupp, 'Irish MPs at Westminster in the Early Nineteenth Century',
Historical Studies VII ed. J. C. Beckett, London 1969, and 'Irish Parlia-
mentary Elections and the Influence of the Catholic Vote, 1801–20',
Historical Journal 10, 2 (1967)

Chapter 12

Notes
1. *Hansard*, 3rd ser., Vol. XXII, col. 94, 4 Feb. 1830.
2. MacDonagh, *The Life of Daniel O'Connell*, London 1903, 401–2.
3. A. Aspinall, ed., *Three Early Nineteenth Century Diaries*, London
   1952, extract from Le Marchant's diary (March 1833)
4. The following is a characteristic passage from the speech: 'And am
   I now to be subjected to the taunts of a briefless barrister . . .? Of
   what use is my success to me? I have wept tears over my lot in
   private . . . and should I not deplore the cruel fate which places the
   Gores and other Protestants above me in my native land?'
      The editor, Mr Brian Farrell, has made the interesting suggestion
   that Andrew Jackson was moved by similar resentments in organising similar popular resistance to an 'Ascendancy'. Much of Jackson's
   political work of the 1820s and 1830s does resemble O'Connell's
   and a comparison between the two would certainly be fruitful and
   suggestive.
5. Jeremy Bentham, *Works*, ed. John Bowring, Edinburgh, 1843–59,
   Vol. XI, 20.
6. These quotations from O'Connell's private correspondence were
   contained in an article by Professor Maurice O'Connell in the *Irish
   Independent*, 27 Jan. 1967.
7. *Daniel O'Connell: His Early Life and Journal, 1795 to 1802*, ed.
   Arthur Houston, London 1906, 174.
8. MacDonagh, *op. cit.*, 404.

Bibliography
Denis Gwynn, *Daniel O'Connell, the Irish Liberator*, London 1929

Michael MacDonagh, *The Life of Daniel O'Connell*, London 1903
Angus MacIntyre, *The Liberator: Daniel O'Connell and the Irish Party 1830–1847*, London 1965
Daniel O'Connell: Nine Centenary Essays, ed. Michael Tierney, Dublin 1947
Seán O'Faolain, *King of the Beggars: A Life of Daniel O'Connell*, London 1938
Professor Maurice O'Connell's forthcoming volumes of O'Connell's collected correspondence will provide a further source of immense value and interest.

Chapter 13

Notes

1. '. . . but none of you can believe what the state of the country really is . . . I will only further observe that it is quite useless, as Mr Trevelyan [Assistant Secretary at the Treasury] appears to do, to compare Ireland with Scotland. There is no capital here among the lower classes and I fear not a great deal among the higher.' Lord Bessborough (Lord Lieutenant of Ireland) to Lord John Russell, 30 Sept. 1846, Russell Papers, Public Record Office, London 30/22/5.
2. Bessborough to Russell, 23 Jan. 1847, Russell Papers, PRO 30/22/6.
3. *Nation*, 8 Jan. 1848.

Bibliography

R. D. Collison Black, *Economic thought and the Irish Question 1817–1870*, Cambridge 1960
K. H. Connell, *The Population of Ireland 1750–1845*, Oxford 1950
Michael Drake, 'The Irish Demographic Crisis of 1740–41', *Historical Studies* VI, ed. T. W. Moody, London 1968
R. Dudley Edwards and T. Desmond Williams, ed., *The Great Famine, Studies in Irish History 1845–52*, Dublin 1956; New York 1957. This work contains a number of valuable and well documented essays on the social and political history of the Famine years
F. S. L. Lyons, *Ireland since the Famine*, London 1971
Lawrence McCaffrey, *Daniel O'Connell and the Repeal Year*, University of Kentucky Press 1966
Angus MacIntyre, *The Liberator: Daniel O'Connell and the Irish Party 1830–1847*, London 1965
Kevin B. Nowlan, *The Politics of Repeal: A Study in the Relations between Great Britain and Ireland, 1841–50*, London and Toronto 1965

N. Redcliffe Salaman, *The History and Social Influence of the Potato,* Cambridge 1949
John H. Whyte, *The Independent Irish Party, 1850–59,* Oxford 1958
Cecil Woodham-Smith, *The Great Hunger, Ireland 1845–9,* London 1962

Chapter 14

Notes

1. This famous 'last link' speech is described as 'alleged' because there is still doubt as to whether or not Parnell actually used these words. They are certainly more explicit than he normally cared to be; on the other hand, Irish nationalists generally found that in America they had to be more raucous if they were to get a hearing.

Bibliography

T. N. Brown, *Irish American Nationalism,* Philadelphia and New York 1966
L. P. Curtis, jr., *Coercion and Conciliation in Ireland, 1880–92,* Princeton and London 1962
J. F. Glaser, 'Parnell's Fall and the Nonconformist Conscience', *Irish Historical Studies* XII (Sept. 1960)
J. L. Hammond, *Gladstone and the Irish Nation,* London 1938; new impression, 1964
Henry Harrison, *Parnell Vindicated,* London 1931
C. H. D. Howard, 'Joseph Chamberlain, W. H. O'Shea and Parnell, 1884, 1891–2', *Irish Historical Studies* XIII (Mar. 1962)
Emmet Larkin, 'The Roman Catholic Hierarchy and the Fall of Parnell', *Victorian Studies* IV (June 1961)
F. S. L. Lyons, 'The Economic Ideas of Parnell', *Historical Studies* II, ed. M. Roberts, London 1959
F. S. L. Lyons, *The Fall of Parnell,* London 1960
F. S. L. Lyons, *Parnell* (Dublin Historical Association), Dundalk 1963; reprinted 1970
F. S. L. Lyons, *John Dillon: A Biography,* London 1968
T. W. Moody, 'The New Departure in Irish Politics, 1878–9' in H. A. Cronne, T. W. Moody and D. B. Quinn, ed., *Essays in British and Irish History in Honour of James Eadie Todd,* London 1949
T. W. Moody, 'Parnell and the Galway Election of 1886', *Irish Historical Studies* IX (Mar. 1955)
T. W. Moody, '*The Times* versus Parnell and Co., 1887–90', *Historical Studies,* VI, ed. T. W. Moody, London 1968

C. Cruise O'Brien, *Parnell and his Party, 1880–90*, London 1957; corrected ed., 1964

R. Barry O'Brien, *The Life of Charles Stewart Parnell*, 2 vols, London 1898

D. A. Thornley, *Isaac Butt and Home Rule*, London 1964

Chapter 15

Bibliography

R. Blake, *The Unknown Prime Minister*, London 1955

P. J. Buckland, 'The Southern Irish Unionists and British Politics', *Irish Historical Studies* XII (Mar. 1961)

J. R. Fanning, 'The Unionist Party and Ireland, 1906–1910', *Irish Historical Studies* XV (Sept. 1966)

D. R. Gwynn, *The Life of John Redmond*, London 1932

D. R. Gwynn, *The History of Partition, 1912–25*, London 1950

J. J. Horgan, *Parnell to Pearse*, Dublin 1948

H. M. Hyde, *Carson*, London 1953

R. Jenkins, *Asquith*, London 1964

F. S. L. Lyons, *The Irish Parliamentary Party, 1890–1910*, London 1951

F. S. L. Lyons, 'The Passing of the Irish Parliamentary Party, 1916–18', in T. Desmond Williams, ed., *The Irish Struggle, 1916–26*, London 1966

F. S. L. Lyons, *John Dillon: A Biography*, London 1968

F. S. L. Lyons, 'The Two Faces of Home Rule' in O. Dudley Edwards and F. Pyle, ed., *1916: the Easter Rising*, London 1968

L. J. McCaffrey, 'Home Rule and the General Election of 1874', *Irish Historical Studies* IX (Sept. 1954)

H. W. McCready, 'Home Rule and the Liberal Party', *Irish Historical Studies*, XIII (Sept. 1963)

R. B. McDowell, *The Irish Convention, 1917–18*, London 1970

F. X. Martin, ed., *Leaders and Men of the Easter Rising: Dublin 1916*, London 1967

C. Cruise O'Brien, ed., *The Shaping of Modern Ireland*, London 1960; paperback ed., 1970

L. Ó Broin, *The Chief Secretary: Augustine Birrell and Ireland*, London 1969

D. C. Savage, 'The Origins of the Ulster Unionist Party, 1885–6', *Irish Historical Studies* XII (Mar. 1961)

A. T. Q. Stewart, *The Ulster Crisis*, London 1967

Chapter 16

Notes
1. On Collins's role, see the memorandum by the first Attorney-General, Hugh Kennedy, to W. T. Cosgrave, 2 Apr. 1923 (Kennedy Papers, UCD). Some indications of Brugha's dissatisfaction can be seen in decisions of the Dáil Cabinet in Sept.–Nov. 1921 (Dáil Éireann Cabinet Minutes, State Paper Office, Dublin) and in de Valera's letter to McGarrity, 21 Dec. 1921 in Sean Cronin, *The McGarrity Papers,* Tralee 1972, 105ff.
2. See A. H. Birch, *Responsible and Representative Government,* London 1965.
3. For an elaboration of this point, see Richard Rose, *Governing without Consensus,* London 1971, especially chap. 13 'The Limits of Leadership'.
4. This group is investigated in detail in A. S. Cohan, *The Irish Political Elite,* Dublin 1972.
5. See Brian Farrell 'Labour and the Irish Political Party System : A Suggested Approach to Analysis', *Social and Economic Review* I, 3 (1970).
6. P. Pyne, 'The Third Sinn Féin Party 1923–26: A Narrative Account', *Social and Economic Review* I, 1 (Oct. 1969), 42.
7. The fullest account is in Frank Munger, 'The Legitimacy of Opposition : The Change of Government in Ireland in 1932', a paper prepared for delivery at the 1966 annual meeting of the American Political Science Association, New York, 6–10 Sept. 1966.

Bibliography
For an overview the authoritative account is F. S. L. Lyons, *Ireland Since the Famine, London* 1971
The discussion of Sinn Féin reorganisation, the role of Labour, the 1918 General Election, the constitutional documents and development of the Dáil is documented in greater detail in Brian Farrell *The Founding of Dáil Éireann: Parliament and Nation-Building,* Dublin 1971.
The most thorough accounts of the Second and Third Sinn Féin are Michael Laffan, 'The Unification of Sinn Féin in 1917', *Irish Historical Studies* XVII (Mar. 1971) and P. Pyne, 'The Third Sinn Féin Party 1923–26', *Social and Economic Review* I, 1–2 (Oct. 1969; Jan. 1970). On the proceedings of the First and Second Dála see *Dáil Debates* including the recently published *Private Sessions 1921–1922,* Dublin n.d.
Useful earlier literature includes: R. M. Henry, *The Evolution of Sinn Féin,* Dublin 1920, and P. S. O'Hegarty, *The Victory of Sinn Féin,*

Dublin 1924. On the Sinn Féin courts see Cahir Davitt, 'The Civil Jurisdiction of the Courts of Justice of the Irish Republic, 1920–1922', *Irish Jurist* V, 2 (Summer 1970). On the Irish Free State constitution, see D. H. Akenson and J. F. Fallin, 'The Irish Civil War and the Drafting of the Irish Free State Constitution', *Éire-Ireland* V, 2 (Summer 1970) and Brian Farrell, 'The Drafting of the Irish Free State Constitution', *Irish Jurist* V–VI (1970–71)

Chapters 17–19

Notes

1. It should also be noted that during 1917 there were serious differences of opinion and clashes of personality within the Sinn Féin movement itself. For these, see M. Laffan, 'The Unification of Sinn Féin in 1917', *Irish Historical Studies* XVIII (Mar. 1971) and Brian Farrell, *The Founding of Dáil Éireann*, Dublin 1971, chap. 2.

2. It is fair to say that even to this day some IRA leaders would dispute this reading of the war situation. The evidence is contradictory and the truth probably is that morale and military capacity varied considerably as between different commands and different parts of the county.

3. Since the above was written, the publication of the then private sessions of the Dáil has revealed that de Valera was prepared to take a very conciliatory attitude towards the North. On 22 August 1921 he remarked that 'They [presumably both his government and the Dáil to which it was responsible] had not the power, and some of them had not the inclination to use force with Ulster.' He himself would not be responsible for such a policy and he added : 'For his part, if the Republic were recognised, he would be in favour of giving each county power to vote itself out of the Republic if it so wished. Otherwise they would be compelled to use force.' (*Private Sessions of the Second Dáil*, Dublin 1972, 29.) De Valera's reference to 'republican doctrinaires' was made in public session. (Dáil Éireann, *Official Report*, 16 August 1921, 7–8.)

4. In private session he argued that as Head of State he was the symbol of the Republic and that that symbol should be kept uncompromised. (*Private Sessions of the Second Dáil*, 95–96). His correspondence at that time pointed in the same direction; see the Earl of Longford and T. P. O'Neill, *Eamon de Valera*, London 1970, 146.

5. Thomas Jones, *Whitehall Diary* III : *Ireland, 1918–1925*, ed. K. Middlemass, London 1971, 161, 187, 189, 234.

6. The first form of the document contained twenty-three clauses, the

second form seventeen. The clauses omitted in the second version all dealt with Northern Ireland and traversed the same ground as the relevant clauses of the Treaty. Their omission meant that the second Document No. 2 contained no direct reference to the North, which must have made it incomprehensible to the already confused deputies. Both versions appear as appendices 17 and 18 in *Private Sessions of the Second Dáil*, Dublin 1972.

7. The one outstanding exception to this generalisation was Seán Mac-Entee, one of the deputies for Monaghan, whose speech was not only a moving plea for the unity of the island but also a remarkably prescient interpretation of the Boundary Commission clause in the Treaty as leading to a recognition of the permanence of partition. (*Debate on the Treaty between Great Britain and Ireland*, Dublin n.d., 152–8.)

8. *Young Ireland*, 31 Dec. 1921.

9. *Ibid.*

10. *Irish Times*, 3 Jan. 1922.

Bibliography

Dáil Éireann, *Minutes of Proceedings of the First Parliament of Ireland, 1919–21* (Official Record), Dublin 1921

Dáil Éireann, *Official Report: Debate on the Treaty between Great Britain and Ireland, signed in London on 6 December 1921*, Dublin 1922

Dáil Éireann, *Official Report for the Periods 16–26 August 1921 and 28 February to 8 June 1922*, Dublin 1922

Dáil Éireann, *Private Sessions of Second Dáil: Minutes of Proceedings, 18 August 1921 to 14 September 1921 and Report of Debates, 14 December 1921 to 6 January 1922*, Dublin 1972

D. G. Boyce, *Englishmen and Irish Troubles*, London 1972

P. J. Buckland, *Irish Unionism* 1: *The Anglo-Irish and the New Ireland, 1885–1922*, Dublin 1972

P. Colum, *Arthur Griffith*, Dublin 1959

M. Comerford, *The First Dáil*, Dublin 1969

B. Farrell, *The Founding of Dáil Éireann*, Dublin 1971

M. Forester, *Michael Collins: the Lost Leader*, London 1971

T. Jones, *Whitehall Diary*, III : *Ireland, 1918–25*, ed. K. Middlemass, London 1971

M. Laffan, 'The Unification of Sinn Féin in 1917', *Irish Historical Studies* XVII (Mar. 1971)

Earl of Longford and T. P. O'Neill, *Eamon de Valera*, London 1970

F. S. L. Lyons, *John Dillon: A Biography*, London 1968

F. S. L. Lyons, *Ireland since the Famine*, London 1971

D. Macardle, *The Irish Republic* (paperback edition) London 1968
R. B. McDowell, *The Irish Convention, 1917–18,* London 1970
E. Neeson, *The Civil War in Ireland* (paperback edition) Tralee, 1969
F. O'Donoghue, *No Other Law,* London 1954
F. Pakenham (Earl of Longford), *Peace by Ordeal,* London 1935
R. Taylor, *Michael Collins* (paperback edition), London 1968
A. J. Ward, *Ireland and Anglo-American Relations, 1899–1921,* London 1969
T. de Vere White, *Kevin O'Higgins* (paperback edition), Tralee 1967
T. Desmond Williams, ed., *The Irish Struggle, 1916–26,* London 1966
C. Younger, *Ireland's Civil War* (paperback edition), London 1970

Appendices

1. Irish Parliaments 1494–1714

The list of parliaments in the Tudor period is taken from David B. Quinn, 'Parliaments and Great Councils in Ireland, 1461–1586', *Irish Historical Studies* III (1942–43). For the remaining period the information is based on the official *Journals of the House of Commons of the Kingdom of Ireland* and on the list of chief governors in Ireland in F. M. Powicke and E. B. Fryde, ed., *Handbook of British Chronology*, 2nd ed., London 1961. A list of parliaments summoned between 1264 and 1494 is given in H. G. Richardson and G. O. Sayles, *The Irish Parliament in the Middle Ages*, Philadelphia 1952, 332–65. Described by its compilers as 'a provisional summary of present knowledge' it is, in fact, the most detailed and accurate record that has yet been prepared and is, as such invaluable.

LL : Lord Lieutenant
LD : Lord Deputy
*Assemblies not summoned under the authority of the Great Seal of England.

Reign	Date	Crown Representative
Henry VII	1494–95	Sir Edward Poynings, LD
	1499	Gerald FitzGerald, eighth Earl of Kildare, LD
	1508–09	Gerald FitzGerald, eighth Earl of Kildare, LD
Henry VIII	1516	Gerald FitzGerald, ninth Earl of Kildare, LD
	1521–22	Thomas Howard, Earl of Surrey, LL
	1531	Sir William Skeffington, LD
	1533	Gerald FitzGerald, ninth Earl of Kildare, LD
	1536–37	Lord Leonard Gray, LD
	1541–43	Sir Anthony St Leger, LD
Mary	1557–58	Thomas Radcliff, Earl of Sussex, LD

Reign	Date	Crown Representative
Elizabeth I	1560	Thomas Radcliff, Earl of Sussex, LD
	1569–71	Sir Henry Sidney, LD
	1585–86	Sir John Perrot, LD
James I	1613–15	Sir Arthur Chichester, LD
Charles I	1634–35	Thomas Wentworth, Viscount Wentworth (later Earl of Strafford), LD
	1640–41	Thomas Wentworth, Earl of Strafford, LL
		[Continued as a 'Rump' until prorogation in 1648]
	*1642–49	[The General Assemblies of the Confederation of Kilkenny]
Interregnum		For Irish representation at Westminster between 1653 and 1659, see Appendix 3
	*1660	[Convention]
Charles II	1661–66	James Butler, first Duke of Ormond, LL
James II	*1689	[The Patriot Parliament]
(in exile)		James II in person, superseding Richard Talbot, Duke of Tyrconnell, LD
William III	1692–93	Henry Sidney, Viscount Sidney, LL
	1695–99	Henry Capel, Baron Capel, LD (d. 1696, followed by a succession of Lords Justices)
Anne	1703–13	James Butler, second Duke of Ormond, LL (1703–07)
		Thomas Herbert, Earl of Pembroke and Montgomery, LL (1707–08)
		Thomas Wharton, Earl of Wharton LL (1708–10)
		James Butler, second Duke of Ormond, LL (1710–13)
	1713–14	Charles Talbot, Duke of Shrewsbury, LL

2. General Elections 1715–97

From the accession of George I to the passing of the Octennial Act in 1768 it was customary for the life of a parliament to be conterminous with the reign of the king. The Octennial Act, which remained in force until 1800, prescribed that a single parliament should not remain in existence for longer than eight years. A list of general elections in these two periods is therefore of greater value than a list of parliaments. The following list is based on the official *Return of Members of Parliament*, Pt 2, London 1880.

After 1768 governments tended to choose an opportune moment for dissolution rather than wait for the latest time allowed under the Octennial Act; as a guide to the complex factors determining the exact dates of elections, references are given to the relevant passages in W. E. H. Lecky, *Ireland in the Eighteenth Century*, London 1892.

Date of Election	Reason for Election
1715	Death of Anne
1727	Death of George I
1761	Death of George II
1769	Octennial Act
1776	Lecky II, 166
1783	Lecky II, 350
1790	Lecky III, 3
1797	Lecky IV, 181–2

Note The term 'Grattan's Parliament', which is generally used to denote the group of assemblies meeting between 1782 and 1800, should be regarded as referring to the sessions meeting under the reformed constitution which was promulgated in 1782 by the curtailment of Poynings' Law and the repeal of the Declaratory Act of 1720 ('the Sixth of George I') and which was operative throughout this period. 'Grattan's Parliament' was formally dissolved in 1800 and, with the exception of the successive parliaments of Northern Ireland and the abortive 'Parliament of Southern Ireland' of 1921, no subsequent assembly was summoned to meet in Ireland under royal authority as vested in a Great Seal.

3. Irish Representation at Westminster
Commonwealth and Protectorate 1649–60

Six MPs sat in the unicameral Barebones Parliament of 1653 as representatives for Ireland. The Instrument of Government (1653), which established the Protectorate, increased the Irish representation to thirty seats; this arrangement was applicable to Oliver Cromwell's Parliaments of 1654–55 and 1656–58 and to Richard Cromwell's Parliament of 1659.

The Union 1801–1921

The Act of Union (1800) provided for four bishops and twenty-eight peers to represent Ireland in the House of Lords, and for 100 MPs to represent Ireland in the House of Commons in the parliament of the United Kingdom. This latter number was increased to 105 by the Reform Act (1832), reduced to 103 by the disfranchisement of the boroughs of Sligo and Cashel in 1870, and increased again to 105 by the Representation of the People Act (1918).

The Government of Ireland Act (1920) provided for twelve Northern Ireland MPs and thirty-three 'Southern Ireland' MPs in the House of Commons. United Kingdom general elections under this act, however, only took place in Northern Ireland.